The DHTML Companion

Robert J. Mudry

Prentice Hall PTR
Upper Saddle River, New Jersey 07458
http://www.phptr.com

ISBN 0-13-796046-8

9 780137 960460

90000

Library of Congress Cataloging-in-Publication Data

Mudry, Robert.
   The DHTML companion / Robert J. Mudry.
      p.   cm.
   Includes index.
   ISBN 0-13-796046-8
    1. DHTML (Document markup language)   I. Title.
  QA76.76.H94M74   1998
  005.7'2—dc21   97–39016
                                        CIP

Acquisitions editor: Jeff Pepper
Cover designer: Scott Weiss
Cover design director: Jerry Votta
Manufacturing manager: Alexis R. Heydt
Marketing manager: Miles Williams
Compositor/Production services: Pine Tree Composition, Inc.

©1998 by Prentice Hall PTR
Prentice-Hall, Inc.
A Simon & Schuster Company
Upper Saddle River, New Jersey 07458

Prentice Hall books are widely used by corporations and
government agencies for training, marketing, and resale.

The publisher offers discounts on this book when ordered in
bulk quantities. For more information contact:

> Corporate Sales Department
> Phone: 800-382-3419
> Fax: 201-236-7141
> E-mail: corpsales@prenhall.com

> Or write:

> Prentice Hall PTR
> Corp. Sales Dept.
> One Lake Street
> Upper Saddle River, New Jersey 07458

Printed in the United States of America

10 9 8 7 6 5 4 3 2 1

ISBN: 0-13-796046-8

Prentice-Hall International (UK) Limited, *London*
Prentice-Hall of Australia Pty. Limited, *Sydney*
Prentice-Hall Canada Inc., *Toronto*
Prentice-Hall Hispanoamericana,S.A., *Mexico*
Prentice-Hall of India Private Limited, *New Delhi*
Prentice-Hall of Japan, Inc., *Tokyo*
Simon & Schuster Asia Pte. Ltd., *Singapore*
Editora Prentice-Hall do Brasil, Ltda., *Rio de Janeiro*

To my wife Ginger,

Her love is a gift I will cherish until the end of time.

Contents

Acknowledgments

A lot of people were involved in making this book possible. I would specifically like to thank the crew at Lockheed-Martin, including Bruce Smith, for all their patience as my work hours slowly dwindled to practically nothing. Linda Lambright, supreme Web goddess, graciously took up much of the slack, and I definitely owe her and her husband a dinner. And of course, my wife, who I forced to suffer through yet another book.

CHAPTER 1

Introduction

Dynamic HTML will change how you design Web pages forever. You will never be forced to compromise your design again. You will never have to rethink your vision because HTML can't handle a specific task. If you can imagine it, Dynamic HTML will allow you to do it. Pretty strong claims, I know, but by the time you finish this book, you will find yourself wondering how you ever managed to get along without it. Dynamic HTML is like trading in your pocket calculator for a high-powered workstation. You will never again be forced to say, "I wish HTML could do that!"

Dynamic HTML is not a new version of HTML, nor is it just a set of a few new tags. It is the marriage of several previously separate Web technologies, expanded to accommodate a new way of thinking about Web page design: style sheets, a scripting language, and a document object model to tie it all together.

- **Style Sheets**, or more specifically Cascading Style Sheets (CSS), will allow you to describe precisely how your pages should look and exactly where and how things should appear.
- **A Scripting Language**, such as JavaScript or VBScript, will give your Web pages the power to follow and react to every click and every mouse movement anywhere in your document, in any way you want.
- **A Document Object Model (DOM)** will make every paragraph, every image, even every single character in your document a distinct, individual entity with the ability to be addressed, manipulated, and even completely changed whenever you want, however you want.

In the following chapters, we will closely examine each of these pieces and see how they can be combined to form what we call Dynamic HTML. But first, let's take a mo-

1

ment to reflect on the reasons behind its creation and to define Dynamic HTML in a bit more detail.

ENOUGH HYPE: WHAT IS DYNAMIC HTML, REALLY?

A level of interactivity has always been missing from our Web pages. Certainly, with some cleverly crafted CGI scripts we can give the illusion of interactive content, but it never managed to get close to the "immediacy" of a real application. The user clicks a link, or enters some data into a form, and the server draws up a completely new document. Once loaded, the document just sits there, like a still frame captured from a motion picture. It is always painfully obvious that the user is querying a server, not interacting with an application.

When Java finally came on the scene, for awhile, it looked like our prayers had been answered. Now our Web pages became applications! But soon after, it was obvious that, while a neat alternative to static Web pages, Java suffered some pretty serious flaws. For one, it's not exactly a simple language to learn and even more difficult to master. You could spend weeks studying thick Java texts and still not be able to create that "dream applet." For many tasks Java was overkill, but when you did try to create a fairly complex applet, Java would fall flat on its face, performance wise. I overheard a conversation between two engineers at work which summed the situation up nicely: "Java is cool, but boy is it slow!" The biggest flaw, however, is not Java's speed or steep learning curve but its inability to truly integrate with your HTML. Java doesn't extend HTML, it bypasses it. Your users were no longer interacting with your Web page but with your Java applet. Obviously something else was needed.

Around the same time technical writers were going into their Java frenzy, Netscape released something called JavaScript. Or to be more precise, Netscape renamed a technology it was working on called "LiveScript" to take advantage of all the hype surrounding Java. Contrary to its name, JavaScript is not even remotely Java. Rather it is a relatively simple scripting language designed to give your Web pages a bit of intelligence. JavaScipt commands are written directly into your HTML documents, right next to your HTML. If you're motivated (or under deadline!) you can learn it in a weekend, without the need for a tree and a half worth of books and instruction manuals. So with high hopes and visions of fully interactive Web pages, thousands of webmasters began learning JavaScript.

The Scripting Language Solution

JavaScript can be a very powerful tool, but it quickly became clear that this wasn't the grand solution we were all looking for either. For one thing, JavaScript could only perform the simplest of tasks. Anything more complex than double-checking a user's form entries was completely out of JavaScript's league. You could replace one image with another using JavaScript, but the images had to be the exact same size. And forget about replacing bits and pieces of HTML once the browser displayed the page. JavaScript is a simple language designed for simple tasks.

Figure 1–1 JavaScript can alert your users when they forget to fill out a form properly.

```
<HTML>
<HEAD>
<TITLE>Figure 1-1</TITLE>
<SCRIPT LANGUAGE="JavaScript">
function checkValue(myForm)
{
  if(myForm.SEARCH.value == "")
{
  alert("Must enter a value!");
  return false;
}
  return true;
}
</SCRIPT>
</HEAD>
<BODY>
<FORM>
Search field
<INPUT TYPE="text" NAME="SEARCH">
<INPUT TYPE="submit" VALUE="Perform Search"
```

Listing 1–1 Shows the simple JavaScript involved.

```
onClick="return checkValue(this.form)">
</FORM>
</BODY>
</HTML>
```

Listing 1–1   *Continued*

Microsoft also tried its hand at the scripting language solution, releasing two new languages of its own: JScript and VBScript. JScript was directly aimed at the JavaScript audience, providing nearly 100 percent compatability with JavaScript. But Microsoft also thought JavaScript was a bit too difficult to learn, so VBScript was offered as a toned-down version of Visual Basic that could be used in lieu of JScript or JavaScript. If you were familiar with Visual Basic and didn't want to learn another language, VBScript was a godsend. But it, too, suffered the same basic drawbacks as JavaScript.

What was the main problem of these scripting languages? You could only access and affect a small fraction of your document. For forms, they were a champ—you could double check user input, pop open an "alert box" if your users entered anything strange, and even change the values of your form fields based on other user input. Anything more complex, however, and you were better off bypassing HTML and struggling with a custom Java applet. But in spite of these shortcomings, these new languages did give us something special that would soon become the basis for what is now known as Dynamic HTML—the concept of a document object model!

Document Object Models

Document object model is a scary term, but in reality it is a very simple concept. Objects are, simply stated, the individual pieces that make up your Web page. A model is the con-

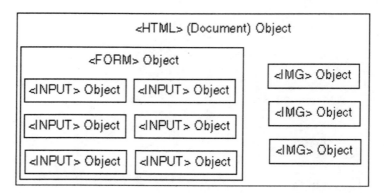

Figure 1–2   Objects can be combined to form other objects. In this example, six <INPUT> objects combine to create a <FORM> object. Three <IMG> objects are also added to ultimately create an <HTML> object.

nection of those objects to make other objects, and ultimately the document itself. For example, a text entry form field is an object and a submit button is an object. Those objects together can create a form object. Now take an image object or two, put them with the form object, and you have your document object. So a document object model is a description of how to put together HTML objects to create a document.

There is, of course, a little more involved in the document object model than pronouncing something an object and slapping together your Web page like normal. After all, even after you call a text entry form field an object, deep down inside it is still just a little snippet of HTML. Obviously if you're giving that little piece of HTML a name as lofty as "an object," there must be more to it than that! The answer is a resounding yes! Objects can also listen for events, such as a mouse click. They can have little pieces of code attached to them, called methods, which define how that object behaves in certain situations. You can query an object, to find out what information it currently contains, and you can give an object new information as well. An object is a piece of HTML with a brain, so to speak.

All this brings us back to the scripting languages. When you use a scripting language, such as JavaScript, to change form elements or images, you're using what is called the JavaScript Object Model. It is similar to the object model I just described in that pieces of your HTML are considered objects, but unfortunately the JavaScript Object Model assigns the object status to only a small subset of your document: regular paragraph text? not an object, the text inside your <H1> tags? not an object. This is a severe limitation that means you can only access the small handful of objects the JavaScript Object Model defines. Your entire document simply isn't accessible. And since JavaScript, JScript, and VBScript follow this same object model, they all suffer the same basic problem.

Now comes the part of the story when Microsoft joins in, and Dynamic HTML is born. Microsoft saw the JavaScript Object Model and realized that in order for a scripting language, any scripting language, to be truly useful, it must have full access to every piece of your HTML document. Everything must be recognized as an object. Every tag, every image, every single piece of text. If it is in your document, it must be given the status of

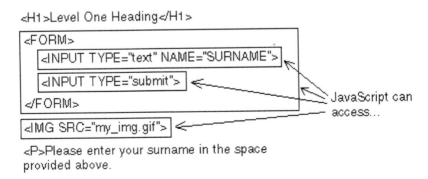

Figure 1–3 The JavaScript Object Model can only access a small subset of your document.

an object, and your script must be allowed to access it. So Microsoft set to work on the Document Object Model specification.

Unlike Netscape's JavaScript Object Model, which only exposes a small subset of your document to the scripting language, Microsoft's Document Object Model exposes the entire document. If it is in your document, your scripting language can access it. Want to examine the contents of your first <H1> tags? With the new object model you can. Change the text inside those tags, even after the document has been displayed? Easy. Tell those tags to respond to a mouse movement or a click? Not a problem. The entire document can be accessed, modified, or made to listen for user events! This is definitely a step in the right direction.

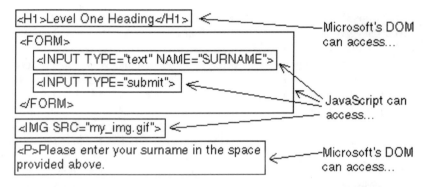

Figure 1–4   Microsoft's DOM can access every part of your document.

That's Neat, but What About Style Sheets?

A style sheet is a little extra code at the top of your HTML that defines precisely how your page should be rendered. Using a style sheet, you can completely redefine the behavior of all your HTML tags. Want all your <H1> headings to appear centered, underlined, in red with a 24-point Courier font? Style sheets make this possible! And that's not all. Style sheets also give you the ability to position elements precisely on your page, control margins, text alignment, spacing and leading, layering and overlapping, and even set different backgrounds for any element.

```
<HTML>
 <STYLE TYPE="text/css">
 H1  { font-family: courier;
       font-size: 24pt;
       color: black;
       text-align: center;
     }
</STYLE>
```

```
<HEAD>
 <TITLE>CSS Example</TITLE>
</HEAD>
<BODY>
 <H1 onMouseOver="this.style.fontSize='32pt';
   this.style.textDecoration='underline'" onMouseOut="this.
   style.fontSize='24pt'; this.style.textDecoration='none'">
 Dynamic HTML</H1>
</BODY>
</HTML>
```

Listing 1–2 Shows how easy style sheets can be to work with.

Figure 1–5 Style sheets allow you to redefine how HTML is rendered. In this example, an <H1> tag is redefined to produce 24-point Courier in red and automatically centered.

Think style sheets sound neat? Now picture what you could do if you could access and change your style sheets, on the fly, with your favorite scripting language! Yes, the Document Object Model extends all the way to style sheets, allowing you to change your document's style on the fly! Just in case it hasn't hit you yet, this means you can change any part of your document in any way you want based on any user event anywhere. On the fly. This is what we mean by Dynamic HTML.

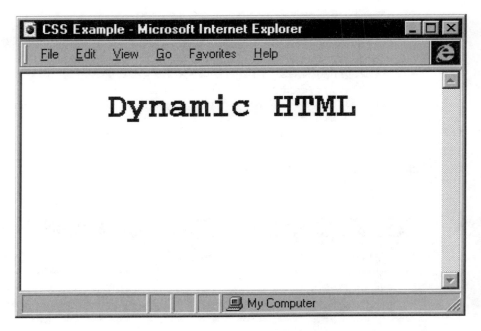

Figure 1–6   The <H1> tag defined as centered 24-point Courier.

Netscape's Little Twist

Everything would be just perfect if it wasn't for one little problem: Netscape. I would like to start by saying that I've been a Netscape supporter from the beginning, quite literally. Netscape has done more than we ever could have hoped to advance Web technology. While the Web standards organization, the World Wide Web Consortium (W3C) was waffling on new standards, Netscape went ahead and implemented them, adding missing pieces on its own. This involved risks, of course, since there was no guarantee that what Netscape did would become the standard, but it also forced W3C to finally make a decision. When it came to Dynamic HTML, Netscape took those same risks and implemented its own vision.

Netscape already had the scripting language, JavaScript. They also committed to style sheets, since that was already well on its way to being an official standard. What was missing was the object model, and here is where Netscape began to stray. Instead of an all-inclusive document object model, like Microsoft proposed, Netscape decided to implement what it called JavaScript Accessible Style Sheets (JASS). But the JASS model didn't allow changes to be made on the fly, so it also developed something called "Layers," which attempted to address some of the positioning and dynamic capabilities that Microsoft offered.

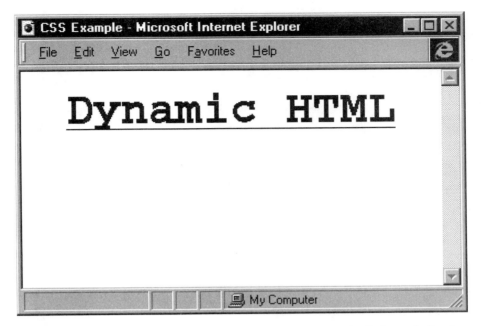

Figure 1–7   With Dynamic HTML, the <H1> tag is redefined on the fly for underlined 32-point Courier with a JavaScript "onMouseOver" event. In other words, when the mouse pointer is brought over the <H1> tag's text, "Dynamic HTML," the font size is automatically increased and underlined!

With the absence of competition, JASS and Layers may well have become standards; but Microsoft was in town this time and was a bit irked at being left out of the Web game for so long. The W3C preferred Microsoft's Document Object Model over JASS and Layers and recommended that Netscape adopt Microsoft's solution instead. But Netscape was stubborn and continued to support its own implementations over Microsoft's. This created quite a public outcry. Webmasters who had been staunch Netscape supporters suddenly found themselves supporting Microsoft's better (and likely to become official) solution.

As of this writing, Netscape seems to have finally gotten the message and promised to support whatever the W3C recommends. But this change of direction came reluctantly, and the status of JASS and Layers is still up in the air. I suspect that Netscape will soon support Microsoft's solution 100 percent, but it may also try to slip JASS and Layers into the mix as well. With this in mind, I have decided to cover primarily Microsoft's solution but cover JASS and Layers to some extent as well.

Let's Get to It, Then!

Before we dive in, there are a few things to take care of. First, you should acquire the latest version of Internet Explorer 4.0 and Netscape Communicator 4.0. Netscape and Microsoft both have their own quirks and bugs, and you should always double check your HTML in each browser before releasing it to the world. Also, Netscape only recently announced its intention to support all of the Microsoft extensions for Dynamic HTML. Until now, Netscape had been pushing its "JavaScript Accessible Style Sheets" (JASS) and "Layers" solutions for Dynamic HTML. When required, I will cover these Netscape specific specifications, but most of this book will be dedicated to the Microsoft version of Dynamic HTML. Since Microsoft's specifications have been blessed as "official" by the W3C and Netscape's haven't, I'm sure these distinctions will soon become moot.

You will also need a very strong understanding of standard HTML. A basic understanding of JavaScript is also required. Microsoft calls this "JScript," but it is essentially the same thing. I picked JavaScript as the language of choice because, unlike VBScript, it is supported by both browsers. If you're not a JavaScript expert, don't worry! I'll keep the examples as simple as possible and explain all the code thoroughly.

Now that you know what Dynamic HTML has to offer, let us dig in and begin learning some of these powerful new techniques! Before long, you will be able to create Web pages like you've never imagined possible!

CHAPTER 2

Dynamic Content

Instead of going into mind-numbing detail on object theory, the document object model, and a half-dozen other less than exciting topics, we're going straight to the practical stuff. Even if you have only limited scripting experience, you probably have at least a passing familiarity with the JavaScript Object Model, which is good enough to create some dramatic effects with Dynamic HTML.

Dynamic content is the ability to make changes directly to your HTML after the document has been displayed and is the basis of Dynamic HTML. You can change the text inside your HTML tags or change the tags themselves. You can add new tags or remove entire chunks of your document that no longer belong. If it is in your document, you can change it, and if it isn't in your document, you can add it. Nothing is written in stone anymore!

ACCESSING YOUR HTML ELEMENTS WITH THE "ALL COLLECTION"

Your entire HTML document might contain dozens of HTML elements. The text of your document is all enclosed in one big <BODY> element. Inside that, you can have a few <H1> elements to highlight important sections of your document and maybe a few <HR> elements to separate those sections. There may be a few words or phrases you've put inside <B> elements to make them stand out and maybe one or two in <I> elements for emphasis. You may even have a few "nonprinting" elements like <HEAD> and <TITLE> so search engines can index your pages properly and users can get a meaningful bookmark of your page. All of these HTML elements are objects inside your HTML document, and your scripting language has access to all of them. But before you can start accessing them, you need some way to tell your script which of these element objects you're talking about.

11

Pointers to the HTML elements in your document can be found in a series of "collections" defined by the Document object. A collection is simply a list of objects, gathered in one convenient location. The Document object defines several collections, but the one of most interest to us right now is the "All" collection, which contains a pointer to every HTML element object in the order they appear in your document.

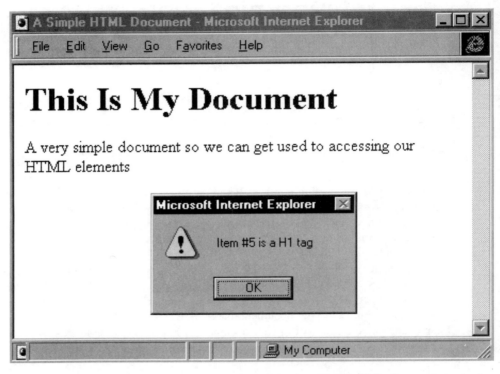

Figure 2–1   Accessing an element using the All collection. The "tagName" property is used to find out what type of HTML element the object contains. In this case, it is an <H1> element.

```
<HTML>
<HEAD>
<TITLE>A Simple HTML Document</TITLE>
<SCRIPT LANGUAGE="JavaScript">
function list_me()
{
  var myText = "Item #5 is a " + document.all(5).tagName +
  "tag";
  alert( myText );
}
</SCRIPT>
</HEAD>
```

```
<BODY onload="list_me()">

<H1>This Is My Document</H1>

<P>A very simple document so we can get
used to accessing our HTML elements</P>

</BODY>
</HTML>
```

Listing 2–1

You can access an individual element by providing the "All" collection with the element's index number. In Figure 2–1, index number 5 is our <H1> element. Notice how elements are counted starting with index number 0, the <HTML> tag! Remember, "nondisplaying" elements such as <HTML> and <HEAD> are elements just the same as <H1> and <P>!

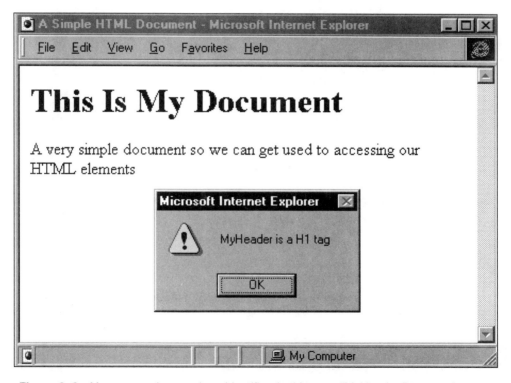

Figure 2–2 You can assign a unique identifier, in this case "MyHeader," to any element you think you'll need to access. This is a bit easier than trying to guess the element's index number!

As you can imagine, trying to pluck the right element out of the "All" collection with an index number can get tedious pretty quickly. A more reliable method is to assign a unique identifier to any elements you may need to access. Identifiers are set using the "ID" attribute. Figure 2–2 is the same as the previous example except this time with an identifier assigned to the <H1> element.

```
<HTML>
<HEAD>
<TITLE>A Simple HTML Document</TITLE>
<SCRIPT LANGUAGE="JavaScript">
function list_me()
{
  var myText = "MyHeader is a " + document.all("MyHeader").
    tagName + " tag";
  alert( myText );
}
</SCRIPT>
</HEAD>
<BODY onload="list_me()">

<H1 ID="MyHeader">This Is My Document</H1>

<P>A very simple document so we can get
used to accessing our HTML elements</P>

</BODY>
</HTML>
```

Listing 2–2

Indexing by number allows you to do neat things like loop through all elements in your document, and indexing by identifier allows you to pick out a single element easily. An alternate syntax to

```
document.all("MyHeader")
```

is to give the indentifier name without the parantheses or quotes:

```
document.all.MyHeader
```

Personally, I like the alternate syntax because I find it keeps my code a bit easier to read, but you should feel free to use either form. My philosophy, however, is the less typing the better!

Just like any other object, the "All" collection has a property and some methods. The "length" property reports how many elements the current document contains. Using the number indexing method combined with the length property makes looping through all your elements easy!

```
for (var x=0; x < document.all.length; x++)
{
    alert( document.all(x).tagName );
}
```

This little snippet of code uses the length property in a for-loop to cycle through your document and return the names of each tag encountered.

The "All" collection also gives you a couple of special methods, item() and tags(), to give you even more options for finding the elements you are looking for. The item() method can be used when your "unique identifiers" aren't unique. If your argument is the name of an identifier, item() will return another collection of all the elements with just those identifiers. Like all collections, you can use the "length" property to determine how many elements were returned. If you give item() a second argument, an index number for your new collection, it will return the element in that position of the new collection. Figure 2–3 shows

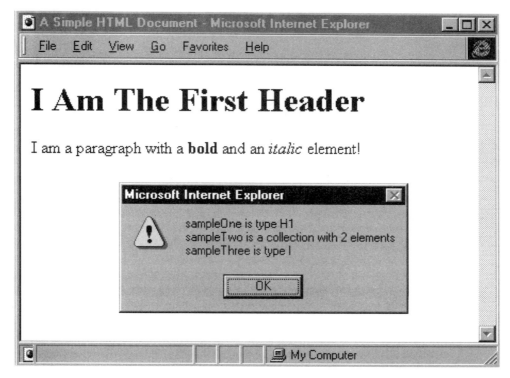

Figure 2–3   The item() method will accept one or two arguments, and returns another collection of elements. Even easier, make your identifiers unique, and you won't have to go through this extra trouble!

the item() method in action. In the function list_me(), there are three examples of using item() to find an element. The first line assigns the element object found at index 5 to the sampleOne variable. The fifth element in the "All" collection is the <H1> element. The second line uses item() to assign a new collection of all the element objects with the not-so-unique identifier "MyItem" to the sampleTwo variable. The last assignment extracts the second element object from the new collection of "MyItem" element objects.

```
<HTML>
<HEAD>
<TITLE>A Simple HTML Document</TITLE>
</HEAD>
<SCRIPT LANGUAGE="JavaScript">
function list_me()
{
  var sampleOne = document.all.item(5);
  var sampleTwo = document.all.item("MyItem");
  var sampleThree = document.all.item("MyItem", 1);

  alert("sampleOne is type " + sampleOne.tagName + "\n" +
    "sampleTwo is a collection with " + sampleTwo.length +
      "elements\n" +
    "sampleThree is type " + sampleThree.tagName);
}
</SCRIPT>
</HEAD>
<BODY onload="list_me()">

<H1 ID="FirstHeader">I Am The First Header</H1>

<P>I am a paragraph with a <B ID="MyItem">bold</B> and
an <I ID="MyItem">italic</I> element!</P>

</BODY>
</HTML>
```

Listing 2–3

The tags() method is a little more interesting. It allows you to get a collection containing only elements of the type you specify. If you want to find all your bold elements, you would use tags() to do it. Figure 2–4 shows the output of Listing 2–4. In the list_me() function, the tags() method is called into action to return all the <B> elements in your document and assign the new collection to the boldItems variable.

```
<HTML>
<HEAD>
<TITLE>A Simple HTML Document</TITLE>
```

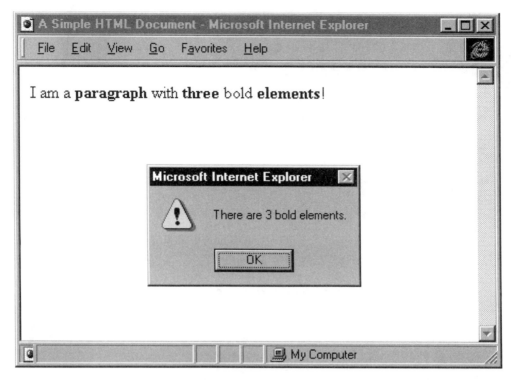

Figure 2–4   The tags() method returns a collection of the type of element you specify.

```
</HEAD>
<SCRIPT LANGUAGE="JavaScript">
function list_me()
{
  var boldItems = document.all.tags("B");
  alert("There are " + boldItems.length + " bold elements.");
}
</SCRIPT>
</HEAD>
<BODY onload="list_me()">

<P>I am a <B>paragraph</B> with <B>three</B> bold
  <B>elements</B>!</P>

</BODY>
</HTML>
```

Listing 2–4

Now that we can pick a single element out of the "All" collection, let's take a look at what's actually inside those elements and how we can change them.

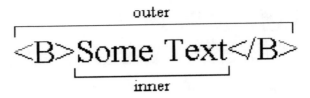

Figure 2–5   innerText and innerHTML are what appear between the start and end tags. outerText and outerHTML actually include the start and end tags.

GETTING INSIDE ELEMENT OBJECTS

Every element object has a full compliment of properties and methods that are used to access and modify the text they contain. While the exact properties and methods that are available depend largely on the type of element, almost all of them give you access to the following four properties and two methods.

- innerText property, for the text between the start and end tags
- outerText property, for the text that includes the start and end tags
- insertAdjacentText() method, for inserting text before and after the start and end tags
- innerHTML propery, like innerText but allows HTML to be used
- outerHTML property, like outerText but allows HTML to be used
- insertAdjacentHTML() method, like insertAdjacentText() but allows HTML to be used

There are two types of properties and methods. The text type allows you to access the text associated with your element as if it were plaintext. Any HTML tags that appear in this text are completely removed, and any HTML tags that are written into this text are converted into plaintext by replacing less-than signs with the < entity and greater-than signs with the > entity. If your <B> element contained an <I> element, the <I> element would be completely removed, though the text that it contained would be left behind.

The HTML type treats any HTML inside your element as if it really were HTML. If your <B> element contains an <I> element, the HTML type won't strip the <I> element out. This is an important distinction when we start making actual changes.

```
<HTML>
<HEAD>
<TITLE>A Simple HTML Document</TITLE>
<SCRIPT LANGUAGE="JavaScript">
function list_me()
{
   var myVar = document.all.boldItalic;
```

```
           alert( "innerText = " + myVar.innerText + "\n" +
             "innerHTML = " + myVar.innerHTML + "\n" +
             "outerText = " + myVar.outerText + "\n" +
             "outerHTML = " + myVar.outerHTML );
       }
       </SCRIPT>
       </HEAD>
       <BODY onload="list_me()">

       <P>A paragraph which contains a
       <B ID="boldItalic">bold and <I>italic</I></B> element.</P>

       </BODY>
       </HTML>
```

Listing 2–5

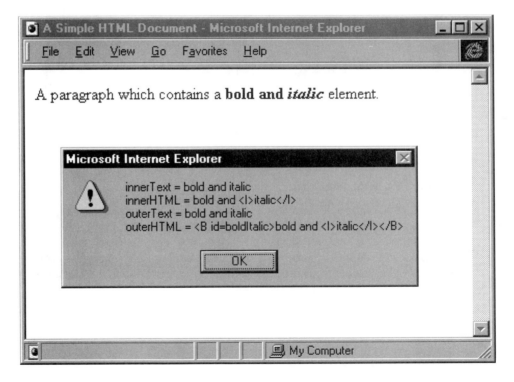

Figure 2–6 The "text" properties treat all the text between the tags as plaintext. The "html" variety recognizes the HTML elements that may be embedded in the "parent" element. Notice how in outerText the original <B> tags are "missing" as well.

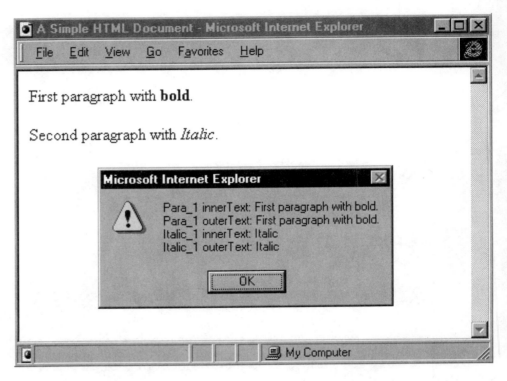

Figure 2–7a   innerText and outerText may look interchangable when read but take a look at Figure 2–7b for what happens when you write to each.

innerText and outerText

The innerText and outerText properties give you direct read and write access to everything that is contained in the element. The difference between these properties is that innerText treats all the text between the start and end tags, while outerText includes the tags as well. This can get you into trouble if you're not careful because anything you write to the outerText property will overwrite the start and end tags, effectively removing that element!

```
<HTML>
<HEAD>
<TITLE>A Simple HTML Document</TITLE>
<SCRIPT LANGUAGE="JavaScript">
function list_me()
{
  alert("Para_1 innerText: " + document.all.Para_1.innerText +
    "\n" +
```

Figure 2–7b   innerText can only be used to read and write text, not HTML. Also notice since I used outerText on Italic_1, I lost the original <I> element!

```
        "Para_1 outerText: " + document.all.Para_1.outerText +
          "\n" +
        "Italic_1 innerText: " + document.all.Italic_1.innerText +
          "\n" +
        "Italic_1 outerText: " + document.all.Italic_1.outerText );

      document.all.Para_1.innerText = "No more <B>bold</B>?";
      document.all.Italic_1.outerText = "no italics";
   }
   </SCRIPT>
   </HEAD>
   <BODY onload="list_me()">

   <P ID="Para_1">First paragraph with <B>bold</B>.</P>
   <P>Second paragraph with <I ID="Italic_1">Italic</I>.</P>

   </BODY>
   </HTML>
```

Listing 2–6

Listing 2–6 shows some examples of reading from and writing to the innerText and outerText properties. Notice, although innerText and outerText may appear interchangable when read, in Figure 2–7a, that when written, to the differences become very apparent! Figure 2–7b shows two pitfalls of the innerText and outerText properties. In the first paragraph, the original <B> element is lost and attempts at replacing it with a new element result in the tags being translated to plaintext. The second paragraph shows the big pitfall with outerText—the original start and end tags are overwriten, and the element is lost! Future attempts at accessing the Italic_1 element will fail because the element no longer exists!

innerHTML and outerHTML

Just like the "text" properties, the innerHTML and outerHTML properties give you direct read and write access to everything that is contained in the element. The innerHTML property gives you access to whatever is between the start and end tags, and outerHTML includes the tags as well. The difference is that any HTML inside the element is kept, instead of being stripped out. This means that any HTML you write into your element will be parsed by the browser and automatically slipped into the "All" collection as a new ele-

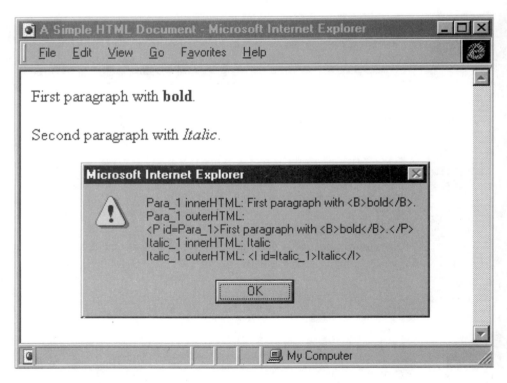

Figure 2–8a   innerHTML shows all the text and also includes any HTML elements embedded in the parent element. outerHTML also includes the start and end tags of the original element.

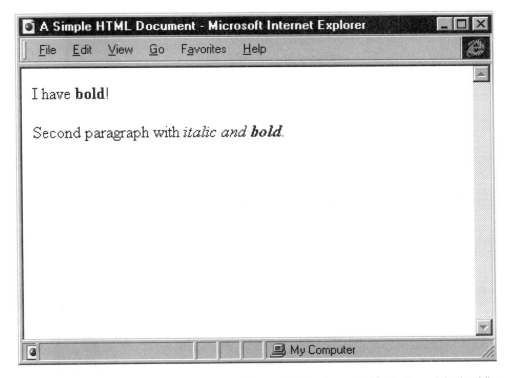

Figure 2–8b   innerHTML allows you to add new HTML elements inside the original, while outerHTML gives you access to the original start and end tags as well. Notice when I wrote the new <I> element in paragraph two, I left out the identifier. This actually changes the element and we won't be able to access the element with the Italic_1 identifier anymore! The element can still be accessed with the more cumbersome "index" method.

ment! Even better, if you use outerHTML you can replace the start and end tags with a completely new element. Of course, this introduces a few complications.

```
<HTML>
<HEAD>
<TITLE>A Simple HTML Document</TITLE>
<SCRIPT LANGUAGE="JavaScript">
function list_me()
{
  alert("Para_1 innerHTML: " + document.all.Para_1.innerHTML +
    "\n" +
    "Para_1 outerHTML: " + document.all.Para_1.outerHTML +
      "\n" +
```

Listing 2–7

```
        "Italic_1 innerHTML: " + document.all.Italic_1.innerHTML +
          "\n" +
        "Italic_1 outerHTML: " + document.all.Italic_1.
          outerHTML );
     document.all.Para_1.innerHTML = "I have <B>bold</B>!";
     document.all.Italic_1.outerHTML = "<I>italic and
        <B>bold</B></I>";
   }
   </SCRIPT>
   </HEAD>
   <BODY onload="list_me()">

   <P ID="Para_1">First paragraph with <B>bold</B>.</P>
   <P>Second paragraph with <I ID="Italic_1">Italic</I>.</P>

   </BODY>
   </HTML>
```

Listing 2–7   *Continued*

The first complication comes about because the browser will try to make sense of any new HTML you jam in your element. If your new HTML is out of context, for example, trying to stick an <LI> element inside a <B> element, the browser will have a bit of trouble coping and you will get a browser error. Also, if you try to insert nonexistent HTML tags, for example, you mistyped "<STRIKE>" as "<STRKE>," the browser will completely ignore the start and end tags, not even bothering to put them into your element. You also may acci-

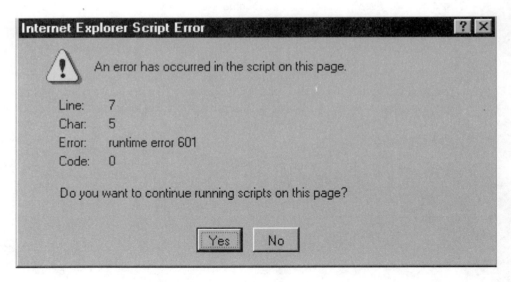

Figure 2–9   Trying to add an <LI> out of context produces a browser error.

dently forget to add an end tag. In this case, the browser will attempt to add one for you automatically. In other words, pay extra attention to your typing when using these properties!

Another even worse complication can occur when using index numbers to access your elements. If you add a new element inside the current element, the new element is automatically inserted into the "All" collection thus shifting around the index numbers. This will cause serious headaches if you attempt to access any elements later in the document, unless you recalculate the index numbers.

```
<HTML>
<HEAD>
<TITLE>A Simple HTML Document</TITLE>
<SCRIPT LANGUAGE="JavaScript">
function list_me()
{
    var oldName = document.all(7).tagName;
```

Listing 2–8

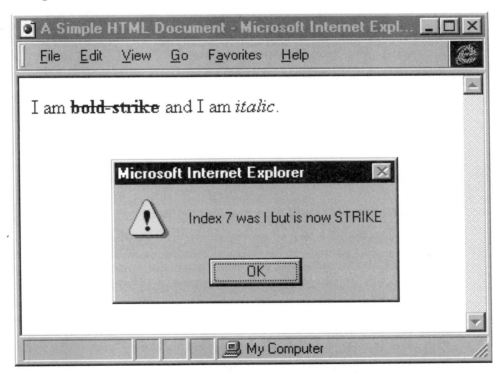

Figure 2–10 Before inserting a <STRIKE> element inside the <BOLD> element at index 6, the element at index 7 was <I>. Now, however, index 7 is the new <STRIKE> instead. The <I> element has been pushed back to index 8. Adding a new element causes all of your index numbers to shift. Be careful!

```
      document.all(6).innerHTML = "<STRIKE>bold-strike</STRIKE>";

      alert( "Index 7 was " + oldName + " but is now " +
        document.all(7).tagName );
    }
    </SCRIPT>
    </HEAD>
    <BODY onload="list_me()">

    <P>I am <B>bold</B> and I am <I>italic</I>.</P>

    </BODY>
    </HTML>
```

Listing 2–8   *Continued*

What else can go wrong? Be very careful when using outerHTML to change the current element! If you accessed your element using an identifier, don't forget to put another identifier into the new element or you won't be able to access it without resorting to index numbers! The very innocent act of changing this element

```
      <B ID="MyElement">I am bold!</B>
```

with the command

```
      document.all.MyElement.outerHTML = "<B>I am still bold!</B>";
```

can create an uncomfortable situation the next time you try to access the, now nonexistent, "MyElement" identifier!

insertAdjacentText() and insertAdjacentHTML()

Occasionally, you may need to insert some text into your element instead of overwriting what is currently there. You could emulate this functionality using the properties discussed above and a bit of clever scripting, however, in anticipation of this requirement two methods have been added to your object element's arsenal: insertAdjacentText() and insertAdjacentHTML(). These methods allow you to insert text or HTML before or after either of your element's start or end tags. This means you can actually affect the text surrounding your element as well.

The "insertAdjacent" methods accept two arguments. The first is the position within your element, and the second is the text you're inserting. There are four positions that are allowed: BeforeBegin, BeforeEnd, AfterBegin, and AfterEnd.

- BeforeBegin inserts your text before the start-tag of your element
- BeforeEnd inserts before the end-tag of your element

Figure 2–11   Insert where? Notice how single-tag elements only allow "BeforeBegin" and "AfterEnd."

- AfterBegin inserts after the start-tag of your element
- AfterEnd inserts after the end-tag of your element

For some elements, not all of these positions make sense. For example, the <BODY> element will only allow AfterBegin and BeforeEnd, for obvious reasons! Another example would be single-tag elements, like <BR> and <HR>, for which there is only a start tag. In this case, however, the only valid options are "BeforeBegin," which will insert before the element, and "AfterEnd," which will insert after the element. At first glance you would think this is illogical, but there is a method to this madness! The position arguments are really relative to the beginning and ending of the element, not the start and end tags. "BeforeBegin" really refers to before the element has begun, and "AfterEnd" means after the element has ended. Subtle logic, but worth noting.

```
<HTML>
<HEAD>
<TITLE>A Simple HTML Document</TITLE>
<SCRIPT LANGUAGE="JavaScript">
function list_me()
{
  document.all.Bold_1.insertAdjacentText("BeforeBegin","Out-
    side Left!");
  document.all.Bold_2.insertAdjacentText("AfterBegin","Inside
    Left!");
  document.all.Bold_3.insertAdjacentText("BeforeEnd","Inside
    Right!");
  document.all.Bold_4.insertAdjacentText("AfterEnd","Outside
    Right!");
}
```

Listing 2–9

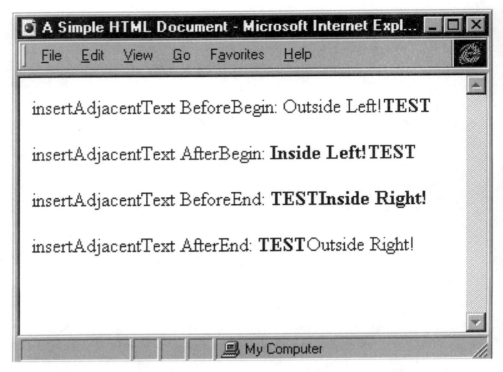

Figure 2–12   All four combinations of the insertAdjacentText() method.

```
</SCRIPT>
</HEAD>
<BODY onload="list_me()">

<P>insertAdjacentText BeforeBegin: <B ID="Bold_1">TEST</B></P>
<P>insertAdjacentText AfterBegin: <B ID="Bold_2">TEST</B></P>
<P>insertAdjacentText BeforeEnd: <B ID="Bold_3">TEST</B></P>
<P>insertAdjacentText AfterEnd: <B ID="Bold_4">TEST</B></P>

</BODY>
</HTML>
```

Listing 2–9   *Continued*

Be careful when using insertAdjacentHTML(), since this method suffers some of the same pitfalls as the innerHTML and outerHTML properties. Invalid HTML is mangled, and you can accidently trip yourself up by adding a new element to your document and throwing off all the index numbers. Another sticky point is that if you forget to close a new element, the browser will automatically close it for you, but not necessarily where you might hope it would! For example, you can't put your bold element into italics using "BeforeBegin" and "AfterEnd," because the italics will be closed automatically before the beginning of your bold element! All tags added with insertAdjacentHTML are closed automatically to prevent the new element from "leaking" past the inserted text. The only way around this problem, right now, is to use the innerHTML property to insert the new element manually. Shortly we'll see how something called a "text range" can present another possible solution. See Figure 2–13 for an example of this problem.

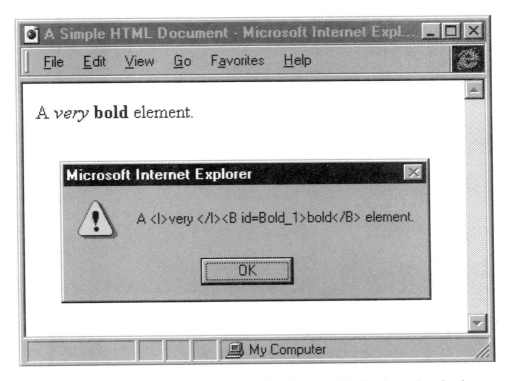

Figure 2–13 insertAdjacentHTML with BeforeBegin automaticallly closes the <I> element before reaching the <B> element. Displaying the HTML for the paragraph shows the automatically added end tag.

```
<HTML>
<HEAD>
<TITLE>A Simple HTML Document</TITLE>
<SCRIPT LANGUAGE="JavaScript">
function list_me()
{
```

Listing 2–10

```
     document.all.Bold_1.insertAdjacentHTML("BeforeBegin","<I>very
     ");
     alert(document.all.Para_1.innerHTML);
   }
</SCRIPT>
</HEAD>
<BODY onload="list_me()">

<P ID="Para_1">A <B ID="Bold_1">bold</B> element.</P>

</BODY>
</HTML>
```

Listing 2–10 *Continued*

Incidently, these two methods bring up an interesting point about paragraphs and the <P> element. Back in ancient times, when text-only Web browsers were still commonplace, the <P> element was one of the few containers that didn't require an end tag. (Can you name another? I'll give you a hint: most webmasters still don't bother giving it an end tag.) This lack of an end tag troubled purists, but it wasn't a problem, technically speaking. Paragraphs were, and still are, automatically closed when the context suggests it. For example, when you start a new paragraph, your last paragraph is automatically closed. But how about now, in this new era of objects and Dynamic HTML? Where does your paragraph officially end for the insertAdjacentHTML() method? The answer, of course, is your paragraph ends in the same place as it always has: where it makes the most sense to the browser. Even if you forget to give your paragraph an end tag, the browser will do it for you. But, you still should remember to close your own paragraphs. It's good style.

EVENTS: GIVING YOUR ELEMENTS EARS

So far, all we've been able to do is make our changes automatically, right after the document is done loading. Neat at first, but not incredibly useful. It would be much better if we could trigger our changes based on a certain user action or event, such as a mouse click or movement. Well, you'll be happy to hear that each and every one of your HTML elements can be told to listen for a wide variety of user actions and events!

An event is programming lingo for "something that happens that might affect your script." When the user clicks a mouse button on your document, we say that "an event has occured." If the user happens to click on one of your HTML elements that you've told to "listen" for mouse click events, your element will "capture" the event and can perform some action in response. For example, if you would like one of your <B> elements to display a message when the user clicks on it, you would tell it that whenever it receives an "onclick" event, to call a function that displays your message.

Previously, the old JavaScript Object Model allowed only certain elements to listen for events. Your form elements could listen for events, as could <A> elements and <BODY> itself. Images also had a few events they could listen for. But the events were few and mostly geared toward form-related issues. Did the user make a change to a text input field? Did she click a button? Submit the form? With the exception of forms, your document was largely unaware of what the user was doing.

The new DOM, on the other hand, allows every one of your elements to listen for dozens of events ranging from mouse clicks to which direction the user is currently moving the mouse. Every part of your document is alive and eager to listen for almost any user action. A whole book alone could be dedicated to the new "event model" and how events interact with each other and your script. Right now, however, I would like to point out a few of the more useful events. Later on we'll examine the event model in a bit more detail.

Every element object can listen for events. Some have specialized events, which only apply to them, such as "onload" for the <BODY> element, however, most will listen for the following four mouse-related events: onclick, ondblclick, onmouseout, and onmouseover. With just these four events you can create some pretty amazing effects!

By the way, since the events are essentially attributes in your HTML, they are not case sensitive. Typically, I like to capitalize every other "word" of the event name, starting with the second word, because I think it makes things a bit more readable. For example, for the onclick event I use onClick. The style you adopt is up to you.

onclick and ondblclick Events

The onclick and ondblclick events are triggered whenever a user clicks on your element with the left mouse button. The onclick event is triggered if the user clicks once, and the ondblclick event if the user double clicks the element. You can tell almost anything to listen for one of these events, including such mundane elements as <B> or <I>!

```
<B onclick="alert('I have just been clicked!')">Click Me</B>
```

This new capability opens a world of neat possibilities! One example we'll show later is an unordered list that can be expanded to show or hide additional list items when any item is clicked.

Believe it or not, there is a lot more involved in the onclick and ondblclick events than this. What happens if you have an onclick event on an <A> element? Does the event trigger, or does the browser follow the link, or both? Do you need to listen for these events on every single one of your elements, or is there a "central location" where all ignored events go that you can examine separately? These are just two of many other issues you may run into later. Right now, however, you know everything you need to use onclick and ondblclick on most of your elements. We'll talk about those other details a bit later, when we cover the event model in more depth and discover the "event object."

Figure 2–14   An onclick event on an <H1> and <B> element. When the element is clicked, in this case the <H1> element, the process_click() function is called and a message is displayed. See Listing 2–11 for details.

```
<HTML>
<HEAD>
<TITLE>A Simple HTML Document</TITLE>
<SCRIPT LANGUAGE="JavaScript">
function process_click(whoWasClicked)
{
  var myTag = whoWasClicked.tagName;
  alert("The " + myTag + " tag was just clicked.");
}
</SCRIPT>
</HEAD>
<BODY>

<H1 onClick="process_click(this)">I can be clicked</H1>
```

```
<P>Please <B onClick="process_click(this)">click me</B>.</P>

</BODY>
</HTML>
```

Listing 2–11

Listing 2–11 shows an example of two elements, an <H1> element and a <B> element, listening for onclick events. If either element is clicked, the process_click function is called with the special "this" variable as its argument. The "this" variable will contain the element object for the function to later process.

One note on the ondblclick event I think you should hear about: your users probably won't expect to have to double click anything on your Web page. Since the start of the Web, links and buttons have always been activated with a single click. At first this caused some confusion among new Web users who were used to double clicking the icons on their desktops to get things working. But after awhile, everyone got used to the single click paradigm. Now your users, if they've been involved with the Web for any length of time at all, understand that single clicking buttons and links is all it takes to get things to happen. But along comes the ondblclick event, and our Web pages now have the ability to react to single or double clicks. I can sense the confusion this is going to cause already! Users who have been single clicking all this time are going to be confronted with well-meaing ondblclick events and are going to find themselves staring expectantly at an unmoving screen after only a single click. I would recommend using ondblclick sparingly, and only with a warning to your users. To prevent confusion, use the single onclick event instead.

onmouseout and onmouseover Events

The onmouseout and onmouseover events work together to let you know when the mouse goes over one of your elements. When the mouse pointer first enters your element, the onmouseover event is called. You can take this opportunity to highlight the current text or maybe change the text to be a bit more descriptive. When the mouse pointer leaves the element again, the onmouseout event is triggered, which you can use to set things back to normal.

These can be two very powerful events, however, you can also annoy your users to no end with them. Try not to make any changes, which these events trigger, too dramatic, or you can end up shocking or confusing your users. Opening a new window or, yet, popping open an "alert" box is even worse. These events are best used to trigger subtle changes such as highlights.

```
<HTML>
<HEAD>
<TITLE>A Simple HTML Document</TITLE>
<SCRIPT LANGUAGE="JavaScript">
function process_over(overWho)
{
```

Listing 2–12

```
    overWho.innerText = "over";
  }
  function process_out(overWho)
  {
    overWho.innerText = "not over";
  }
  </SCRIPT>
  </HEAD>
  <BODY>

  <P>The mouse is currently
  <B onMouseOver="process_over(this)" onMouseOut ="process_out
    (this)">
  not over</B> me.</P>

  </BODY>
  </HTML>
```

Listing 2–12   *Continued*

Listing 2–12 shows an example of how to use the onmouseover and onmouseout events on a <B> element. When the mouse goes over the element, the process_over() function is called and the message "not over" is changed to "over." When the mouse is moved out of the element, the process_out() function is called and the message is changed back to "not over." If you type this one in, watch the position of your pointer! If the pointer "goes over" the element near its right edge, the element will actually shrink and the pointer will suddenly be "not over" the element! This causes the element to flicker between "over" and "not over" rapidly. It's one of those little pitfalls that can drive you crazy if you're not expecting it! There is no screen shot to go with this listing, because the effect is largely lost when printed out.

There are of course plenty of other events, but these four will serve you well through the rest of this chapter. Later on, we'll have a look at most of the important events at your disposal for a variety of other elements and how they fit in with the "event model."

SPAN AND DIV: CONTEXT INDEPENDENT ELEMENTS

Our HTML elements can now be modified, deleted, and new ones added. We can even have elements listen for events such as mouse clicks or the mouse pointer brushing past. But not all your text is inside <B> or <I> elements, and sometimes you may want to perform these amazing feats on plain, regular text. One possibility is accessing the text directly inside your <P> element, but that can be very inconvenient or even impossible. Take the following HTML as an example:

```
  <P>I am some example HTML!</P>
```

What do you do if you want to take the word "example" and have it listen for events or change to all capital letters without affecting the rest of the paragraph? Well, you can't have just that one word listen for events without the entire paragraph listening as well, and it would be rather a pain to have to change the entire paragraph just to modify that one word's capitalization. You could place it inside a <B> or <I> element, but you don't want it bold or in italics. Making it a paragraph of its own won't work either, since that will break up the flow of your text. The solution? The "context independent" <SPAN> and <DIV> elements!

Context independent is just a fancy way of saying "they don't make special changes to your text." By using <SPAN> or <DIV>, you can create a separate little element that can be accessed just like your other elements, but without making them bold, or italics, or starting a new paragraph. In other words, they act like containers that can hold some text for you to access a bit easier with your script. You can put as many <SPAN> or <DIV> elements anywhere you want in your document, and your users will never be the wiser for it.

```
<P>I am some <SPAN>example</SPAN> HTML!</P>
```

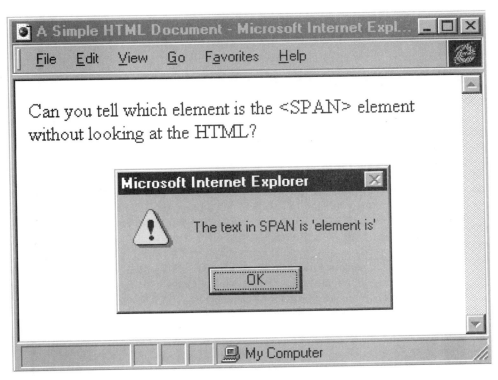

Figure 2–15 Can you spot the <SPAN> element without looking at the HTML in Listing 2–13?

The <SPAN> Element

The <SPAN> element was originally designed as a "generic" tag that could be cus-
tomized using style sheets. We'll learn about style sheets later. Right now, <SPAN> gives
us an excellent vehicle for specifying an arbitrary chunk of text for dynamic content. Use
<SPAN> whenever you need an element but don't want to affect how the text is dis-
played. The code in Listing 2–13 shows an example of <SPAN>.

```
<HTML>
<HEAD>
<TITLE>A Simple HTML Document</TITLE>
<SCRIPT LANGUAGE="JavaScript">
function show_message()
{
  alert("The text in SPAN is '" + document.all.MySpan.inner-
    Text + "'");
}
</SCRIPT>
</HEAD>
<BODY onLoad="show_message()">

<P>Can you tell which <SPAN ID="MySpan">element is</SPAN> the
&lt;SPAN&gt; element without looking at the HTML?</P>

</BODY>
</HTML>
```

Listing 2–13

The <DIV> Element

You're probably familiar with <DIV> from its use as an alternate to <CENTER>. Or if you're
an HTML purist you know <CENTER> as shorthand for <DIV ALIGN=CENTER>. Either
way, the official HTML 3.2 specifications say <DIV> is a way to "structure HTML documents
as a hierarchy of divisions," whatever that means. In practice, without its "ALIGN" attribute,
it does absolutely nothing to the text it contains. It does differ from <SPAN> in one way, however; it is a block element while <SPAN> is inline. What this means to you is that <DIV> will
automatically "terminate" your <P> element, or technically any other block elements, causing
a line break before and after it. Inline elements like <SPAN> don't do this.

```
<HTML>
<HEAD>
<TITLE>A Simple HTML Document</TITLE>
<SCRIPT LANGUAGE="JavaScript">
function show_message()
{
```

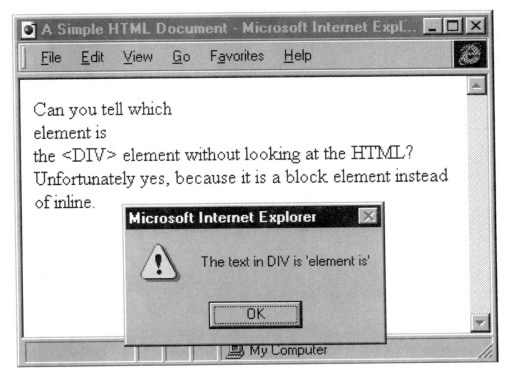

Figure 2–16 The <DIV> element can be used as a context independent element, however, it is a block element so it will terminate your paragraphs.

```
        alert("The text in DIV is '" + document.all.MyDiv.innerText +
          "'");
}
</SCRIPT>
</HEAD>
<BODY onLoad="show_message()">

<P>Can you tell which <DIV ID="MyDiv">element is</DIV> the
&lt;DIV&gt; element without looking at the HTML? Unfortunately
yes, because it is a block element instead of inline.</P>

</BODY>
</HTML>
```

Listing 2–14

What use is <DIV> over <SPAN>? Not much, from what I can tell, but I see <DIV> used as a context independent element frequently so I thought I'd mention it. I guess if you want to use a block element for dynamic content, this is what you would use.

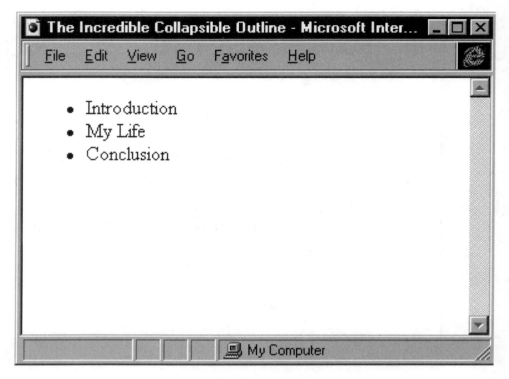

Figure 2–17a   The initial outline.

THE INCREDIBLE COLLAPSIBLE OUTLINE

One of the trendier uses of dynamic content has been the creation of collapsible menus and "outlines" for your Web pages. In retrospect, this was the trendy use for Java as well. I wonder if all webmasters really want are collapsible outlines? In any event, let's put some of this new knowledge to use and design a simple collapsible outline script. We'll make the design criteria very simple for now and later expand the script as we discover new techniques. The outline should start collapsed, with only the top level headings showing at first. When the user clicks on one of the headings, that part of the outline should expand to show more detail. When the user clicks the heading again, that part of the outline should collapse back to its original state. Let's also make sure the user knows that the headings can be clicked by having them become bold when the mouse pointer goes over them.

```
<HTML>
<HEAD>
<TITLE>The Incredible Collapsible Outline</TITLE>
<SCRIPT LANGUAGE="JavaScript">
var first = 0; // Is 0 if the list is collapsed, 1 if
  expanded.
```

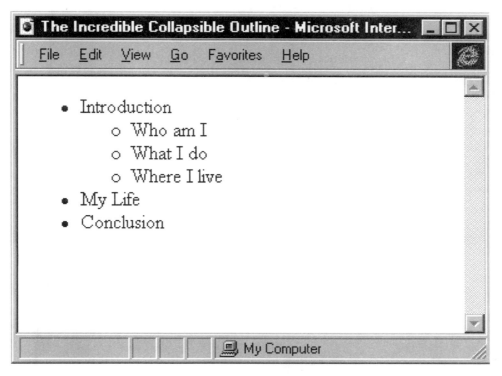

Figure 2–17b   The outline after the user clicks on the first "Introduction" heading.

```
function expander(whichOne)
{
  if (whichOne == 1) // The user clicked the first item
  {
    var secondList = document.all.Expand_1; // The "sublist"
      element
    if (first)   // "first" is 1, so the list should be
      collapsed
    {
      secondList.innerHTML = "";
      first = 0; // So we know the list is collapsed
    }
    else
    {            // The list needs to be expanded
```

Listing 2–15

```
        secondList.innerHTML = "<LI>Who am I";
        secondList.insertAdjacentHTML("BeforeEnd","<LI>What I
          do");
        secondList.insertAdjacentHTML("BeforeEnd","<LI>Where I
          live");
        first = 1; // So we know the list is expanded
      }
    }
    else
    {
      alert("Under construction!");
    }
  }

</SCRIPT>
</HEAD>
<BODY>

<UL>
<LI><SPAN ID="Title_1" onClick="expander(1)">Introduction</
  SPAN><UL ID="Expand_1"></UL>
<LI><SPAN ID="Title_2" onClick="expander(2)">My Life</SPAN>
 <UL ID="Expand_2"></UL>
<LI><SPAN ID="Title_3" onClick="expander(3)">Conclusion</SPAN>
 <UL ID="Expand_3"></UL>
</UL>

</BODY>
</HTML>
```

Listing 2–15 *Continued*

For the first pass of the problem, I've created a short HTML outline using an unordered list, in Listing 2–15. Ignore the script for a moment and take a look at the HTML
in the <BODY>. There are three list items, which will act as our top headings. Each item
is inside a <SPAN> element, which have been given the identifiers "Title_1" through
"Title_3." This is where the user will click to expand and collapse the outline. See the
onclick event? That is where we call our expander() function, with the number of the item
to expand or collapse. I could have put the onclick event directly on each <LI> element,
or the <UL> element for that matter, but I want the click to work only on the headings.
Anyway, it's a good excuse to show <SPAN> in action.

Under each list item is also another, currently empty, unordered list. This is where
we will build the expanded part of our expanding outline. When the user clicks on the first
list item, the unordered list "Expand_1" will be populated with additional items. When

the user clicks on the second item, the unordered list "Expand_2" will be expanded, and so forth. Figures 2–17a and 2–17b show the list before expanding and after.

The script itself consists of only one function, expander(), which will expand and collapse the lists. There is also a single global variable, "first," which will allow us to track the state of the list—if it is currently expanded or collapsed. When the user clicks on one of the items, our expander() function is called with a sort of index number, "whichOne," indicating which item was clicked. To simplify things at first, our function will only work on the first item. If the others are clicked (whichOne is 2 or 3) an alert with the message "Under construction!" is displayed. Actually, there is a bit of irony there, when you look at the items that give the message: My Life and Conclusion!

The first thing that happens when the right item is found, in our case item 1, is the variable "secondList" is assigned the element object for the second unordered "sublist." Once done, the value of the global variable "first" is checked. We're using "first" to record the state of the list. In other words, if that part of the outline is currently expanded and needs to be collapsed, or is collapsed and should be expanded. If "first" is true (equal to 1) the list is already expanded and should be collapsed. If it is false (equal to 0), as is the case when the outline is first displayed, we need to expand. Let's look at expanding first.

Expanding is as simple as inserting new <LI> elements into the appropriate unordered list. The first command uses the innerHTML property to insert the first <LI> element. The next two use insertAdjacentHTML() to insert the remaining two items. I could have used innerHTML to insert the new list all at once:

```
secondList.innerHTML = "<LI>Who am I\n<LI>What I
do\n<LI>Where I live";
```

I could also have also used insertAdjacentHTML() for all three items. But this way, we get to see how innerHTML and insertAdjacentHTML can be used together in an actual application. The final action is to set the "first" variable to 1, so the next time the user clicks we know that this part of the outline is already expanded and needs to be collapsed again, instead. Figure 2–17b shows the outline with the first item expanded.

Collapsing is even easier than expanding. Look back up at the section of code directly above the expanding code, before that first "else." To collapse the outline, all we need to do is delete all of the <LI> elements. Assigning a null to the list element object in this manner:

```
secondList.innerHTML = "";
```

does the trick. All the elements and their text are deleted and the list appears to "disappear." We then assign 0 to the "first" variable, so the script knows it needs to expand the list next time around, and we're done. Incidently, we could have used innerText as well—things would have been deleted just the same. Don't use the outerText or outerHTML properties here, though, because that would delete the <UL> element as well as its contents, and we wouldn't be able to expand the list again!

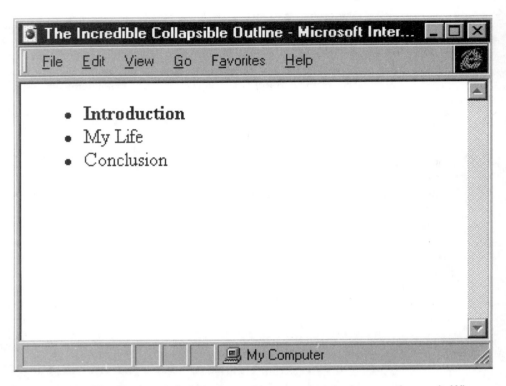

Figure 2–18   The first item is bold because the mouse pointer is currently over it. When the mouse leaves the element, it will return to normal text.

```
<HTML>
<HEAD>
<TITLE>The Incredible Collapsible Outline</TITLE>
<SCRIPT LANGUAGE="JavaScript">
var first = 0; // Is 0 if the list is collapsed, 1 if
  expanded.

function expander(whichOne)
{
  if (whichOne == 1) // The user clicked the first item
  {
    var secondList = document.all.Expand_1; // The "sublist"
      element
    if (first) // "first" is 1, so the list should be
      collapsed
    {
      secondList.innerHTML = "";
      first = 0; // So we know the list is collapsed
    }
    else
```

```
    {         // The list needs to be expanded
      secondList.innerHTML = "<LI>Who am I";
      secondList.insertAdjacentHTML("BeforeEnd","<LI>What I
        do");
      secondList.insertAdjacentHTML("BeforeEnd","<LI>Where I
        live");
      first = 1; // So we know the list is expanded
    }
  }
  else
  {
    alert("Under construction!");
  }
}
// sets the element bold
function gotMouse(whichOne)
{
  var myElement = document.all(whichOne); // Get element based
    on ID
  var theText = myElement.innerText; // Get the element's text

  myElement.innerHTML = "<B>" + theText + "</B>"; // Make it
    bold
}

// returns the element to normal
function lostMouse(whichOne)
{
  var myElement = document.all(whichOne); // Get element based
    on ID
  var theText = myElement.innerText; // Get the element's text

  myElement.innerText = theText; // Write text back to element
}

</SCRIPT>
</HEAD>
<BODY>

<UL>
<LI><SPAN ID="Title_1" onClick="expander(1)"
        onMouseOver="gotMouse('Title_1')"
        onMouseOut="lostMouse('Title_1')">Introduction</SPAN>
  <UL ID="Expand_1"></UL>
<LI><SPAN ID="Title_2" onClick="expander(2)"
        onMouseOver="gotMouse('Title_2')"
        onMouseOut="lostMouse('Title_2')">My Life</SPAN>
```

Listing 2–16

```
  <UL ID="Expand_2"></UL>
<LI><SPAN ID="Title_3" onClick="expander(3)"
          onMouseOver="gotMouse('Title_3')"
          onMouseOut="lostMouse('Title_3')">Conclusion</SPAN>
  <UL ID="Expand_3"></UL>
</UL>

</BODY>
</HTML>
```

Listing 2–16   *Continued*

With all that said and done, Listing 2–16 adds the two new functions and extra HTML needed to implement our "bold" feature. If you look back down at the <SPAN> elements, you will see that each list item now has an onmouseover and onmouseout event. Now, whenever the mouse goes over the <SPAN> element, onmouseover will call the gotMouse() function, and when the mouse leaves the element, the lostMouse() function will be called. One interesting thing is that this time, instead of using an arbitrary index number to represent the list item we're dealing with, I actually send the ID name. Let's look at the two new functions and see why.

The first function is gotMouse(), which is triggered by an onmouseover event. When gotMouse() is called, the first thing it does is take that ID name and use the "All" collection to retrieve the actual element object directly and assign it to the "myElement" variable. We then take "myElement" and retrieve its innerText property. Now all we need to do is use the innerHTML property to put a <B> element around the text and we're done. When the user moves the mouse over the element, the text will suddenly become bold!

I decided to pass the name of the element ID and use the "All" collection to get the object, to show the versatility the "All" collection gives you to retrieve element objects. But this isn't the only way we could have done this—it isn't even the most efficient. If we wanted to really get to the point quickly, it would have been much easier to pass the "this" variable to our function, instead of the ID name. The "this" variable stands for "the current element object," and we could have used it directly instead of resorting to an "All" lookup. Take this variation of the gotMouse() function:

```
function gotMouse(myElement)
{
    var theText = myElement.innerText;

    myElement.innerHTML = "<B>" + theText + "<\B>";
}
```

If we replace the old onmouseover with the following one:

```
onMouseOver="gotMouse(this)"
```

then "myElement" would contain the element object directly, and there would be no reason to use the "All" collection to translate the ID name into an actual object. As they say, there's more than one way to do it. What makes a good programmer a great programmer is the ability to find the most efficient way to perform a specific task. But even that is somewhat subjective—sometimes the best code is simply the code that works.

The lostMouse() function is called by onmouseout, when the user moves the mouse pointer of the element. It works much like gotMouse(), except instead of adding a <B> element it removes it. When first called, lostMouse() does the exact same thing as got-Mouse(). First it takes the ID name and uses the "All" collection to retrieve the associated object. The innerText property is then used to fetch the text that needs to be unbolded. Only the final line of code is different. Instead of wrapping a <B> element around the retrieved text using the innerHTML property, the text is written directly back using inner-Text and the <B> element disappears!

How the <B> element gets stripped out is actually so simple it is elusive. At first glance, it appears as though the work is happening in the last line, where we use innerText to write the text back instead of innerHTML. Since innerText won't write HTML, the text will end up with the <B> element stripped out. But on second glance, if the <B> element was still in the text, innerText would actually include the <B> and </B> tags with the rest of your text creating a big mess. Obviously the <B> element is being stripped out before they ever get to this point. Where is this happening? In the second line, where we read the text:

```
var theText = myElement.innerText;
```

Remember, when you use innerText to read from your element, all your HTML tags are automatically stripped out. So, the <B> element is removed because you use innerText to read the element, not because you use innerText to write the text back!

```
<HTML>
<HEAD>
<TITLE>The Incredible Collapsible Outline</TITLE>
<SCRIPT LANGUAGE="JavaScript">
var first = 0; // Is 0 if the list is collapsed, 1 if
  expanded.
var second= 0; // Same as "first" except for second list
var third = 0; // Same as "first" except for third list

function expander(whichOne)
{
   if (whichOne == 1) // The user clicked the first item
   {
```

Listing 2–17

```
  var secondList = document.all.Expand_1; // The "sublist"
    element
  if (first) // "first" is 1, so the list should be
    collapsed
  {
    secondList.innerHTML = "";
    first = 0; // So we know the list is collapsed
  }
  else
  {          // The list needs to be expanded
    secondList.innerHTML = "<LI>Who am I";
    secondList.insertAdjacentHTML("BeforeEnd","<LI>What I
      do");
    secondList.insertAdjacentHTML("BeforeEnd","<LI>Where I
      live");
    first = 1; // So we know the list is expanded
  }
}
else if (whichOne == 2) // The user clicked the second item
{
  var secondList = document.all.Expand_2; // The "sublist"
    element
  if (second) // "second" is 1, so the list should be
    collapsed
  {
    secondList.innerHTML = "";
    second = 0; // So we know the list is collapsed
  }
  else
  {          // The list needs to be expanded
    secondList.innerHTML = "<LI>I was born";
    secondList.insertAdjacentHTML("BeforeEnd","<LI>I got
      married");
    secondList.insertAdjacentHTML("BeforeEnd","<LI>I paid
      taxes");
    secondList.insertAdjacentHTML("BeforeEnd","<LI>Wrote a
      book");
    secondList.insertAdjacentHTML("BeforeEnd","<LI>More tax
      joy");
    second = 1; // So we know the list is expanded
  }
}
else // By default, the user must have clicked the third item
{
  var secondList = document.all.Expand_3; // The "sublist"
    element
  if (third) // "third" is 1, so the list should be
    collapsed
  {
```

```
        secondList.innerHTML = "";
        third = 0; // So we know the list is collapsed
      }
      else
      {          // The list needs to be expanded
        secondList.innerHTML = "<LI>Not done here yet!";
        third = 1; // So we know the list is expanded
      }
    }
}
// sets the element bold
function gotMouse(whichOne)
{
  var myElement = document.all(whichOne); // Get element based
    on ID
  var theText = myElement.innerText; // Get the element's text

  myElement.innerHTML = "<B>" + theText + "</B>"; // Make it bold
}

// returns the element to normal
function lostMouse(whichOne)
{
  var myElement = document.all(whichOne); // Get element based
    on ID
  var theText = myElement.innerText; // Get the element's text

  myElement.innerText = theText; // Write text back to element
}

</SCRIPT>
</HEAD>
<BODY>

<UL>
<LI><SPAN ID="Title_1" onClick="expander(1)"
          onMouseOver="gotMouse('Title_1')"
          onMouseOut="lostMouse('Title_1')">Introduction</SPAN>
  <UL ID="Expand_1"></UL>
<LI><SPAN ID="Title_2" onClick="expander(2)"
           onMouseOver="gotMouse('Title_2')"
           onMouseOut="lostMouse('Title_2')">My Life</SPAN>
  <UL ID="Expand_2"></UL>
<LI><SPAN ID="Title_3" onClick="expander(3)"
           onMouseOver="gotMouse('Title_3')"
           onMouseOut="lostMouse('Title_3')">Conclusion</SPAN>
```

Listing 2–17

```
    <UL ID="Expand_3"></UL>
  </UL>

  </BODY>
  </HTML>
```

Listing 2–17   *Continued*

The completed code for the entire outline can be found in Listing 2–17. In this version, two new global variables are added, "second" and "third," which are used to keep track of the state of their respective parts of the outline. The expander() function has also been expanded to take care of the second and third parts of the outline.

The Incredible Collapsible Outline was designed to show most of the things we've learned in a real application, but I admit it isn't the most efficient way to accomplish the task and there are a number of problems that would need to be addressed before using it on your own Web pages. The most glaring problem to me is that even with the "bold" feature, it still isn't clear that the outline can be clicked on to be expanded because the mouse pointer does not change like it does when over a link. Another problem is that the outline isn't very customizable—anything longer or more complex than this will become tedious to program using this method. But hopefully it has served its purpose and shown how dynamic content works in a real application. Later we will revisit the expanding outline with some more advanced techniques.

TEXT RANGES AND SELECTIONS: THE TEXTRANGE OBJECT

Using the properties and methods above, you have an incredible amount of control over your document. Sometimes, however, you may be interested in working with text that is not necessarily associated with any one element or that is otherwise difficult to get at with the means discussed so far. For example, how do you access that text you just inserted outside your element with insertAdjacentText? Text Ranges gives you control over an arbitrary chunk of text, from the entire document down to a single character. At the same time, it also supplies a mechanism for performing searches for a specific text string inside your range.

To create a text range, you will first need to create a TextRange object. The TextRange object has two properties: to hold your range's contents, and over two dozen methods to manipulate the range. Typically, you will use the createTextRange() method, found on the "body object," to create your range. You can also access the createTextRange() method from a text-type <INPUT> element, a <TEXTAREA> element, and Internet Explorer's <BUTTON> element, but we will concentrate on the body object.

The body object can be found on the document object directly, or from the "All" collection as the HTML <BODY> element. I prefer accessing it from the document object since there is less typing involved, and the less typing required to accomplish a task, the better!

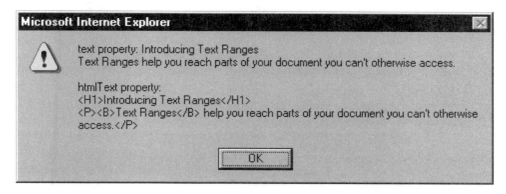

Figure 2–19 The output from the text and htmlText properties of our range.

When you call the createTextRange() method, it will return a TextRange object on success, or null on failure. You will want to assign the results to a variable, or you'll end up with a TextRange object you can't do anything with! Your new object will contain everything inside your document's body.

```
var myRange = document.body.createTextRange();
```

Now that you have your TextRange object, you can examine its contents using the "text" and "htmlText" properties. Like the "innerText" property on element objects, the "text" property contains text with the HTML elements stripped out. The "htmlText" property includes the HTML with the text, just like the "innerHTML" property.

```
<HTML>
<HEAD>
<TITLE>Text Ranges</TITLE>
<SCRIPT LANGUAGE="JavaScript">
function show_range()
{
  var myRange = document.body.createTextRange();

  alert("text property: " + myRange.text + "\n\n" +
  "htmlText property: " + myRange.htmlText );
}
</SCRIPT>
</HEAD>
<BODY onLoad="show_range()">

<H1>Introducing Text Ranges</H1>
```

Listing 2–18

```
<P><B>Text Ranges</B> help you reach parts of your document
you can't otherwise access.</P>

</BODY>
</HTML>
```

Listing 2–18   *Continued*

The "text" property can be written to as well as read from, just like "innerText." Right now, however, this isn't terribly useful, unless your goal is a document with no HTML formatting! The "htmlText" property won't help us much, either, because unlike "text," this property is read-only. Instead of writing directly to "htmlText," we'll have to use the TextRange object's pasteHTML() method. If you're wondering why things were implemented this way, so am I. In any event, attempting to write to "htmlText" directly will produce an error.

pasteHTML() method

The pasteHTML() method is pretty simple. It accepts only one argument, the HTML and text you want to paste into the range, and has no return code because it never fails.

```
myRange.pasteHTML("<B>I am some text and HTML</B>");
```

Make sure that your HTML is valid and properly formatted since pasteHTML() actively tries to make sense out of it before pasting it into your range. The result is usually interesting but rarely what you were hoping for. Read on for some examples of the pasteHTML() method.

Redefining the Scope of Your Range

Text ranges aren't terribly exciting without the ability to redefine where the range starts and stops. Fortunately the TextRange object comes armed with several methods just for this purpose. After creating your range object with createTextRange(), use one or more of these methods to fine tune precisely which part of the document your range encloses.

moveToElementText() method

The moveToElementText() method redefines your range to enclose any given element object. It accepts one argument, the target element object. Be certain you give it the actual object, as found in the "All" collective and not just its index number or identifier name. For example, to set the range for the element

```
<H1 ID="MyElement">Hello There!</H1>
```

you would say

```
myRange.moveToElementText( document.all.MyElement );
```

where "myRange" is whatever you called the range created with createTextRange(). Now, instead of the entire document, your range will include only this element. You can use pasteHTML() or the range's "text" property to modify this fragment of your document.

```
<HTML>
<HEAD>
<TITLE>Text Ranges</TITLE>
<SCRIPT LANGUAGE="JavaScript">
function show_range()
{
  var myRange = document.body.createTextRange();

  myRange.moveToElementText( document.all.Level_1 );
  myRange.text = "An Introduction to Text Ranges";

  myRange.moveToElementText( document.all.Bold_1 );
  myRange.pasteHTML( "<I>Text Ranges</I>" );
}
</SCRIPT>
</HEAD>
<BODY onLoad="show_range()">

<H1 ID="Level_1">Introducing Text Ranges</H1>

<P><B ID="Bold_1">Text Ranges</B> help you reach parts of your
document you can't otherwise access.</P>

</BODY>
</HTML>
```

Listing 2–19

After you've made changes to your text range through the text property or the paste-HTML() method, your range is automatically "collapsed" and must be reset before attempting to use it again. A range is said to be collapsed when its starting point and ending point are set to equal the same spot in your document. In other words, the range because "one-dimensional." I'll cover this in a bit more detail later.

One pitfall I've noticed is that even though the documentation suggests that only the text inside the tags, and not the start and end tags themselves, are included in the range, this isn't necessarily the case. Displaying the contents of the range using the "htmlText" property, sometimes shows both start and end tags and sometimes only the start tag, but using pasteHTML() or editing the "text" property directly seems to include neither. Whether this is a bug or an "undocumented feature" is unclear and one of the pitfalls of working with beta software, I suppose. In any event, I'm sure this odd behavior will be fixed soon.

In spite of the strange behavior mentioned above, moveToElementText() is a good way to define a "rough" position for your range.

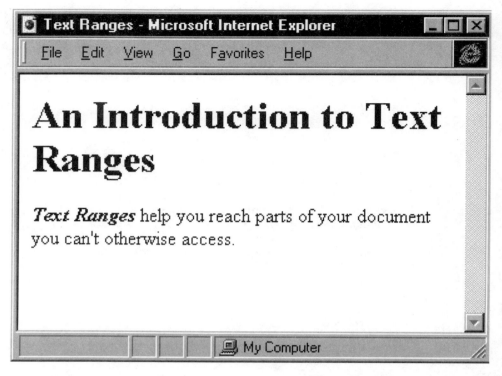

Figure 2–20 You can write to the text property of your range directly, but if you want to write to the htmlText property, you need to go through the pasteHTML() method. The moveToElementText() method allows us to move our ranges between elements.

moveStart() and moveEnd() Methods

You can then refine things a bit using the moveStart() and moveEnd() methods. As the names imply, moveStart() moves the starting point of your range, and moveEnd() moves the ending point. Both methods accept two arguments. The first argument is a keyword defining what units to use in determining how far to move the start or end point. The second argument is the count, or number of units to move. If omitted, it defaults to one.

- "character" will move on a character by character basis.
- "word" will move this number of words.
- "sentence" will move this number of sentences, a sentence being a group of words ending with a puncuation mark.
- "textedit" moves back to the original range.

The count can be negative or positive. A negative count with moveStart() will expand the range's scope by that many units to the left of the range's original start point, and a pos-

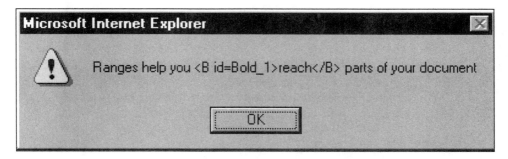

Figure 2–21 Moving the starting and ending points of a text range. Notice how the end point appears to have moved one less word to the right then we requested? That is because the space right after the <B> element "tricks" the moveEnd() method into thinking there is an extra word. It's a feature.

itive count will shrink the range to the right. With the moveEnd() method, a negative count shrinks the range by moving the end of the range closer to its start, and a positive number expands the range to the right. If you're curious, if you "shrink" the range too much you'll end up with an "empty" range. Try not to overlap your start and end points—your browser will get a headache. Both methods return the number of units actually moved.

```
<HTML>
<HEAD>
<TITLE>Text Ranges</TITLE>
<SCRIPT LANGUAGE="JavaScript">
function show_range()
{
  var myRange = document.body.createTextRange();

  myRange.moveToElementText( document.all.Bold_1 );
  myRange.moveStart("word", -3);
  myRange.moveEnd("word", 5);

  alert(myRange.htmlText);
}
</SCRIPT>
</HEAD>
<BODY onLoad="show_range()">
<H1>Introducing Text Ranges</H1>

<P>Text Ranges help you <B ID="Bold_1">reach</B> parts of your
document you can't otherwise access.</P>

</BODY>
</HTML>
```

Listing 2–20

When your units are "word" or "sentence," sometimes moveEnd() may not behave exactly as you would expect. The problem occurs when a space, in the case of "word," or punctuation mark when using "sentence," is already at the end of your range. In this case, moveEnd() will count that space or punctuation mark as one unit, making it appear as though your range didn't move at all. If it looks like you're getting one less unit than you're asking for, make sure this isn't what's happening!

collapse() and expand() Methods

Collapsing a range refers to making the start point of your range equal the end point, essentially creating a range that contains nothing. The collapse() method does just this. It takes one boolean argument. If the argument is "true," the range is collapsed to the start of the range. If the argument is "false," the range is collapsed to the end of the range. With no arguments, the method defaults to "true."

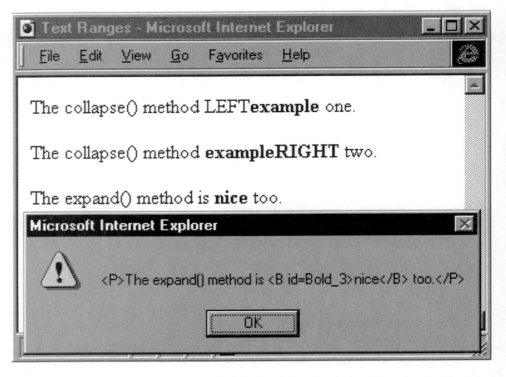

Figure 2–22 Collapsing to the start point, collapsing to the end point, and expanding to an entire sentence. *Note* when collapsing to the start point, the inserted text is pasted outside the element, but when collapsing to the end point, the inserted text is pasted just inside the element.

Why you would want to collapse a range is another question. Basically, it provides a convenient way to insert text or HTML at the beginning or end of your range. Collapse the range with "true," and any text or HTML that is pasted into your collapsed range is actually inserted at the point where your range had previously started. Collapse the range with "false," and you can insert at the point where your range had previously ended.

Now that your range is collapsed, you can use the expand() method to make it bigger again. It accepts one argument, the type of unit it should expand to: "character," "word," "sentence," or "textedit." Expand is nice because you can tell it to expand your range to contain just the word your collapsed range is on or the entire sentence. If your range already contains a word or two, but you really want it to contain the entire sentence, you can use the expand() method for that as well.

```html
<HTML>
<HEAD>
<TITLE>Text Ranges</TITLE>
<SCRIPT LANGUAGE="JavaScript">
function show_range()
{
  var myRange = document.body.createTextRange();

  myRange.moveToElementText( document.all.Bold_1 );
  myRange.collapse( true );
  myRange.pasteHTML( "LEFT" );

  myRange.moveToElementText( document.all.Bold_2 );
  myRange.collapse( false );
  myRange.pasteHTML( "RIGHT" );

  myRange.moveToElementText( document.all.Bold_3 );
  myRange.expand( "sentence" );
  alert( myRange.htmlText );
}
</SCRIPT>
</HEAD>
<BODY onLoad="show_range()">

<P>The collapse() method <B ID="Bold_1">example</B> one.</P>
<P>The collapse() method <B ID="Bold_2">example</B> two.</P>
<P>The expand() method is <B ID="Bold_3">nice</B> too.</P>

</BODY>
</HTML>
```

Listing 2–21

move() method

If you need to move your range a few units to the left or right, another method at your disposal is the move() method. Like most of the other movement methods, the first argument is the type of unit and the second is the count. The default count is one. When you perform the move() method, your range is collapsed to the start point of the range. The range is then moved the number of units specified. You can then use one of the other movement methods to redefine your end point, including expand().

moveToPoint() method

The methods up to this point have all based their movement on characters, words, and sentences, and other elements. The moveToPoint() method gives you control at the pixel level. The two arguments are the x and y coordinates relative to the upper left corner of the browser window. Both the start and end points of your range are set to the coordinates, so you are left with an empty range. You should then use the expand() method to "snap" your range to the nearest text.

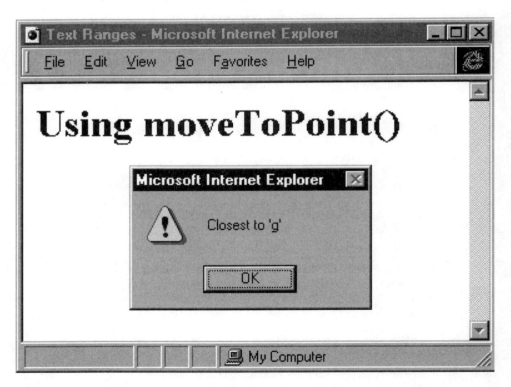

Figure 2–23   The closest character to the x,y coordinate 75,5 is apparently the letter *g*. The coordinates are measured from the upper-left corner of the document.

```
<HTML>
<HEAD>
<TITLE>Text Ranges</TITLE>
<SCRIPT LANGUAGE="JavaScript">
function show_range()
{
  var myRange = document.body.createTextRange();

  myRange.moveToPoint(75,5);
  myRange.expand("character");

  alert( "Closest to '" + myRange.htmlText + "'" );
}
</SCRIPT>
</HEAD>
<BODY onLoad="show_range()">

<H1>Using moveToPoint()</H1>

</BODY>
</HTML>
```

Listing 2–22

Trying to position a range using x and y coordinates may appear cumbersome at first; however, it becomes extremely useful when using information returned from other methods and events, such as the position of the user's mouse pointer. We'll examine some of those techniques later.

Range Bookmarks

Sometimes you might want to move a range for a minute and then snap back to the original range. Or perhaps you want to set up several ranges and flip between them without going through all the trouble of redefining the start and end points every single time. The concept of "range bookmarks" allows you to take a snapshot of your range's position and return to the same position later with a single command.

To create a range bookmark, you will use the getBookmark() method and assign its return value to a variable. The method doesn't require any arguments and returns a string if successful, or a null on failure. If you view the string, you'll find it full of random garbage. This is because the string actually contains a specially encoded representation of the range that the browser will use to reconstruct your range later.

When you're ready to restore your range, you will use the moveToBookmark() method. It accepts one argument, the string returned by getBookmark(). It returns true on success or false on failure. Your range's start and end positions will both be restored, however, if the contents of the original range have been modified, the range will be collapsed to the start point.

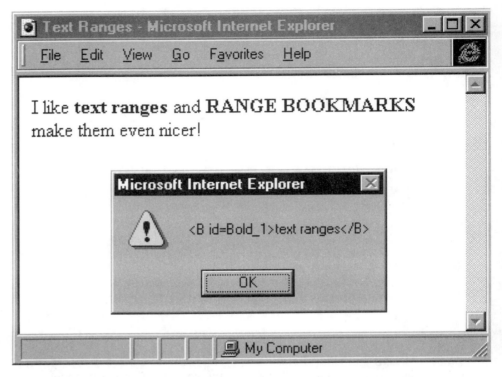

Figure 2–24   The getBookmark() and moveToBookmark() methods in action.

```
<HTML>
<HEAD>
<TITLE>Text Ranges</TITLE>
<SCRIPT LANGUAGE="JavaScript">
function show_range()
{
  var myRange = document.body.createTextRange();
  var myBookmark = "";

  myRange.moveToElementText( document.all.Bold_1 );
  myBookmark = myRange.getBookmark();

  myRange.moveToElementText( document.all.Bold_2 );
  myRange.text = "RANGE BOOKMARKS";

  myRange.moveToBookmark( myBookmark );
  alert( myRange.htmlText );
}
</SCRIPT>
```

```
</HEAD>
<BODY onLoad="show_range()">

<P>I like <B ID="Bold_1">text ranges</B> and <B
ID="Bold_2">range bookmarks</B> make them even nicer!</P>

</BODY>
</HTML>
```

Listing 2–23

In Listing 2–23, a single text range is created and set to enclose the first <B> element, "Bold_1." A bookmark is then taken with the getBookmark() method and assigned to the string "myBookmark" so it can be retrieved later. The range is then moved to the second <B> element, "Bold_2," so we can change that text to all capitals. The moveToBookmark() method is then used to set the range back to "Bold_1," and the contents of the range are displayed. All this excitement is captured in Figure 2–24.

Manipulating Multiple Ranges

There are no rules that say you can't define more than one range at a time. Every time you call createTextRange(), you're creating another range completely independent of all your other ranges. There are even several methods at your disposal for performing such tasks as duplicating, comparing, and combining your ranges.

duplicate() method

One quick way of creating a new range, besides createTextRange(), is using the duplicate() method. By performing a duplicate() on your original range, you can create an exact copy to move and manipulate separately. The duplicate() method doesn't require any arguments, and returns a new range which is a copy of the original. You may be wondering why you can't just use the JavaScript equals (=) operator to make a copy.

```
myRange = myRange2; // Doesn't do what you might expect!
```

The equals operator may give the illusion of copying your range, but in reality what you end up with is two variables pointing to the exact same range! Everything you do to the first range will be done to the second. The duplicate() method, on the other hand, actually creates an entirely new and separate range object that can be operated on independently.

```
<HTML>
<HEAD>
<TITLE>Text Ranges</TITLE>
<SCRIPT LANGUAGE="JavaScript">
```

Listing 2–24

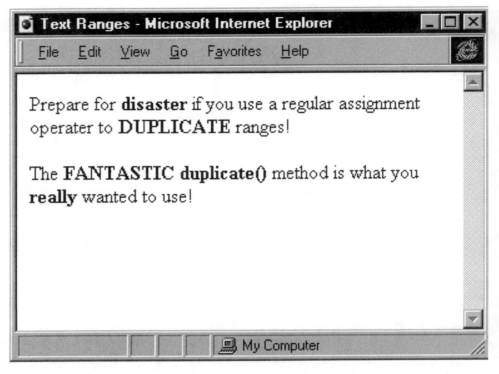

Figure 2–25 A failed attempt at duplicating a range with an assignment operator and a successful attempt using the duplicate() method.

```
function show_range()
{
  var myRange = document.body.createTextRange();
  var myBookmark = "";

  myRange.moveToElementText( document.all.Bold_1 );
  myBookmark = myRange.getBookmark();

  myRange.moveToElementText( document.all.Bold_2 );
  myRange.text = "RANGE BOOKMARKS";

  myRange.moveToBookmark( myBookmark );
  alert( myRange.htmlText );
}
</SCRIPT>
</HEAD>
<BODY onLoad="show_range()">

<P>I like <B ID="Bold_1">text ranges</B> and <B
ID="Bold_2">range bookmarks</B> make them even nicer!</P>
```

```
</BODY>
</HTML>
```

Listing 2–24 *Continued*

Look at Listing 2–24 carefully. First, a single text range is created, "myRange," and the variable "myRange2" is also declared but not initialized. The "myRange" range is then set for the element "Bold_1" and an attempt at "duplicating" the range with an assignment operator is then made. But as you'll soon see, instead of duplicating the range, all I've done is make two variables, "myRange" and "myRange2" point to the same range! In the next two lines of code, I move "myRange2" to the element "Bold_2," but when I write to the "myRange" variable's range, with the assumption that it will write to the "Bold_1" element's text, it actually modifies the "Bold_2" element! Oops!

Trying again, "myRange" is now moved to the "Bold_3" element and is then duplicated with the duplicate() method to "myRange2." I now have two variables each pointing to a completely separate text range object. Much better. After moving "myRange2" to the "Bold_4" element, I write to the "myRange" range, and the "Bold_3" element is modified, as expected. Whew!

Even with two separate ranges, occasionally something you do to one can affect the other. Sometimes, when changing the HTML or text in a range, you may end up adding new elements or shuffling your document around a bit. In these cases, your other ranges usually readjust themselves to make up for your changes and continue to enclose the same area they previously covered. However, if two ranges overlap and you change the contents of one of them, the other range may find itself covering slightly less ground than before. So be careful when overlapping your ranges!

Merging Your Ranges with the setEndPoint() method

Two ranges can also be merged together to form a single range; however, there are no methods specifically designed to do this. If you want to join two ranges, the easiest way is to use the setEndPoint() method to create overlapping ranges, then discard the range you no longer need. The setEndPoint() method is used to take one of the endpoints of one range and reposition it to one of the endpoints of another range. It accepts two arguments. The first argument identifies which endpoints are to be manipulated, and the second is your other range. To specify endpoints, use the following keywords:

- "StartToEnd" moves the start point of the current range to the end point of the second range.
- "StartToStart" moves the start point of the current range to the start point of the second range. This is one way to "merge" your ranges, creating one range that covers the same area as both ranges combined. Be careful, though, because anything between the two ranges will be included as well!
- "EndToStart" moves the end point of the current range to the start point of the second range.

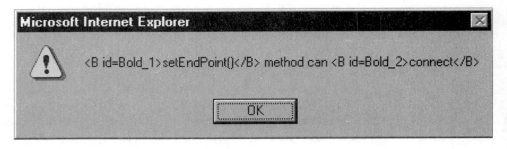

Figure 2–26   The "myRange" range contains all of the original text, plus all the text from the "myRange2" range and everything in between. The end of "myRange" has been moved to the end of "myRange2."

- "EndToEnd" moves the end point of the current range to the end point of the second range. Like "StartToStart," this is another way to merge your ranges.

```
<HTML>
<HEAD>
<TITLE>Text Ranges</TITLE>
<SCRIPT LANGUAGE="JavaScript">
function show_range()
{
  var myRange = document.body.createTextRange();
  var myRange2 = myRange.duplicate();

  myRange.moveToElementText( document.all.Bold_1 );
  myRange2.moveToElementText( document.all.Bold_2 );

  myRange.setEndPoint( "EndToEnd", myRange2 );
  alert( myRange.htmlText );

}
</SCRIPT>
</HEAD>
<BODY onLoad="show_range()">

<P>The <B ID="Bold_1">setEndPoint()</B> method can <B
ID="Bold_2">connect</B> ranges together.</P>

</BODY>
</HTML>
```

Listing 2–25

Be careful not to "bend the range over itself." In other words, if the current range is to the left of the second range, performing a "StartToEnd" would bend the start of the range over its end, which will result in browser strangeness. If the current range is to the left, use the "EndToStart" and "EndToEnd" keywords. If the current range is to the right, use the "StartToEnd" and "StartToStart" keywords.

Comparing Ranges' Endpoints: compareEndPoints(), isEqual(), and inRange()

A companion to the setEndPoints() method is compareEndPoints(). If you're not sure where your ranges are relative to each other, use this method to find out. Like setEnd-Points(), it accepts two arguments. The first specifies which endpoints to compare, and the second argument is the range you're comparing to.

- "StartToEnd" compares the start of your current range to the end of the second range.
- "StartToStart" compares the start of your current range to the start of the second range.
- "EndToStart" compares the end of your current range to the start of the second range.
- "EndToEnd" compares the end of your current range to the end of the second range.

The method returns −1 if the current range's endpoint is to the left of the second range's, a 0 if they are equal, and 1 if the current range's endpoint is to the right.

With compareEndPoints(), you can tell if the two ranges cover the same area; however, it would require two checks. First you would compare "StartToStart" and then "EndToEnd." A more straightforward way to see if two ranges cover the same area is to use isEqual(). This method accepts one argument, the range you're comparing to and returns *true* if they cover the same area and *false* otherwise. If the ranges overlap, then isEqual() will return *false*.

If you want to see if a second range is inside of the current range, you can use the inRange() method. Like the isEqual() method, it returns *true* if the ranges are equal but also returns *true* if the second range is contained inside the first. The second range must be completely contained inside the current range. If they simply overlap, inRange() will return *false*.

```
<HTML>
<HEAD>
<TITLE>Text Ranges</TITLE>
<SCRIPT LANGUAGE="JavaScript">
function show_range()
{
  var myRange = document.body.createTextRange();
  var myRange2 = myRange.duplicate();
```

Listing 2–26

```
myRange.moveToElementText( document.all.Bold_1 );
myRange2.moveToElementText( document.all.Bold_2 );

if ( myRange.isEqual( myRange2 ))
{
  alert( "The ranges start and end points match.");
}
else if ( myRange.inRange( myRange2 ))
{
  alert( "myRange2 is completely inside myRange.");
}
else
{
  var ret = myRange.compareEndPoints( "StartToStart",
  myRange2 );

  if (ret < 0)
  {
    alert( "myRange's start point is left of myRange2's
    start point");
  }
  else if (ret > 0)
  {
    alert( "myRange's start point is right of myRange2's
    start point");
  }
  else
  {
    alert( "The start points are equal.");
  }
}
}
</SCRIPT>
</HEAD>
<BODY onLoad="show_range()">

<P>You can <B ID="Bold_1">compare</B> range start and end
points with these <B ID="Bold_2">three</B> methods.</P>

</BODY>
</HTML>
```

Listing 2–26   *Continued*

Listing 2–26 is a rather complex demonstration of the usage of all three methods. Two
methods are created, and one is moved to the "Bold_1" element, the other to the "Bold_2"
element. Next, the isEqual() method is applied, but since the end points of both ranges are
completely different, the test fails. The code then checks to see if "myRange2" is completely

inside "myRange." Once again, not even close. Failing that, the compareEndPoints() method is applied for the start of each range, and the results saved to the "ret" variable. Since the start of the "myRange" range is to the left of the start of the "myRange2" range, the next test succeeds immediately, and a message is printed in an alert.

What is In Your Range?: parentElement() and findText()

While it is true that ranges can be used to modify parts of your document directly, one of their more exciting applications is the ability to discover what a certain part of your document contains. For example, does the current range contain a certain element? Does it contain a particular block of text? Two important methods for examining the contents of your range are parentElement() and findText().

The parentElement() method returns the element object of whichever element completely encloses your range. If the range is inside more than one element, the smallest element that encloses the entire range is used. For example, if your range is completely inside a <B> element, which itself is inside a <P> element, the parent element is the <B> element because that is the smallest element that encloses the entire range. On the other hand, if your text range was a little larger than the <B> element, the parent element would be the <P> element.

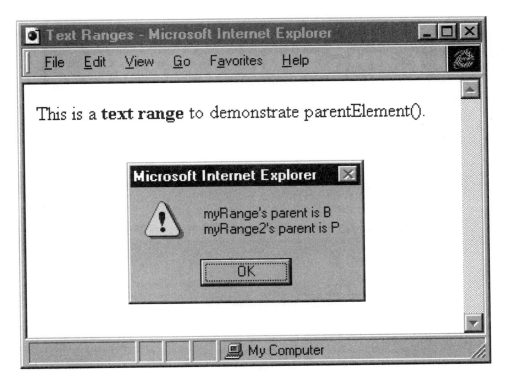

Figure 2–27   The first range is completely enclosed by the <B> element, so its parent element is <B>, but the second range is a little bit larger, so its parent element is <P>.

```
<HTML>
<HEAD>
<TITLE>Text Ranges</TITLE>
<SCRIPT LANGUAGE="JavaScript">
function show_range()
{
  var myRange = document.body.createTextRange();
  var myRange2;

  myRange.moveToElementText( document.all.Bold_1 );
  myRange2 = myRange.duplicate();

  myRange2.moveEnd( "word",3);

  var myElement = myRange.parentElement();
  var myElement2= myRange2.parentElement();

  alert( "myRange's parent is " + myElement.tagName + "\n" +
    "myRange2's parent is " + myElement2.tagName );
}
</SCRIPT>
</HEAD>
<BODY onLoad="show_range()">

<P>This is a <B ID="Bold_1">text range</B> to demonstrate par-
entElement().</P>

</BODY>
</HTML>
```

Listing 2–27

If you need to know whether your range contains a certain string of text, you can use the findText() method to find out. This method requires one argument, the string of text to check for, and returns *true* if the text exists inside the range, or *false* if it doesn't. See Listing 2–28 for an example.

```
<HTML>
<HEAD>
<TITLE>Text Ranges</TITLE>
<SCRIPT LANGUAGE="JavaScript">
function find_it()
{
  var myRange = document.body.createTextRange();

  myRange.moveToElementText( document.all.Para_1 );
```

```
      if ( myRange.findText( "seen" ) )
      {
        alert( "I see you saw 'seen'..." );
      }
      else
      {
        alert( "I didn't see 'seen'..." );
      }
    }
    </SCRIPT>
    </HEAD>
    <BODY onLoad="find_it()">

    <P ID="Para_1">Has anyone seen my car?</P>

    </BODY>
    </HTML>
```

Listing 2–28

These two methods might not seem like a big deal, since you wrote the HTML, created the ranges, and probably know what elements or text are inside. But there is a type of range for which this might not be true: the user defined range.

USER DEFINED RANGES: THE SELECTION OBJECT

The power of text ranges really becomes apparent when you start manipulating user defined ranges, more commonly known as "selections." A user creates a selection when highlighting a section of your document with the mouse. Up until now, the only use for selections was copying text from your document into the clipboard, and then pasting it into another application. But with text ranges and the selection object, your scripts also have access to the user's selections!

The selection object is located on the document object and contains information on the user's current selection. Accessing this data is accomplished by checking the "type" property to check the status of the selection, then applying the createRange() method to convert the selection to a form you can manipulate. If the "type" property contains the string "Text," there is a selection ready to be retrieved. If the property contains the string "None," there is currently no selection. This is quickly illustrated by the code fragment below:

```
    if ( document.selection.type == "Text" )
    {
        var myRange = document.selection.createRange();
    }
```

It looks straightforward at first; however, the actual implementation can be a bit tricky. The big question is, *how* do you know the user just made a selection?

There are two events directly related to selections. The onselectstart event, which generally goes on the <BODY> element, is triggered when the user begins a selection. More specifically, a selection is said to start when the user holds down the left mouse button your the document and begins moving the mouse. The problem is, this event triggers before the user has actually made the selection, so it doesn't solve our problem. The other event, onselect, which is triggered when the user changes the current selection, sounds more useful. Unfortunately, this doesn't quite work out either because as soon as the change starts the event is triggered. In other words, the event triggers for every new character that is selected, or deselected, without waiting for the user to actually finish making the selection. Once again, we know we're about to have a new selection to work with, but we have no idea when the selection is ready for our meddling.

What we really need is an event that is triggered when the user finishes making a selection, but that is exactly what we don't have. My theory is that this part of the specification is not quite finished, and I would guess that we'll see the event we're hoping for in the next release or two of Internet Explorer. For the time being, there is an event that can help us out, even though it wasn't specifically designed for the purpose: the onmouseup event.

The onMouseUp event is triggered when the user releases one of the mouse buttons. It just so happens that to create a selection, the user has to hold down the left mouse button, drag, and then—release the button! Not an ideal solution, but I'll take it! When the script detects an onmouseup event, it will check the selection's "type" property. If the property is "Text," or in the case of Listing 2–29, if it isn't "None," then the user probably just finished making a new selection. After that, we can use the createRange() property to convert the selection into a text range. This new range can be read, modified, or moved just like any other.

```
<HTML>
<HEAD>
<TITLE>A Simple HTML Document</TITLE>
<SCRIPT LANGUAGE="JavaScript">
function process_selection()
{
  if ( document.selection.type != "None" )
  {
    var myRange = document.selection.createRange();

    alert( myRange.htmlText );
  }
}
</SCRIPT>
</HEAD>
<BODY onMouseUp="process_selection()">
```

```
<P>This is a test of the <B>selection</B> events, methods, and
properties.</P>

</BODY>
</HTML>
```

Listing 2–29

Clearing and Emptying Selections: the clear() and empty() methods

The selection object defines two more methods, which you may find useful. The empty()
method deselects the current selection, and the clear() method deletes the current selection. Their functions sound similar, but they really do completely different things.

When the empty() method is used, whatever the user currently has selected is deselected, and the selection object's "type" property is reset to "None." Attempting to use
createRange() after a call to empty() will have unpredictable results. The clear() method,
on the other hand, removes whatever the user selected from the document. The "type"

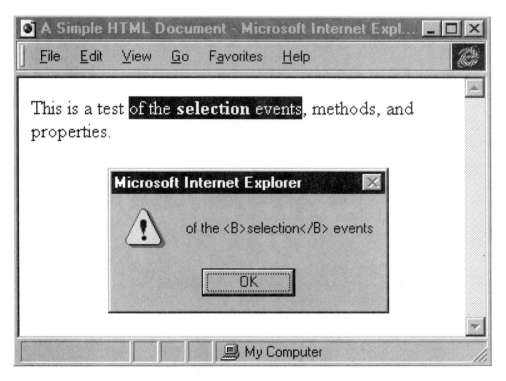

Figure 2–28   Displaying our new text range created directly from the user's selection.

property is also reset to "None"; however; this time createRange() can be used. Ranges created from a cleared selection are collapsed at the point where the selection was cleared.

```
<HTML>
<HEAD>
<TITLE>A Simple HTML Document</TITLE>
<SCRIPT LANGUAGE="JavaScript">
function process_selection()
{
  if ( document.selection.type != "None" )
  {
    var myRange = document.selection.createRange();

    document.selection.clear();
  }
}
</SCRIPT>
</HEAD>
<BODY onMouseUp="process_selection()">

<P>This is a test of the <B>selection</B> events, methods, and
properties.</P>

</BODY>
</HTML>
```

Listing 2–30

If you type in the code from Listing 2–30, you can see the clear() method in action. All your selections will disappear as soon as you release the mouse button. Be careful with this in your own applications! Everything is deleted, including any elements stuck inside the selection. This actually raises an interesting question: what happens when you clear part of an element, in particular half an unordered list or the beginning of a <B> element? Thankfully, the browser is smart enough not to let your elements "go bad." If you clear the front half, and therefore the start tag, of a <B> element, the start tag is replaced to cover the remainder of the element. Deleting the top of an unordered list results in a new <UL> start tag being inserted just above the remaining <LI> elements, keeping the list valid. Still, you may want to double check that you're not clearing something vital before executing this method!

Converting Text Ranges to Selections: the select() method

Often I've wished there was a way to instruct the browser to select some text for the user. For example, to highlight a word or phrase in response to a search query, much as the browser does, when the user uses the browser's built-in "find" command. It was a pleasant surprise when I discovered the select() method, which does just that.

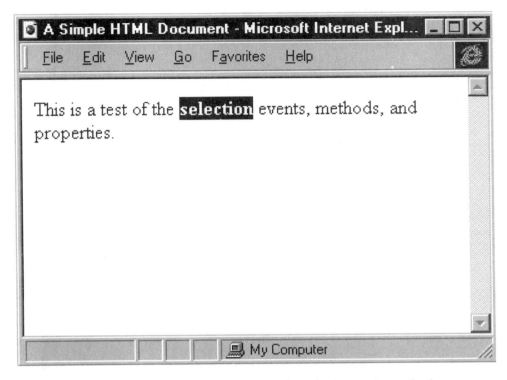

Figure 2–29 Using the text range select() method to create a selection.

The select() method is actually a method of the text range object, not selection. It does, however, directly affect the selection object. When used on a text range, that range is automatically selected for the user. Incidentally, this method isn't new. In the old object model, select() could be applied to the <INPUT TYPE="text"> element as well as <TEXTAREA>. But in the new DOM, select() has been married with text ranges, greatly increasing its scope and utility. Look at Listing 2–31, where select() is used with a text range to highlight the <B> element "Bold_1."

```
<HTML>
<HEAD>
<TITLE>A Simple HTML Document</TITLE>
<SCRIPT LANGUAGE="JavaScript">
function create_selection()
{
  var myRange = document.body.createTextRange();

  myRange.moveToElementText( document.all.Bold_1 );
  myRange.select();
```

Listing 2–31

```
    }
    </SCRIPT>
    </HEAD>
    <BODY onLoad="create_selection()">

    <P>This is a test of the <B ID="Bold_1">selection</B> events,
    methods, and properties.</P>

    </BODY>
    </HTML>
```

Listing 2–3   *Continued*

RANGE COMMANDS

You may have already guessed that with all the complexity behind text ranges, there must be something else they can be used for. In fact, there is a slew of commands that can be used to reformat or carry out other special actions on your text ranges. These commands, one shy of fifty last count, are applied using a special text range method execCommand(). There are also six other methods used in conjunction with execCommand() to ensure that the command can be executed in the current context, that the command did actually execute, and a few other obscure functions.

The key method is execCommand(). It always accepts at least one argument, the command to execute. If the specific command executed requires, execCommand() may also take one or two additional arguments. The types of commands available vary widely, from the "bold" command, which automatically makes your text range bold, to the "copy" command, which copies your range to the clipboard. I have noticed a pattern, however, and have separated the commands into five catagories: commands that wrap or remove HTML elements around your range (Bold, Italic, Underline, etc.), commands that insert an HTML element into your range (InsertHorizontalRule, InsertOrderedList, Insert-TextArea, etc.), commands that apply a "style" to your range (BackColor, ForeColor, FontName, Indent, etc.), commands that deal with the clipboard or selections (Copy, Cut, Paste, SelectAll, etc.), and finally, the four remaining miscellaneous commands.

With the exception of their arguments, all the commands are used in basically the same way. A text range is created, and the execCommand() method is then applied to the range. This is demonstrated in Listing 2–32 with the very simple "Bold" command. Ironically, while the end result is a bold range, Internet Explorer decided to use the <STRONG> element instead of <B>.

```
    <HTML>
    <HEAD>
    <TITLE>Text Range Commands</TITLE>
    <SCRIPT LANGUAGE="JavaScript">
    function do_command()
```

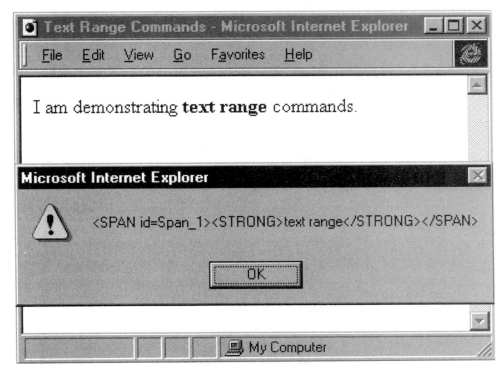

Figure 2–30   The "Bold" command makes our range bold via the <STRONG> element.

```
{
 var myRange = document.body.createTextRange();

 myRange.moveToElementText( document.all.Span_1 );
 myRange.execCommand( "Bold" );

 alert( myRange.htmlText );
}
</SCRIPT>
</HEAD>
<BODY onLoad="do_command()">

<P>I am demonstrating <SPAN ID="Span_1">text range</SPAN>
commands.</P>

</BODY>
</HTML>
```

Listing 2–32   *Continued*

The first argument of the execCommand() method is a string identifying the command to execute. Some commands require an additional argument or two. The second argument, if needed, is a boolean value (*true* or *false*) that, if set *true,* requests the command to display an optional user interface. What exactly this means is beyond me, since none of the commands seem to offer said user interface. In any event, it should always be set to *false*. The final argument is the "value," usually a string, if the command requests one. For example, the CreateLink command needs to be provided a URL, and the value argument would be used to give it one:

```
myRange.execCommand( "CreateLink", false, "/index.html" );
```

I'm not sure why "they" decided to put this mysterious and never used boolean argument before the often used value argument, forcing us to always have to type the rotten thing in. But they did, and you do. Hopefully sometime soon we'll have a few commands that offer this user-interface the documentation talks about, and then we'll get to type the occasional "true." Until then, we're stuck with it.

In the following pages you will find five sections, detailing the five categories of commands. Each section will contain a brief description of the nature of that particular group of commands, along with a table listing each command and any value argument it may expect. Any quirks or subtle nuances will also be reported, along with a listing or screen shot as appropriate.

Commands That Wrap and Remove: Bold, Italic, Underline . . .

Of these nine commands, six of them will wrap your range in whichever HTML element they specialize in, and three will remove a specific kind of element from your range.

Don't get confused by the name of the CreateBookmark command—it has nothing to do with your "favorite sites" list or range bookmarks. What it creates is what we called a "named anchor" in the old days. Just to jog your memory, a named anchor is used to jump to a certain point within a Web page. Typically, you would set up an <A NAME=> element, with a unique name, and then refer to that name at the end of a URL preceded by a hash mark. When the Web page is loaded with this special URL, the document would open and jump to the point where you placed that particular named anchor. Anyway, if you give the CreateBookmark command a value, it will use that value as the name for the anchor. If you neglect to give it a value, the anchor will be removed instead.

The CreateLink command is also somewhat misnamed. They should have called it CreateAnchor instead, because that is what it does. The value argument is the URL your new anchor should point to. If you would like to remove the anchor instead, use the Unlink command.

FormatBlock is another interesting command. If you give it the name of a block element, for example, ADDRESS for an <ADDRESS> element, it will convert the block element your range is currently in to the block element you just specified. Unfortunately, this command doesn't work quite as advertised either. The only block element I was able to get it to accept was the <ADDRESS> element—every other attempt failed.

The rest of the commands are rather straightforward, with the exception of the RemoveParaFormat command, which doesn't seem to behave properly at all. According to all the documentation, it should remove the paragraph formatting, meaning the <P> element, from your range. What it actually appears to do is put a </P> end tag right before any <P> opening tags in your range. Hopefully this will be fixed in a future release.

Command Name	Additional Argument(s)	Description
Bold	None	Makes the range bold with the <STRONG> element.
CreateBookmark	boolean: false value: A name for the anchor	Creates a named-anchor with the <A NAME=> element.
CreateLink	boolean: false value: A URL for the link	Creates a link with the <A HREF=> element.
FormatBlock	boolean: false value: A string specifying the block element to use	Applies the given block element to the block element closest to the range. Unfortunately, doesn't work yet.
Italic	None	Makes the range italic with the <EM> element.
RemoveFormat	None	Removes all HTML formatting from the range.
RemoveParaFormat	None	Places a </P> tag in front of any <P> tags in your range. Yeah, it's broken.
Underline	None	Underlines the range with the <U> element.
Unlink	None	Removes any <A> elements from the range.

Commands That Insert: InsertHorizontalRule, InsertOrderedList . . .

In a brilliant attempt at making an already complex topic even more complex, we have been graced with the following twenty commands, each of which has been painstakingly crafted to provide the same functionality of the pasteHTML() method, without any of the flexibility whatsoever. The reason I was kinder to the nine previous commands has since eluded me; however, one possible explanation is that at least those commands would have required a moderate quantity of thought to emulate manually. This bunch, on the other hand, actually puzzles me with its existence.

All the commands here will insert an HTML element into your range. They are best used in a range that has been collapsed as an insertion point. They all expect two additional arguments, though apparently none of them actually bother to use them. Take the InsertButton command, for example. It should insert an <INPUT TYPE=button> element in your document; and, presumably, if given a value, it will use that value as an identifier name so you can access the element more easily in the future. And you are going to want to access the element because there is no way to set its attributes through the command. Incidently, as a testament to its own utility, there is also an InsertInputButton command that does the same thing.

The InsertOrderedList and InsertUnorderedList commands did amuse me, somewhat. If your range is inside a block element, such as <P>, these commands will convert the element to an <OL> or <UL>, respectively, and convert any text inside the element to a <LI>

element. I was also amused when I discovered that InsertInputHidden and InsertParagraph usually crashed Internet Explorer. Maybe some of these commands do have a use after all...

In any event, I am sure I'm being a bit too harsh. It is obvious these commands are currently *under construction,* so to speak, and I'm sure their usefulness will either improve or they will be removed. I list them here for completeness and your convenience.

Command Name	Additional Argument(s)	Description
InsertButton	boolean: false value: An identifier name (ID)	Insert <INPUT TYPE=button>.
InsertFieldset	boolean: false value: An identifier name (ID)	Insert a <FIELDSET> element.
InsertHorizontalRule	boolean: false value: The size of the rule	Insert an <HR> element. Whatever size you use, it just does 100%.
InsertIFrame	boolean: false value: A URL	Insert an <IFRAME> element.
InsertInputButton	boolean: false value: An identifier name (ID)	Insert <INPUT TYPE="button">.
InsertInputCheckbox	boolean: false value: An identifier name (ID)	Insert <INPUT TYPE="checkbox">.
InsertInputFileUpload	boolean: false value: An identifier name (ID)	Insert <INPUT TYPE="file">.
InsertInputHidden	boolean: false value: An identifier name (ID)	Insert <INPUT TYPE="hidden">.
InsertInputPassword	boolean: false value: An identifier name (ID)	Insert <INPUT TYPE="password">.
InsertInputRadio	boolean: false value: An identifier name (ID)	Insert <INPUT TYPE="radio">.
InsertInputReset	boolean: false value: An identifier name (ID)	Insert <INPUT TYPE="reset">.
InsertInputSubmit	boolean: false value: An identifier name (ID)	Insert <INPUT TYPE="submit">.
InsertInputText	boolean: false value: An identifer name (ID)	Insert <INPUT TYPE="text">.
InsertMarquee	boolean: false value: An identifier name (ID)	Insert a <MARQUEE> element.
InsertOrderedList	boolean: false value: An identifier name (ID)	Inserts an <OL> element and an <LI> element if required.
InsertParagraph	boolean: false value: An identifier name (ID)	Inserts a <P> element.
InsertSelectDropdown	boolean: false value: An identifier name (ID)	Insert a <SELECT> element.
InsertSelectListbox	boolean: false value: An identifier name (ID)	Insert a <SELECT multiple> element.
InsertTextArea	boolean: false value: An identifier name (ID)	Inserts a <TEXTAREA> element.
InsertUnorderedList	boolean: false value: An identifier name (ID)	Insert a <UL> element and an <LI> element if required.

Commands That Apply Style: BackColor, ForeColor, FontName, Ident . . .

These commands will change the "style" of your range. I define style as anything that affects colors, fonts, or positioning. In other words, I'm being completely arbitrary. I think you will find the first four the most useful of the bunch, the others being a little less exciting than they sound.

The BackColor command changes the background color of the text only in the current range. The value argument is the color, and it can be in any valid color format. I've always been a hexadecimal triplet kind of guy, but you are also free to use color names if that suits your fancy. The neat thing about this command is that it actually makes use of what we call an "in-line style," a feature of style sheets. Without going into style sheets right now, what is going on is that a <FONT> element is wrapped around your range, with an in-line style to set the background color. Figure 2–31 shows what I mean.

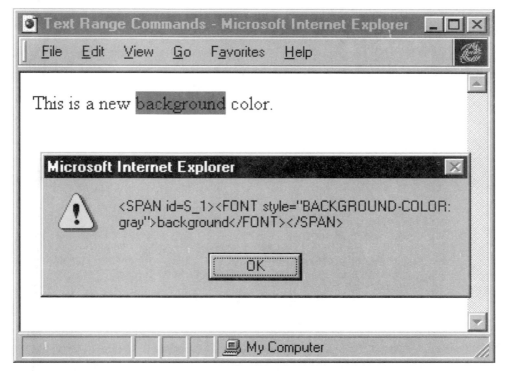

Figure 2–31 The BackColor command in action. Notice how only the color of our range was affected.

```
<HTML>
<HEAD>
<TITLE>Text Range Commands</TITLE>
<SCRIPT LANGUAGE="JavaScript">
function do_command()
{
  var myRange = document.body.createTextRange();

  myRange.moveToElementText( document.all.S_1 );

  myRange.execCommand( "BackColor", false, "gray" );

  alert( document.all.S_1.outerHTML );
}
</SCRIPT>
</HEAD>
<BODY onLoad="do_command()">

<P>This is a new <SPAN ID="S_1">background</SPAN> color.</P>

</BODY>
</HTML>
```

Listing 2–33

The FontName command wraps a <FONT> element around your range and uses the "face" attribute to change the font name. The FontSize command uses the <FONT> element with the "size" attribute, and the ForeColor command uses the "color" attribute. I could dedicate an entire chapter to fonts, but for now I'll just give one example and move on:

```
myRange.execCommand( "FontName", false, "courier" );
```

Executing the above command on your range will change the font to Courier. Can you use your favorite font instead of Courier? Sure, but the odds of your users having "SuperMegaCool" font are slim to none, so try to avoid very strange fonts. I'll talk more about fonts and colors a bit later on.

The Indent and Outdent commands sound intriguing, but they turn out to be rather uninteresting at second look. Indent wraps a <BLOCKQUOTE> element around your range, and Outdent appears to break your range out of a <BLOCKQUOTE> element if it is in one. I'm a bit disappointed, actually, because with style sheets these commands could really indent and outdent, instead of relying on the <BLOCKQUOTE> element. When we look into style sheets, I'll show you how to do this for real.

The "Justify" commands are just a fancy way to change the alignment of your text. To obtain their effect, they set the "align" attribute of the nearest <P> or <DIV> element. If you're curious, JustifyFull is the same as JustifyRight.

Command Name	Additional Argument(s)	Description
BackColor	boolean: false value: A color name or value	Changes background color of current range.
FontName	boolean: false value: A font name	Changes the font of the current range.
FontSize	boolean: false value: A font size	Changes the font size of the current range.
ForeColor	boolean: false value: A color name or value	Changes the color of the font in the current range.
Indent	None	Indents the range's text.
JustifyCenter	None	Centers your range's text.
JustifyFull	None	Fully justifies your range's text.
JustifyLeft	None	Left justifies your range's text.
JustifyRight	None	Right justifies your range's text.
Outdent	None	Outdents the range's text.

Commands for the Clipboard or Selections: Cut, Copy, Paste, SelectAll . . .

These six commands are arguably the most interesting. The Copy, Cut, Delete, and Paste commands mirror any good application's normal clipboard functions. The Copy command will copy the current range directly into the user's clipboard. The data can then be pasted directly into another application. The Cut command does the same thing as Copy, except that the range is then deleted from your document. Delete removes the data from your document without copying it to the clipboard.

The most controversial of these is the Paste command, which takes the contents of the clipboard and pastes it into your range, or at an insertion point created by a collapsed range. Before you start worrying about Web pages stealing the contents of your clipboard, Paste will only work if the clipboard has been populated by your script with the Copy or Cut commands.

The SelectAll command is unique in that it is one of the few commands that does not operate on a range. Instead, it is called directly from the document object:

```
document.execCommand( "SelectAll" );
```

When called on your document object, the entire document will be selected for the user. It can then be cut, copied, or accessed through the Selection object. The Unselect command unselects the selection and is called from the document object like SelectAll.

Command Name	Additional Argument(s)	Description
Copy	None	Copies the range to the clipboard.
Cut	None	Copies the range to the clipboard and then deletes it from your document.
Delete	None	Deletes the range from your document.
Paste	None	Pastes the clipboard into your range. *Only data that was copied into the clipboard by the browser can be pasted!*
SelectAll	None	Selects entire document.
UnSelect	None	Unselects your selection.

Miscellaneous Commands

The final four commands don't fit into any other catagory since they really don't affect the text of your ranges. I'd rather not go into the PlayImage and StopImage commands, and I'm sure you can figure out what the Refresh command does. OverWrite, on the other hand, is rather interesting.

The default mode of input for the <TEXTAREA> and <INPUT TYPE=text> elements is "insert" mode. In other words, whatever you type is inserted at that point. If you turn on OverWrite mode, however, any text you type will overwrite any text underneath. You can simulate this effect by typing something, then backing up your cursor and continuing to type. The new text will insert itself at that point and push the rest of the text to the right. Now pressing the "insert" key on your keyboard will toggle the insert mode off, and your subsequent keystrokes will overwrite the following characters instead of inserting before them. This command will toggle that OverWrite mode if called on a <TEXTAREA> or <INPUT TYPE=text> range.

Now unfortunately, it doesn't work yet. But I'm sure it will at some point, and when it does, I'd like to warn against using it often, if at all. Most users know when they want insert or overwrite mode and will press their "insert" key to change the mode, if they so desire. Changing it for them, unless you have a darn good reason, will just create confusion. So when this command finally does work, please be careful with it!

Command Name	Additional Argument(s)	Description
OverWrite	boolean: false value: true for overwrite mode, false for insert mode	Sets the overwrite mode for user input.
PlayImage	None	Start playing a dynamic image that has been specified with <IMG dynsrc=>.
Refresh	None	Reload the current document. Call from the document object.
StopImage	None	Stops playing a dynamic image.

Other Command Methods: the queryCommand methods

There are a handful of other methods that work with execCommand(), but unfortunately none of them appear to be implemented yet. I will describe them here, briefly, to give you an idea of what is to come. Don't count on these descriptions being completely accurate, as I am sure the details will change. It is for this reason I am being particularly vague.

The queryCommandEnabled() and queryCommandSupported() commands each accept a single argument and will normally be called before execCommand() to determine if the command you are about to execute will work in the current context. Call these methods on the range in question and give them the command name as their argument. If the command is enabled (available) or supported in the current context, the methods will return *true*, otherwise they will return *false*. A good example of when you would use this is after converting a selection into a range when you're not sure what the range contains.

The queryCommandState() and queryCommandIndeterm() methods are used to keep track of the state of the command you just executed. These, too, take one argument, the name of the command you are querying. If the command was successfully executed by execCommand(), queryCommandState() will return *true*. If the command failed or was not executed for some other reason, it will return *false*. If it doesn't know one way or the other, it will return *null*. You can then use queryCommandIndeterm() to find out if the reason a *null* was returned was because the state really was indeterminate or for "some other reason," for example, you never did call execCommand() on your range.

If you're not sure whether the command you are about to call is a valid command, you can use queryCommandValue() to look it up. Give it the proposed command name as its argument. If it is a real command, the command's name will be returned, otherwise a *null* will be given. A similar method is queryCommandText(), which accepts two arguments. The first is the name of a command and the second is an action to take. If the action is "Name" and the command exists, the method will return "the short name of the command." That implies that these commands will all have short aliases, but I cannot confirm this assumption. If the action is "StatusText" and the command exists, the method will return "the string that appears on the status bar." Don't ask—I have no idea. When these methods are finally implemented, I'll explore them in more detail.

CONCLUSION

In this chapter, you were introduced to the concept of dynamic content. You learned how to use the "All" collection to access the element objects in your documents and how to use their properties and methods to manipulate the data they contain. You were also introduced to events, which allow your element objects to react to certain user actions, including mouse movements and clicks. We also discussed two context independent elements, <SPAN> and <DIV>, which can be used when you need to create an element object but don't want to change the formating of your text. We then took this knowledge and created a collapsible outline.

We also learned how to create text ranges and use their properties and methods. When married with the Selection object, text ranges can be powerful tools to communicate with your document as well as with the user. Add to that range commands, and you now have unprecedented control over your document and its components.

CHAPTER 3

Getting A Handle
On Events

Our object model certainly has grown up since the early days of browser scripting! Where there were only a few properties and methods, there are now hundreds. But with this added robustness has come a need for a more complex event model. At last count, there were thirty-nine events, but with concepts such as "event bubbling," the possibilities are nearly endless. The event model explains how events are listened for, what happens when an event is encountered, and how events trigger and react to other events. While it isn't required that you understand every aspect of the event model, a basic understanding can help prevent frustration and will allow you to take advantage of some pretty advanced techniques.

BACK TO BASICS: BINDING EVENT HANDLERS TO OBJECTS

An event handler is, simply stated, a function that is called when the browser detects an event. For example, in the following code, there is a <SPAN> element listening for onclick events. If the user clicks on the "click me" text, that event will be processed by the alert() function. In this case, the alert() function is the event handler. Or stated another way, the alert function handles the event.

```
<SPAN onClick="alert('You clicked me!')">click me</SPAN>
```

The binding part of this story is in the so-called "onClick=" attribute. In this case, the "onClick=" attribute has bound the alert() function to the <SPAN> element object. When you use one of these "event attributes," you are binding an event handler to an element object. This is called binding an event handler "inline," and you've probably noticed by now that we've been doing this all along. You can bind as many different event handlers to a single element object as you need. Each handler will be called individually when the appropriate event is received.

An event handler doesn't have to be a function. You can also use an expression, such as incrementing a variable or setting another object's properties. In the following example, an onclick event handler has been bound to a form button. When the button is clicked, a variable is incremented and the innerText property of a <SPAN> element is updated to reflect the new number of clicks. Obviously, this technique is geared to only simple tasks. Anything more complex than what we've done here probably requires its own function, instead of being jammed into the event attribute.

```
<HTML>
<HEAD>
<TITLE>Event Handlers</TITLE>
<SCRIPT LANGUAGE="JavaScript">
var num=0;
</SCRIPT>
</HEAD>
<BODY>

<CENTER>
<H1>You clicked the button <SPAN ID="MyNum">0</SPAN> times.
  </H1>

<FORM>
<INPUT TYPE="button" VALUE="Click Me" LANGUAGE="JavaScript"
       onClick="num++; document.all.MyNum.innerText = num;">
</FORM>
</CENTER>

</BODY>
</HTML>
```

One interesting point is the use of the "LANGUAGE=" attribute. This tells the browser that the code fragment in the event attribute is JavaScript. The language attribute is optional, and if you forget to include it the browser will assume the language is whatever language it last encountered. In this case, it would have used JavaScript. The documentation claims that if there was no previous script defined, the browser will choose the "default" language. What is the default language? Personally, my philosophy is to assume it is the opposite of whichever language I'm trying to use. But this does imply something fairly interesting: using the language attribute, you can mix and match different scripting languages in the same document. Why you would want to do this is another question, but it is possible to have some of your scripting in JavaScript, and some of it VBScript. If you are interested in this kind of pain, be my guest, but I personally will be using only a single scripting language in my documents.

There is another technique for binding event handlers, other than the inline technique. However, I think it is a bit cumbersome. It is called, for lack of a better name, the "for-event" method. Your event handler is coded alone inside its own <SCRIPT> element. You then use the <SCRIPT> element's "FOR=" attribute to set the identifier name of the element object to which this handler is to bind, and the "EVENT=" attribute is given the event's name. The example below does the same thing as the previous example, except this time we bind our event handler with the for-event technique. Notice how there are two <SCRIPT> elements. The first merely initializes our variable, and the second is the event handler.

```
<HTML>
<HEAD>
<TITLE>Event Handlers</TITLE>

<SCRIPT LANGUAGE="JavaScript">
    var num=0;
</SCRIPT>

<SCRIPT FOR=MyButton EVENT=onclick LANGUAGE="JavaScript">
    num++;
    document.all.MyNum.innerText = num;
</SCRIPT>

</HEAD>
<BODY>

<CENTER>
<H1>You clicked the button <SPAN ID="MyNum">0</SPAN> times.</H1>

<FORM>
<INPUT TYPE="button" VALUE="Click Me" ID="MyButton">
</FORM>
</CENTER>

</BODY>
</HTML>
```

As you can imagine, with many event handlers this technique can get rather cumbersome quickly. But there is a benefit to using one technique over the other. Event handlers bound using the for-event technique will begin listening for events only after the entire document has been loaded. For inline binding, the events begin listening as soon as the element object is created, which is not necessarily when the document has finished loading. This difference could be a great benefit in some situations: if you want to guarantee an event won't be triggered until the document is done loading, you can use the for-event technique, otherwise your event handlers may start working before the document is finished loading and strange results can occur.

There will be times when this little feature will become critical, and it is absolutely necessary to ensure there is no possibility that an event occurs before the document is done loading. For example, any time you use the dynamic content features to modify your document, it is imperative that the document finishes loading completely before you start twiddling with text and HTML. Normally, I don't worry about the stray event triggering before the document is ready because most of my documents load fast enough so it isn't an issue. But if my page contains a few large images, or a bunch of small ones, I do start to get a little concerned about events triggering prematurely. In these cases, I will use the for-event technique instead of inline, just to make sure that impatient users don't start clicking before everything is nice and ready.

You can mix and match your binding techniques in the same documents. For events that absolutely must wait for the document to finish loading before being triggered, you can bind using the for-event technique. For other less critical event handlers, you can use the less cumbersome inline technique.

THE EVENT LIFE CYCLE AND EVENT BUBBLING

When an event is triggered, there are a number of steps it will take from the initial user action to the execution of your event handler. These steps are called the event's "life cycle," and understanding what is going on will really help you get the most out of the event model.

1. **An action is detected.** The user does something that causes an event, such as clicking somewhere on the document or moving the mouse.
2. **The "event object" is updated.** The event object is created whenever an event occurs and is updated to contain detailed information about the event.
3. **The event "fires."** The script is officially notified of the event.
4. **Event handlers are called.**
5. **The event "bubbles" up the element hierarchy.** Some elements may contain other elements. If an "inside" element receives an event, that event is also "bubbled" to the parent element.
6. **Default actions are executed.** Some element objects have certain default actions associated with them. For example, an <A HREF=> element object's default action is to load a new document.

An event starts its life with the user's action. This is the actual mouse click, or the mouse pointer's entry into an element's space before it has been associated with any particular object or event handler. At this step, the browser knows *something* happened, and from this point it will determine what happened, where, and how to deal with it.

Introducing the Event Object

Once the browser receives an event, its next task is to update the "event object" with everything it knows about the current event. If there was a mouse click, in what element object did the click occur? Where exactly was the mouse at the time, and was the user pressing any keys? Some events require that specific information is also recorded. For example, the on-mouseover and onmouseout events also record in which element object the mouse was pre-viously and to which it is currently moving. Every aspect of the event is recorded in the event object, and that information is made available for your event handlers.

The event object is located on the "window" object and is only available when an event has occurred. Your event handlers can access the event object from the window ob-ject directly, as is seen in the following line of code.

```
var theName = window.event.srcElement.tagName;
```

In this example, we are retrieving the srcElement property of the event object. The srcElement is the element object where an event occurred, for example, where the user clicked. The tagName property of the element object is then checked and the results are assigned to a variable for future reference. We'll learn all about the event object and its properties later. There are some really neat things you can find out using the event object, and I would like to devote a separate section to its discussion when we're done with the event life cycle.

After the event object has been updated, the event officially "fires," and the script is notified of the event handlers that will need to be executed. The event handlers are then called, and your script can now "do its thing." You might think this would be the end of the life cycle. Your event handlers have finally been called, and that should be the end of it, right? If objects couldn't contain other objects, then yes, this would be the end of it. But your objects can contain other objects, and in order for each object to get a shot at handling the event, the events must know how to "bubble."

Event Bubbling

Element objects can, and usually do, contain other element objects. When an element ob-ject contained in another element object receives an event, the event will "bubble" to the parent element, and so on, all the way up to the window object. This bubbling gives each object a chance to respond to the same event. Not only is this a useful feature, but in some cases essential.

```
<P onClick="myHandler()">Click me <B>anywhere</B>!</P>
```

In the above line of HTML, a user would expect that anywhere he clicked would produce some result. But without event bubbling, if the user clicked on the bold text "any-where," nothing would happen. This is because the <B> element does not have an event handler bound to it, and without bubbling the event would never be captured. Fortunately, with event bubbling, the event will bubble to the <B> element's parent, the <P> element, which does have an event handler bound to it. An event on the <B> element will bubble to the <P> element.

The event doesn't stop bubbling when it finds an event handler. Even if every element the event bubbles to has an event handler, the event will continue to bubble, triggering handlers as it goes. The event won't stop bubbling until either you specifically tell it to stop, or it finally bubbles up through the <BODY> element and into the window object, every step of the way triggering event handlers where it finds them.

```
<P onClick="alert('P')">Click me <B onClick="alert('B')
">anywhere</B> to explore event bubbling!</P>
```

In this example, clicking on the text "Click me" or "to explore event bubbling!" will trigger the event handler on the <P> element and display an alert box with the letter *P*. But clicking on the text "anywhere" will first trigger the <B> element's event handler, displaying an alert box with the letter *B,* then bubble up to the <P> element's event handler and send another alert box with the letter *P*.

Event bubbling is a really great feature, but occasionally it can create unwanted results. Maybe you don't want your event to bubble. Thankfully, you can "pop" an event bubble, so to speak, and stop parent objects from receiving the event. This is accomplished with the cancelBubble property of the event object. If your event handler doesn't want the event to bubble, it should set the cancelBubble property of the event object to *true,* as shown in the listing below. Now, when the event handler is finished, so is the event.

```
<HTML>
<HEAD>
<TITLE>Event Bubbling</TITLE>
<SCRIPT LANGUAGE="JavaScript">
function myHandler(myElement,cancelMe)
{
    myElement.innerHTML = "<U>" + myElement.innerHTML + "</U>";

    window.event.cancelBubble = cancelMe;
}
</SCRIPT>
</HEAD>
<BODY>

<P onClick="myHandler(this,true)">Click me <B
  onClick="myHandler(this,false)">here</B>
to explore event bubbling.</P>

<P onClick="myHandler(this,true)">Click me <B
  onClick="myHandler(this,true)">here</B>
to see an event bubble being cancelled.</P>

</BODY>
</HTML>
```

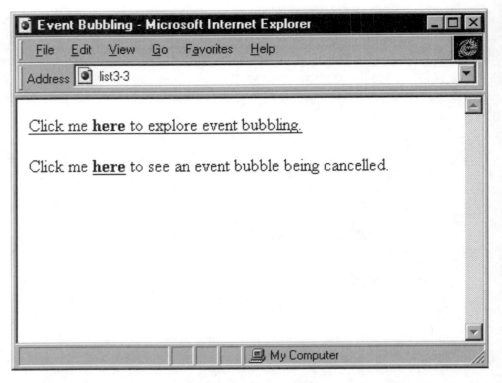

Figure 3–1 In the first line of text, event bubbling is not cancelled at the <B> element, and everything gets underlined; but the second line of text does cancel the bubble at the <B> element, and only that element is underlined.

Figure 3–1 contains two lines of text, both of which have the word "here" clicked. In the first line, the function myHandler() on the <B> element is called in response to the onclick event. Two arguments are passed to the handler. The first is the special "this" variable, which represents the current object. The second is the value *false*, which will tell the handler *not* to cancel the event bubble. The event handler will underline the <B> element, then bubble to the <P> element where it will once again trigger the myHandler() event handler. Now the entire <P> element is also underlined, and event bubbling is finally cancelled. With event bubbling, both the original element and its parent react to the event and both are underlined.

The second line of text calls the myHandler() function a little differently. This time, it sends the *true* value, telling our handler to cancel the bubble. When the <B> element is clicked, the event handler underlines the <B> element, but the cancelBubble property is set to *true* and the bubbling stops. The <P> element never receives the event, and thus the <P> element is not underlined, because the event bubble was cancelled.

Default Actions

The final phase of the event life cycle is where any default actions are taken. A default action is a response to an event that the browser automatically takes, even if the user hasn't defined an event handler for that situation. Some objects don't have default actions, but many do. Most notable of these is the <A HREF=> element, which will respond to an onclick event by loading a new document—that is, this element's default action.

    Just because a default action exists, doesn't mean you can't provide an event handler as well. Any event handler on an element object that already has a default action is executed as normal. When the life cycle reaches the default action phase, the default action is then executed as well. But this behavior may sometimes defeat the purpose of providing your own event handler. In these cases, you can tell the default action not to execute using your event handler's "return value." In the listing below, an <A HREF=> element object has been given the myHandler() event handler bound to the onclick event. When the anchor is clicked, the event handler is first executed and a confirmation box is displayed for the user, asking if the link should really be visited. If the user selects "OK," the event handler returns *true* and the default action is allowed to proceed, taking the user to the new document. However, if the user selects "Cancel," the event handler returns *false* and the default action is interrupted, preventing the new page from loading.

```
<HTML>
<HEAD>
<TITLE>Event Bubbling</TITLE>
<SCRIPT LANGUAGE="JavaScript">
function myHandler()
{
    if (! confirm( "Are you sure you want to visit this site?" ))
    {
        return false;
    }
    return true;
}
</SCRIPT>
</HEAD>
<BODY>

<P>The <A HREF="http://www.prenhall.com/" onClick="return
myHandler()">Prentice-Hall
website</A> is cool!</P>

</BODY>
</HTML>
```

    It is very important that not only does the event handler return *false,* to cancel the default action, but you also return *false* to the onclick= attribute. If you forget the "return"

Figure 3–2   If the user selects "Cancel," the default action is interrupted and the new document is not loaded.

in the line below, the default action will never receive the request to abort and the new page will happily load.

```
<A HREF="http://my.new.url/" onClick="return myHandler()">
```

Another way to cancel a default action is to set the returnValue property of the event object to *false*. If the returnValue property is set to *false*, the default action will be cancelled even if the event handler itself returns *true*! Also, since setting the returnValue property does not end your event handler like using the "return" statement does, you can set the returnValue property to *false* at any time and be sure the default action will be cancelled, regardless of what or when your event handler returns. The listing below is identical to the previous example, except this time it uses the returnValue property to cancel the default action. Notice that the event handler will always return *true,* but this doesn't matter because the default action will listen to the returnValue property instead.

```
<HTML>
<HEAD>
<TITLE>Event Bubbling</TITLE>
<SCRIPT LANGUAGE="JavaScript">
function myHandler()
{
    if (! confirm( "Are you sure you want to visit this site?" ))
    {
        window.event.returnValue = false;
    }
    return true;
}
</SCRIPT>
</HEAD>
<BODY>

<P>The <A HREF="http://www.prenhall.com/"
onClick="myHandler()">Prentice-Hall
website</A> is cool!</P>

</BODY>
</HTML>
```

Notice this time, I didn't bother putting the "return" in the onclick= attribute because the returnValue property will communicate with the default action directly. By the way, don't confuse returnValue with cancelBubble! Their settings are completely independent of each other. Setting returnValue to *false* does not affect event bubbling in any way.

THE EVENT OBJECT DETAILED

The event object offers quite a few other useful properties. We've already seen the cancel-Bubble and returnValue properties. There is also the srcElement property, which we briefly saw as well. The srcElement property reports the element object that initiated the event. For example, if the event was captured in a <B> element, the srcElement property will return the <B> element. One thing that can throw you off is when examining this property during an event bubble.

```
<P onClick="myHandler()">Click <B>anywhere</B> for a message.</P>
```

In the example above, if the user clicks in the <B> element, when the event bubbles up to the <P> element the srcElement property will indicate the <B> element, not the <P> element. Even though the event handler for the <P> element caught the event, since it started in the <B> element the srcElement property will report the <B> element. Remember, srcElement is the entire element object.

Another interesting property is the "type" property, which returns the name of the event minus the "on" prefix. For example, if the event is "onclick," the type property will

Figure 3–3   Clicking in the <B> element returns the <B> element, even though the <P> element's event handler responded to the event.

contain the word "click." This information might allow you to create a "generic" event handler, which could be used in a number of situations, for example, a single event handler that would underline an element if triggered by an onmouseover event or remove any underlining if triggered by an onmouseout.

Mouse Related Events

There are seven events directly related to the mouse, and the event object contains several special properties that contain extra information on these events. The mouse events can be broken down even farther into two groups: things that happen when a mouse button is clicked, and things that happen when the mouse is moved.

The onclick event is one of the most familiar of all the events but is a bit more complex than it first appears. One misconception is that the only way to trigger an onclick event is by clicking the mouse button. Actually, an onclick event can also occur when a key on the keyboard that affects a form element is pressed. For example, pressing the ENTER or RETURN key when a submit button has focus will cause an onclick event. Pressing the ESC key will also cause an onclick event if any part of a form has focus. So will the spacebar if a radio button, checkbox, submit or reset button has focus in a form. In other words, if pressing the key will affect a form the same way as if it were clicked with the mouse, an onclick event will occur.

When caused by a mouse click, the onclick event is always accompanied by two other events: onmousedown and onmouseup. The onmousedown event occurs whenever the mouse button is pressed. When the user releases the button, the onmouseup event is then triggered. Only after these two events have been fired, and if the mouse was not moved off the element, will an onclick event occur. So the exact sequence of an onclick event is actually:

1. An **onmousedown** event, when the user first presses the mouse button but hasn't released it yet.
2. An **onmouseup** event, after the user has released the mouse button.
3. An **onclick** event, if the mouse didn't move to another element during the onmousedown and onmouseup events.

The final clicking event is ondblclick, when a user double clicks an element. This is really just an extension of the sequence shown above:

1. Another **onmouseup** event, once again with the mouse remaining on the same element. Notice that there is no onmousedown event!
2. The **ondblclick** event, if the user clicks fast enough.

If the user clicks too slowly, then instead of an ondblclick event, another onclick event will be fired instead. To illustrate this point, and since I finally found a great example of the "type" property, take a look at the listing below and Figure 3–4.

```
<HTML>
<HEAD>
<TITLE>Event Bubbling</TITLE>
<SCRIPT LANGUAGE="JavaScript">
var eventSequence = "";

function myHandler()
{
    var eventName = window.event.type;

    if (eventName == "dblclick")
    {
        alert("The event sequence was:\n" + eventSequence +
"dblclick" );
        eventSequence = "";
    }
    else
    {
```

```
            eventSequence += eventName + "->";
      }
}
</SCRIPT>
</HEAD>
<BODY>

<H1 onClick="myHandler()"
    onMouseDown="myHandler()"
    onMouseUp="myHandler()"
    onDblClick="myHandler()">Double click please!</H1>

</BODY>
</HTML>
```

Figure 3–4   When double clicked, the <H1> element's impressive arsenal of event handlers records the sequence of events to create the dblclick event and then displays the event names in the order it received them.

The <H1> element is listening for all four events involved in creating an ondblclick event, and each calls the myHandler() event handler. When any of these events is fired, the myHandler() event looks at the "type" property of the event object. If the type is not "dblclick," the event name is appended to a global variable and a make-shift arrow "—>" is tacked on as well. When the type is "dblclick," an alert box displays the contents of our global variable, showing the order of the events it has received to create a dblclick event.

Whenever one of the mouse click events occurs, the event object records information on the position of the mouse at that time in a series of properties. Not only do you know that the user clicked the mouse, and what the user clicked on, but the exact coordinates of the click as well! The clientX and clientY properties report the X and Y coordinates of the mouse pointer relative to the upper left corner of the document. If you're curious about the coordinates relative to the user's entire screen, you can check the screenX and screenY properties.

```
<HTML>
<HEAD>
<TITLE>Event Bubbling</TITLE>
<SCRIPT LANGUAGE="JavaScript">
function myHandler()
{
    alert( "clientX,Y: " + window.event.clientX + "," +
                          window.event.clientY +
           "\nscreenX,Y: " + window.event.screenX + "," +
                          window.event.screenY );
}
</SCRIPT>
</HEAD>
<BODY onClick="myHandler()">

<H1>Click anywhere on the document for coordinates</H1>

</BODY>
</HTML>
```

There are also four other "coordinate" properties, but they are only useful in conjunction with style sheets, which we will discuss later. They are offsetX, offsetY, x, and y.

The event object also stores the state of the mouse buttons at the time of the onmousedown and onmouseup events. By checking the "button" property after one of these two events, you can discover if the user pressed (or released) the left, right, or both mouse buttons. If the left mouse button caused the event, the property will contain 1. For the right mouse button, the property will contain 2, and for both buttons it will contain 3. If no buttons were pressed, the property will contain 0.

The other group of mouse related events reports the location the mouse has moved from or to: onmouseover, onmouseout, and onmousemove. When the mouse pointer moves over an element, the onmouseover event is fired. Invariably, the user will end up moving the

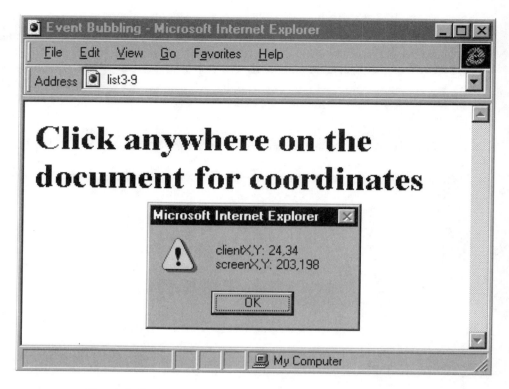

Figure 3–5   In this example, I just clicked on the "C" in "Click."

mouse pointer inside the element, even if it is just to move the pointer over another element. While the pointer is moving inside the element, the onmousemove event will start firing like crazy. As soon as the pointer leaves the element, an onmouseout event is fired, probably followed by another onmouseover event as the pointer enters another element.

Whenever the onmouseover or onmouseout events are fired, the event object records which element the mouse pointer is moving to in the toElement property and where the mouse pointer was coming from in the fromElement property.

```
<HTML>
<HEAD>
<TITLE>Mouse Events</TITLE>
<SCRIPT LANGUAGE="JavaScript">
var moveNum = 0;

function catch_out()
{
    var wentTo = window.event.toElement;
    var cameFrom = window.event.fromElement;
```

```
        alert("onMouseMove triggered " + moveNum + " times.\n" +
            "Just entered the " + wentTo.tagName + " element from\n" +
            "the " + cameFrom.tagName + " element.\n");
        moveNum = 0;
}
function count_move()
{
        moveNum++;
}
</SCRIPT>
</HEAD>
<BODY>

<H1 onMouseOut="catch_out()" onMouseMove="count_move()">The Mouse
Events</H1>

</BODY>
</HTML>
```

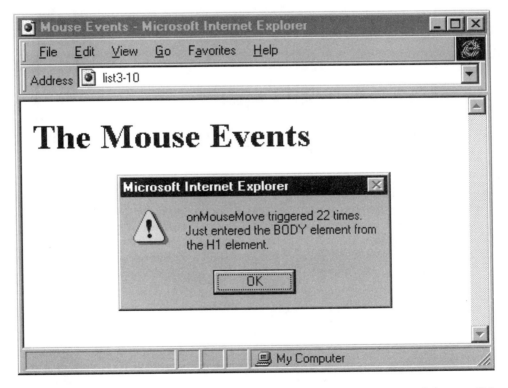

Figure 3–6 Starting from the top of the "M," the mouse pointer was moved down until it left the <H1> element.

In this example, an <H1> element is listening for onmouseout and onmousemove events. As soon as the mouse pointer enters the <H1> element and starts moving, the onmousemove event handler count_move() is called, which increments a counter by one. When the mouse pointer finally leaves the element, the catch_out() event handler is called, which displays where the pointer was, where it is going, and how many times it moved while it was in the element.

In Figure 3–6, I did a little experimentation to try to determine how often the onmousemove event is fired. I started from the top of the "M" and slowly moved the mouse pointer down until it left the element. The faster I moved the mouse, the fewer times onmousemove fired. The results ranged from a count of one, when the mouse was moved as quickly as I could, all the way to forty-nine when moved very slowly.

Keyboard Events

The event object also keeps track of the user's keystrokes. Whenever the user presses a key or releases it, that information is stored in a series of properties on the event object and one or more events are fired.

The onkeydown event fires whenever any key, including CTRL, ALT, SHIFT, and so on is pressed. This event is best bound to the <BODY> element or any of the form elements that require typing. For example, if bound to an <INPUT TYPE="text"> element, onkeydown will fire whenever the user presses a key when that element has focus.

The onkeypress event is much like onkeydown, except that it will not fire when the SHIFT key, or other "modifier keys," such as ALT or CONTROL, are pressed. This allows onkeypress to distinguish between upper and lower case letters, numbers versus symbols, and other special characters produced by combinations of keystrokes.

The last two keyboard events are onkeyup, which fires when the user finally releases the key, and onhelp, which fires when the user presses the "F1" or "Help" key on the browser.

Any time a key is pressed on the keyboard, a number of properties on the event object are updated. If the SHIFT key is pressed, the shiftKey property will contain *true*. When released, the shiftKey property is reset to *false*. The CONTROL key is also tracked by the ctrlKey property, and the ALT key by the altKey property. But if you really want to know what the user is doing, check the keyCode property.

The keyCode property will contain different information depending on which keyboard event was triggered. In the case of onkeypress, keyCode contains the UNICODE value of the currently pressed key. If no keys were pressed, as the case may be if you check this property for an event other than one of the keyboard events, the property will contain zero.

UNICODE is a standard for encoding keystrokes. In particular, the UNICODE standard was developed in response to the fact that, believe it or not, everyone in the world doesn't use the same alphabet. So, the folks at the UNICODE Consortium tackled the task of making sure every language has a standard way of being represented in digital form. Luckily, for our purposes, the UNICODE character set for the English language is very similar to the ASCII character set, so if you're familiar with ASCII, you shouldn't have any problems interpreting the contents of keyCode. If, on the other hand, I've just introduced you to a brand new acronym, take a look at Table 3–1. This describes how the values in the keyCode property relate to actual keystrokes. If you're interested in more information on UNICODE, check out the UNICODE Consortium's website at http://www.unicode.org.

Table 3–1   Part of the UNICODE Basic Latin Character Set

Value	Key	Value	Key	Value	Key
0	NULL	62	>	95	—
13	ENTER	63	?	96	`
27	ESC	64	@	97	a
32	SPACE	65	A	98	b
33	!	66	B	99	c
34	"	67	C	100	d
35	#	68	D	101	e
36	$	69	E	102	f
37	%	70	F	103	g
38	&	71	G	104	h
39	'	72	H	105	I
40	(	73	I	106	j
41	)	74	J	107	k
42	*	75	K	108	l
43	+	76	L	109	m
44	,	77	M	110	n
45	-	78	N	111	o
46	.	79	O	112	p
47	/	80	P	113	q
48	0	81	Q	114	r
49	1	82	R	115	s
50	2	83	S	116	t
51	3	84	T	117	u
52	4	85	U	118	v
53	5	86	V	119	w
54	6	87	W	120	x
55	7	88	X	121	y
56	8	89	Y	122	z
57	9	90	Z	123	{
58	:	91	[	124	|
59	;	92	\	125	}
60	<	93	]	126	~
61	=	94	^		

Unfortunately, the onkeydown and onkeyup events use a slightly different encoding scheme for keyCode. A bit of experimentation produced Table 3–2; however, your keyboard may be able to produce more or less key codes than mine. The keyCode property will contain the currently pressed key when responding to an onkeydown event, and the previously released key for onkeyup.

Table 3–2   Some of the Key Codes Reported from onkeydown and onkeyup

Value	Key	Value	Key
8	BACKSPACE	74	J
9	TAB	75	K
13	ENTER	76	L
16	SHIFT	77	M
17	CONTROL	78	N
18	ALT	79	O
19	PAUSE	80	P
20	CAPS LOCK	81	Q
27	ESC	82	R
32	SPACE	83	S
33	PAGE UP	84	T
34	PAGE DOWN	85	U
35	END	86	V
36	HOME	87	W
37	LEFT ARROW	88	X
38	UP ARROW	89	Y
39	RIGHT ARROW	90	Z
40	DOWN ARROW	112	F1
45	INSERT	113	F2
46	DELETE	114	F3
48	0	115	F4
49	1	116	F5
50	2	117	F6
51	3	118	F7
52	4	119	F8
53	5	120	F9
54	6	121	F10
55	7	145	SCROLL LOCK
56	8	186	;
57	9	187	=
65	A	188	,
66	B	189	-
67	C	190	.
68	D	191	?
69	E	192	`
70	F	219	[
71	G	220	\
72	H	221	]
73	I	222	"

One really neat thing about the keyboard events is that you can use keyCode to determine if the user typed an acceptable key, and if not, your event handler can return *false* to cancel the keystroke's default action—the keystroke itself! In other words, if the user types a "bad key" inside an <INPUT TYPE="text"> element, you can catch that keystroke and cancel it before it ever gets into the element!

In this example, an <INPUT TYPE="text"> element is listening for onkeypress events. Whenever the user attempts to type anything in the text box, the is_good_key() event handler is called to check which keys the user just typed. If anything other than a number was pressed, the returnValue property is set to *false,* cancelling the keystroke. Only numbers will be allowed in the text entry box.

```
<HTML>
<HEAD>
<TITLE>Keyboard Events</TITLE>
<SCRIPT LANGUAGE="JavaScript">
function is_good_key()
{
    var key_pressed = window.event.keyCode;

    // Check if the user pressed key 0 - 9. If any other key
    // was pressed, set the returnValue to false.
    if (key_pressed < 48 || key_pressed > 57)
    {
        window.event.returnValue = false;
    }
}
</SCRIPT>
</HEAD>
<BODY>

<FORM>
Enter a number: <INPUT TYPE="text" onKeyPress="is_good_key()">
</FORM>

</BODY>
</HTML>
```

Speaking of cancelling keystrokes, you can't cancel the default action of function keys. I find this a rather unfortunate circumstance, as sometimes it would be nice to override the function keys. But since "the browser" uses the function keys as shortcuts for browser actions, we're stuck.

Document and Object Loading Events

When documents, images, and other objects are loaded into your browser, a number of events can be triggered. The onload event is fired when your document or another object has completed loading. During the loading process, the onreadystatechange event will fire at various important stages. When the user decides to load a new document, the onbefore-unload event fires so your script can complete any last minute actions or prompt the user to see if anything needs attention before the current document is unloaded and replaced with the new one. After onbeforeunload, the document receives one last chance to complete any clean-up activities when the onunload event fires.

When used to detect if your document has completed loading, the onload event should be bound to the document's <BODY> tag. You can also use the for-event technique, but there is a special twist: the onload event actually belongs to the window object, not the document object! This means you should specify the window object in the "FOR=" attribute, not the document's body! Only for convenience does the inline technique of event handler binding allow you to bind to the <BODY> tag.

```
<SCRIPT FOR=window EVENT=onload LANGUAGE="JavaScript">
```

The onload event handler can also be bound to the <IMG> element, and other objects that load data. For example, when bound to an <APPLET> element, the event handler will fire when the applet has completed loading.

Your object will pass through several stages as it loads and before the onload event is triggered. For example, an <IMG> element's first stage is "uninitialized," meaning the browser knows that an image needs to be loaded but hasn't done anything about it yet. The second stage is "loading," when the browser starts downloading the image from the server. Your object may then enter an "interactive" stage, when it is still loading but the user can begin to interact with it. In the final stage, the load is "complete." These stages of loading are recorded in a property, directly on the object, called "readyState."

As the object loads, the readyState property is updated to reflect the new status, and the onreadystate event is fired to notify your script that the state has changed. Thus, you can use the onreadystate event and the readyState property of the object to determine what phase of loading the object is currently in. Unfortunately, the onreadystatechange event isn't currently implemented, so I can't show an example. Hopefully, by the time you read this the latest version of your browser will respond to this event as described by the documentation.

At some point, the user is going to want to move on to another document. When the user clicks the browser's back button, selects another link, accesses one of their bookmarks, or even attempts to shutdown the browser, an onbeforeunload event will be fired. Like onload, the onbeforeunload event is actually part of the window object but can be bound inline to the <BODY> tag. When the browser detects a request for the current document to be unloaded and before it complies, your onbeforeunload event handler will have an opportunity to do any final cleanup work, and even attempt to persuade the user not to unload the document if something was left in an incomplete state. For example, if the user filled out a form but neglected to actually submit it, an onbeforeunload event handler can be used to detect this situation and warn the user.

```
<HTML>
<HEAD>
<TITLE>Events</TITLE>
<SCRIPT LANGUAGE="JavaScript">
function quit_or_not()
{
```

```
        return "I don't want you to quit!";
}
</SCRIPT>
</HEAD>
<BODY onBeforeUnload="return quit_or_not()">

<CENTER>
<H1>Please Don't Leave This Page!</H1>
</CENTER>

</BODY>
</HTML>
```

One really neat thing about this event is that if the event handler returns a text string, like the one in the example above, that message is automatically displayed and the user is asked to confirm the decision to unload the document. Check out Figure 3–7 to see what this custom confirmation box looks like.

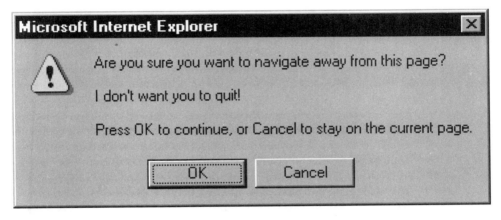

Figure 3–7   The onbeforeunload event handler's custom confirmation box.

I should take this time to mention that asking the user to confirm unloading your document for no other reason than you don't want them to leave is rather annoying. Make sure you have a good reason and back that reason up with a clear text message. For example, if the user forgot to submit a form, the message "Are you sure?" is unacceptable. Be as descriptive as possible: "You forgot to submit the form after making changes."

There is one last annoying detail: right now, even if the user decides not to unload the page, the browser does it anyway. Ironically, the only time onbeforeunload's "don't go away" feature worked for me was when I attempted to reload the current document. For home, back, following another link, choosing a new bookmark, or even turning off the browser, I received the special confirmation box, but the document unloaded regardless of my selection. Before relying on this feature, double check that this bug has been fixed.

After the onbeforeunload event, you have one last chance to do any cleanup or last minute actions: the onunload event. When your document is this far gone, don't try performing any fancy tasks! The document is on the verge of unloading, and that's final. Like onload, this event is part of the window object but you can bind to the <BODY> tag for convenience.

Focus and Blur Events

An object is said to have focus when it is first in line for the user's attention. For example, a window has focus when it is on top of every other window, and its "menu bar" is active. A text entry box has focus when the cursor is flashing inside it and the next characters the user types will affect its content. A button can have focus if the user tabs to it or clicks on it.

Objects can get focus in a number of ways. When a user clicks on a window, that window gets the focus. When the user clicks in or tabs to a text entry field, that field has focus. On Unix, a window can get focus if the mouse pointer simply passes over it, while on the Macintosh focus can be acquired through the use of the "Finder." However an object gets focus, when it gets it, the onfocus event is fired.

The onfocus event can be bound to the browser's window via the <BODY> tag. You can also bind onfocus to a form element. Once the onfocus event handler is bound to an object and when that object gets the focus, the event handler is fired. Only one window can have focus at a time. When another window gets the focus, the current window immediately losses it. The same thing goes for form elements—only one can have focus at a time.

When an object loses the focus, it is said to have been "blurred." This can be detected with the onblur event. Like onfocus, you can bind onblur to the browser's window via the <BODY> tag or a form element. On object becomes blurred if the user tabs away from it, clicks on another object, or even switches to another application. A form element will lose the focus if its window loses focus.

The onfocus and onblur events can be a bit dangerous when bound to a window. In particular, avoid creating alert boxes, confirm boxes, or prompt boxes when the window is listening for onfocus or onblur events! When your alert box opens, the current window will lose focus temporarily. As soon as the user finishes with the alert box, the window will regain focus. If you're not careful, you can put the browser into a rather painful blur-focus-blur loop that can be a bear for the user to break. As a matter of fact, just a few minutes ago I ended up rebooting my laptop after testing some code designed to illustrate this danger. Needless to say, there won't be a screen shot of the code below!

```
<BODY onFocus="alert('I am in a focus loop!')">
```

Do not type the line of code above! As soon as the document containing this ill-fated <BODY> element is loaded, an alert box will steal away its focus. When you click "Ok," the document will regain focus and the alert box will be created again, stealing the focus once more. Endless loop.

Form Related Events

There are three events specific to forms and form elements. They are the onsubmit, onreset, and onchange events and are only useful in the context of forms.

When a user submits a form, usually, but not necessarily, via the submit button, the onsubmit event on the <FORM> element is fired just prior to the data being sent to your CGI script. This allows you the opportunity to double check the user's input, and if necessary cancel the default action of submitting the form. For example, if your form requests the user's mailing address but the city is missing, onsubmit can be used to warn the user and cancel the form submission. I must stress, however, that it is still your CGI script's responsibility to verify whatever data your form has sent, regardless of any protections gained from onsubmit! The user could easily bypass your safety checks by disabling the browser's scripting language, creating another form instead of yours, or even connecting directly to your server and entering incorrect data manually.

```
<FORM onSubmit="return check_form_data()">
```

My philosophy is to precheck all data using the onsubmit event but also to check again when the data reaches the CGI script. The benefit in using onsubmit to precheck the data is that the user won't be forced to wait for my CGI script to notify them of the error—it happens before the script is submitted. On the other hand, I don't feel obligated to provide robust error recovery in my CGI either. A simple "catch all" error message will usually suffice for the users who managed to bypass my onsubmit checks.

You can also check the user's input right after they've modified a field, without waiting for the form to submit. The onchange event is fired right after the user has committed to a change, for example, by tabbing away from the field or performing some action that causes the field to lose focus after a change was made. To use it, bind your onchange event handler directly to the <INPUT>, <SELECT>, or <TEXTAREA> element you are checking.

Since an onchange event is almost always accompanied by an onblur event, and if you're listening for both, you will first receive the onchange, then the onblur. If onchange was fired because the user submitted the form, the onsubmit event will be fired last.

The onreset event is fired when the user resets the form with the "reset" button. Like onsubmit, the onreset event handler should be bound to the <FORM> element. The event is fired just prior to the browser performing the reset action, so it is possible to cancel the reset by returning *false*. On occasion, I have had the need for a reset button that would only "reset" part of my form. Using onreset to override the normal reset action would be an excellent way to achieve this.

Generally speaking, I would not recommend using onsubmit or onreset to display an "Are you sure?" confirmation box. These are, without a doubt, patently annoying! How many times have you yelled in frustration at the computer "If I didn't want to [insert action], I wouldn't have clicked the button?!" You should use these events to double check data or reset the form in a nondefault fashion, not annoy the user.

Selection Events

We had a brief look at the two main "selection" events in chapter two: onselectstart and onselect. The first of these, onselectstart, is fired when the user first begins a selection by holding down the mouse button and dragging the pointer across the document. The event starts as soon as the drag starts but before anything is actually selected. When the user changes the selection by moving the mouse with the button still held, the onselect event will begin to fire. Every time the mouse moves, as little as one character, onselect will fire again and again. If the user changes the selection by clicking elsewhere in the document or otherwise clears the selection, the onselect event will also fire. Unfortunately, there are no events that fire when the user finally finishes the selection by releasing the mouse button, so we'll have to fake it as we did in chapter two using the onmouseup event.

The onselectstart event can be bound to almost any element that contains text or images that can be selected by the user. If bound to a <B> element, for example, the event will fire only when the user starts the selection inside that element. When bound to the <BODY> element, the event will fire anywhere inside the document. You can also bind the event to <INPUT> or <TEXTAREA> elements. The onselect event, on the other hand, is a little more limited. You can only bind it to the <INPUT>, <TEXTAREA>, or the <BODY> element.

If you don't want the user to be able to perform a selection, the onselectstart event's default action, starting a selection, can be canceled by returning *false*. Now the user won't be able to start their selection. I don't recommend this technique as a way to stop users from "copying" data from your document to their clipboard. For one, it would be quite annoying to try selecting some information on your document, like an email or postal address, only to be stopped by your script. Second, it is a poor "security" precaution because a determined user could save the document to their desktop and copy the information that way, cut the information from a "view document source" window, or even print it out and retype it by hand.

After the user has managed to make a selection, he can then "drag" that selection to be pasted into an <INPUT> or <TEXTAREA> element. Images from the <IMG> element can also be dragged and dropped on the desktop as well as links from the <A HREF=> element. When the user attempts to drag a selection or object, an ondragstart event is fired. The ondragstart event can be bound to any element for which a drag might occur. You can bind it to the <BODY> element if you want to know when anything is being dragged or to an individual <IMG> element if you only want to know when the user is trying to drag an image around. You can even bind it to a "regular" element, for example, <B>, if you want to be alerted when the user attempts to initiate drag from that element. If your ondragstart event handler returns *false,* you can cancel the default dragging action and prevent the user from doing any sort of dragging whatsoever. What's very frustrating is that there isn't an event to signify when the user has finished dragging.

Miscellaneous Events

The rest of the events I've classified as miscellaneous. These include a few events for the <MARQUEE> element, some "filter" events, a few "data binding" events, onabort, onerror, onscroll, and onresize.

As all Web designers know, or at least should know by now, the user has ultimate control over the size of the browser window. When the user changes the size of the browser window, an onresize event bound to the <BODY> element will fire. Right now, there's not much you can do with this information, but in the next chapter we'll explore some ways you can find out more about the browser's current setup, including the exact window size. The onresize event can also be bound to a table and the table elements, letting you know if the resize affected the layout of the table. You cannot stop the user from resizing the window by returning *false*.

Users have also been known to take advantage of scrollbars and scroll a document or element. If it has a scrollbar, rest assured that your users are going to scroll it. If you want to know when the user is scrolling around your document, you can bind onscroll to your <BODY> element. Anytime the user scrolls, horizontally or vertically, the onscroll event will fire. You can also bind onscroll to the <TEXTAREA> element, but take care because the event will fire even if the scrolling occurred because the user typed past the boundaries of the <TEXTAREA>. Note that onscroll is one of the few events that will not bubble, so if the user scrolls a <TEXTAREA> and you are bound to <BODY>, onscroll will not fire on the <BODY> element! You cannot cancel a scroll either.

Occasionally things go wrong. An image won't load, a script fails—whatever the reason, an error message may be generated. Nothing is more embarrassing than a user being presented with a broken image or an error message. Fortunately, there is hope: the onerror event. When there is a problem, the onerror event will let you try to recover as gracefully as possible. Right now, onerror only applies to elements failing to load external files, the prime example being an <IMG> element with a bad image. By binding an onerror event handler to the <IMG> element, a bad image URL can be detected and dealt with in a non-embarrassing fashion. For example, you can try to load another image in its place.

Speaking of failure to load an image, the onabort event, if bound to an <IMG> element, will alert your script if the user stops the transfer of an image before it is complete. A good use for onabort is replacing aborted images with a text description of what would have been displayed.

Your marquees also have a few events. When a marquee defined by the Internet Explorer <MARQUEE> element begins to scroll, the onstart event is fired. If the behavior is not "alternate," onstart will also fire whenever the text "restarts" from the start position. When the scrolling is finished, if a "loop" of less than infinite is set, an onfinish event is fired. If the behavior is set to "alternate" when the marquee text bounces off either side of the marquee, an onbounce event is fired. You can't stop the marquee by returning *false* from any of these event handlers.

The <MARQUEE> element is only supported by Internet Explorer and is not in any of the "official" specifications. I really don't want to get into an argument about the "evils" of using a nonstandard element like <MARQUEE>, mainly because I won't have a leg to stand on since, right now at least, only Internet Explorer supports most of the stuff I've talked about up to this point anyway. But I still feel obligated to mention that non-Internet Explorer users won't see your marquee text scrolling. It will just sit there, static and unmoving. Even when other browsers finally support dynamic HTML properly,

<MARQUEE> will likely remain Internet Explorer only, so you may want to investigate the various "marquee" Java applets if you really want scrolling text.

Speaking of things that may or may not be supported by other browsers, "filters" are a really neat feature of style sheets that allow you to modify in some very creative ways how your objects are displayed. For example, you can tell an <IMG> to "glow," automatically create various "shadow" affects, and flip vertically or horizontally. You can even do fades and transitions with filters. Of course, I would rather discuss the specifics when we talk about style sheets later on, but while we're looking at events I thought I would bring up one filter-related event, just for your information. The onfilterchange event is fired whenever a filter does its thing. You can also check out what filter just triggered the event by examining the event object's "srcFilter" property. I'll leave the details of this event and property for later.

One last little group of events I would like to mention are the "data binding" events. Data binding allows you to "attach" data from someplace else directly into your document. For example, you can attach a database entry to a table cell and have your document automatically retrieve that database entry when the document loads. As you can imagine, there are quite a few events that are needed to coordinate and track these data binding transactions. Unfortunately, this topic is beyond the scope of this book, and I won't have the opportunity to discuss the details. However, for completeness I decided to list the events and event object properties associated with data binding.

There are eight events associated with data binding. They are onafterupdate, onbeforeupdate, onerrorupdate, ondatasetcomplete, ondatasetchanged, ondataavailable, onrowexit, and onrowenter. The event object also has one property, "reason," which is updated with additional information when one of these events is fired. More information on data binding can be found on the Microsoft web site at http://www.microsoft.com.

CONCLUSION

The event model allows you to listen in as the user interacts with your document. Without it, your scripting language would be severely crippled and dynamic HTML would not be possible! In this chapter we took an in-depth look at the event model. We reviewed the basics of event handler binding and maybe even learned a new trick or two. We also examined the six steps in an event's life cycle and how you can take advantage of them in designing your event handlers. Most importantly, we examined the event object itself, where you can learn and modify additional information about the current event. The event object contains a number of properties, which are listed in Table 3–3. Another important feature is event bubbling, which gives an element's parent the opportunity to respond to events as well. We learned how to take advantage of event bubbling and how to cancel a bubble if the need arises. We also learned about default actions and how to cancel them with the returnValue property.

Table 3–3 The Event Object Properties

Property	Description
altkey	Contains true if the ALT key was pressed during the event.
button	Mouse button held down during a mouse event. Will contain the following values: 0 = no button, 1 = left button, 2 = right button, 3 = both buttons.
cancelBubble	When set to true, the current event will stop bubbling.
clientX	The mouse's X position relative to the browser window at the time of the event.
clientY	The mouse's Y position relative to the browser window at the time of the event.
ctrlKey	Contains true if the CTRL key was pressed during the event.
fromElement	Set during onmouseover or onmouseout with the element you are moving from.
keyCode	The UNICODE value of the event's key press for onkeypress, or a special key code for onkeyup or onkeydown.
offsetX	The mouse's X position relative to the container position at the time of the event.
offsetY	The mouse's Y position relative to the container position at the time of the event.
reason	For data binding events, the current status of the data transfer.
returnValue	When set to false, will cancel the default action.
screenX	The mouse's X position relative to the user's screen at the time of the event.
screenY	The mouse's Y position relative to the user's screen at the time of the event.
shiftKey	Contains true if the SHIFT key was pressed during the event.
srcElement	The element where the event originated.
srcFilter	For "filter" events, the filter which triggered onfilterchange.
toElement	Set during onmouseover or onmouseout with the element you are moving to.
type	The name of the event without the "on" prefix. (i.e., "onclick" is "click")
x	X position of mouse to the element positioned using CSS positioning.
y	Y position of mouse to the element positioned using CSS positioning.

The new event model gives us a bunch of wonderful events to listen for. These events can be split into groups, based on what they respond to. Mouse related events handle things that happen with the mouse. Keyboard events deal with keystrokes. There are also events that handle document and object loading, focus and blur, form elements, and user selections. The miscellaneous category contains events that perform unique functions: events for the <MARQUEE> element, filters, data binding, onabort, onerror, onscroll, and onresize. A complete list of the events covered appears in Table 3–4.

Table 3–4 A List of Events

Event	Cause
onabort	The loading of an image was aborted.
onafterupdate	When a databound object has completed its data transfer, after onbeforeupdate.
onbeforeunload	The document is about to be unloaded, before the onunload event.
onbeforeupdate	When an object is about to go databound.
onblur	The object (window, form field, etc.) has lost focus.
onbounce	The marquee's text reached the side of the marquee and is about to reverse direction.

Table 3–4   *Continued*

Event	Cause
onchange	The data in a form field has changed and the user committed to that change.
onclick	A mouse click was detected.
ondataavailable	Data has arrived for a data source object.
ondatasetchanged	Data in a data source object has changed.
ondatasetcomplete	All data from a data source object has been transferred.
ondblclick	A mouse double-click was detected.
ondragstart	User began to drag a selection.
onerror	An error has occurred. Used to determine if an <IMG> loaded properly.
onerrorupdate	The onbeforeupdate event handler canceled the data transfer.
onfilterchange	The filter has modified an object.
onfinish	The marquee text is done looping.
onfocus	An object (window, form field, etc.) has gained focus.
onhelp	User attempted to access the browser's help feature.
onkeydown	User pressed a key. Returns a special key code in the keyCode property.
onkeypress	User pressed a key. Returns the UNICODE value of the character generated.
onkeyup	User released a key.
onload	Document or object has loaded.
onmousedown	A mouse button was pressed.
onmousemove	The mouse was moved.
onmouseout	Mouse pointer has left the area of the element.
onmouseover	Mouse pointer has entered the area of the element.
onmouseup	A mouse button was released.
onreadystatechange	The object has changed to another state while loading.
onreset	Form is about to be reset.
onresize	User resized the browser window.
onrowenter	A databound object's current row has changed.
onrowexit	A databound object's current row is about to be changed.
onscroll	User scrolled a scrollbar.
onselect	The user has changed the selection by dragging the mouse while holding the mouse button or by clearing the selection.
onselectstart	The user started a selection.
onstart	The marquee text has begun scrolling or reset to the starting position for another cycle.
onsubmit	A form is about to be submitted.
onunload	Document is about to unload.

Knowing when to use one event over another will keep your code simple and robust, but without an understanding of event bubbling and how your events interact, your code can get confusing and your job frustrating. A solid understanding of the event model will assist in script writing and the creation of compelling dynamic HTML "applications."

CHAPTER 4

More Object Model Details

It's finally time to finish our look at the new object model and tie up some loose ends before moving into the wonderful world of style sheets. In this chapter, we will concentrate on the window object and do a quick review of the object hierarchy. We'll also take another look at the document object, this time concentrating on additional properties, methods, and collections. Finally, we'll round out our knowledge of element objects.

THE WINDOW OBJECT

The new object model looks remarkably similar to the "old" one, so if you've been heavily into the JavaScript or VBScript programming for awhile, this should all seem very familiar. Of course, there are some differences, most notably new objects like "screen" and "event," but for the most part the new model is just an expansion of the old.

The window object is still at the top level, with all other objects underneath. The one exception is the "TextRange" object, which we learned before, only exists when explicitly created and basically floats outside of the model proper. Underneath the window object, you will find the location, history, navigator, screen, event, and document objects. You will also find the frames collection in which any frames are indexed. The window object also gives you access to a few special properties and methods, which we'll look at a bit later.

The Location Object

Everything you ever wanted to know about the window's current URL can be found in the location object's eight properties: hash, host, hostname, href, pathname, port, protocol, and search. The href property contains the entire URL, and the other properties hold the

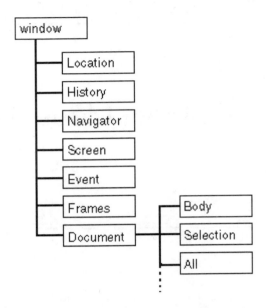

Figure 4–1 The top levels of the new object model. Notice the similarities to the old model.

individual pieces. Each of these properties can be written to as well, allowing you to change either the entire URL or just individual pieces on the fly. The document will be reloaded or updated based on your changes. For example, you can change only the pathname to load a new document on the server, without reforming the entire URL.

Figure 4–2 shows a URL, split into its components. The href property includes the entire URL. The protocol is the method used to retrieve the document, usually "http:." The protocol property includes the ending colon. Next is the host property, which includes the server's name as well as the port number. This is further split into the hostname and port properties. The pathname property is the path of your document or script. More specifically, it is the information after the third slash in the URL. The hash property follows the pathname and is anything after the hash in your URL that represents a named anchor. If this is a URL for a CGI script using the "GET" method, you can also retrieve the

Figure 4–2 A URL dissected. The "search" portion is not shown.

name=value pairs after the question mark. This is called the "search" portion because way back "in the beginning," data after a question mark went straight to a search engine, a remnant of the long forgotten <ISINDEX> element. If the current URL doesn't contain the specified portion, accessing that property will return an empty string.

The location object also gives us access to three methods. The assign() method accepts one argument, the URL, and is equivalent to setting the "href" property. If the URL is valid, the current document is replaced with the document at the new URL. The replace() method also accepts one URL argument; however, the current document is replaced without adding a new entry to the user's history. In other words, if you use assign() to set the URL, the user can click the "back" button to go back to the previous document, but with the replace() method, the old document is gone forever. The final method, reload(), simply reloads the current document, as if the user clicked the "reload" button.

The History Object

The history object has always been shrouded with controversy, even in the old object model. This object represents the user's history list—those documents the user has visited since starting the browser—and some users have serious privacy concerns. Fortunately, these concerns are largely unfounded: the history object does *not* allow your scripts to learn which sites the user has visited. Instead, it gives your script the opportunity to "press" the browser's forward or back buttons. There is *no way,* using the history object, for a script to retrieve a list of sites or documents the user has visited.

There is only one property on this object, "length," that indicates how long the user's history list is. Basically, with this information, you can tell if this is the first document the user has visited since starting the browser (you wish!) or if the user was browsing for awhile before hitting your pages. There is no other practical use for this information, except perhaps to determine how far back in the history you can force the browser to go.

The three methods, back(), forward(), and go(), allow you to pretend you're pressing the browser's back or forward buttons. This could be useful for a custom "back" button, but most uses more extensive than this are unreliable since you really have no idea where in the history your page is. The back() method accepts no arguments and simply simulates pressing the browser's back button once. If you try to go past the start of the user's history, nothing will happen. The forward() method simulates pressing the browser's forward button once. If you go past the end of the history—if this is the last page the user visited—nothing will happen. The go() method gives a little more control, but not much.

The go() method accepts one argument, either a number representing how far in the history list to go or a URL to bring the user back to that URL in her history. When given a positive number, the browser will move that many "units" forward through the history. A negative number moves backwards. For example, go(-1) is the same as the back() method and go(1) is the same as the forward() method. Attempting to move past the boundaries of the history list will result in nothing happening. If you give go() a URL, either whole or part, the browser will attempt to go to the history entry that matches that URL as closely as possible.

The Navigator Object

Some general information about the browser, like the name and version, can be found in the navigator object. If you know your document or scripts will only function with a certain browser version, this is a great way to find out what kind of experience the user is about to have. For example, if you know for a fact that your pages won't work at all using Netscape Communicator, you can check the navigator object and find out which browser the user is using. If the browser is Netscape's, you can send a warning to the user or redirect the browser to a set of pages that will work for Netscape. Incidentally, this object was originally named by Netscape after their older Navigator browser. Microsoft didn't change the name of the object to maintain compatibility. I'm actually a bit upset the object wasn't named something more generic like "browser," but we're stuck with it now so no sense in complaining. In the future, I would hope that browser manufacturers will be more sensitive to the long term. But in this light, Microsoft decided to add an alias to the navigator object called "client." You can use the client object as a substitute for the navigator object, however this will eliminate compatibility with some other browsers until they become compliant with these new specifications.

Four of the navigator object's read-only properties distinguish the name and version of the current browser. The appCodeName property is the "code name" of the browser. This is supposed to represent the name of the browser as it is known to the browser's development team. For example, the Netscape browser was known as "Mozilla" to Netscape, a cartoonish green fire-breathing monster. It is interesting to note that Microsoft has set the appCodeName property to "Mozilla" as well. I hesitate to speculate on the significance of this. A more formal description of the browser can be found in the appName property. This is the browser's official name. The version number of the browser can be found in appVersion. There is also a userAgent property, which is the value sent to your CGI scripts in the HTTP headers. The values of these four properties for two important browsers are noted in Table 4–1.

Table 4–1   The Navigator Object's Browser Identification Properties for Two Browsers

	Microsoft Internet Explorer 4.0	Netscape Navigator 3.0
appCodeName	Mozilla	Mozilla
appName	Microsoft Internet Explorer	Netscape
appVersion	4.0 (compatible; MSIE 4.0b2; Window 95)	3.0 (Win95; I)
userAgent	Mozilla/4.0 (compatible; MSIE 4.0b2; Windows 95)	Mozilla/3.0 (Win95; I)

The final navigator object property is "cookieEnabled," which will contain *true* if the browser has cookies enabled, or *false* if they are disabled. This is a read-only property. Cookies are another subject of debate among users and webmasters. Your script can set a "cookie" on the user's browser, which can contain information of your choosing that will remain persistent even after the user turns off the browser. For example, if your site only allows members to join, you can use a cookie to store the user's membership information so it doesn't have to be retyped every time. There are several problems with this. First, these "cookies" are written directly to the user's harddrive. Personally, I don't like anything being written to my harddrive without my permission, and many others feel exactly the same way. Second, there is still a question of who can access these cookies other than the original site. In theory, only the original site has access, but some people believe that if there is any possibility of this information being leaked, then it is a bad feature. Finally, there is the marketing connection: cookies can be used by marketing firms to track your web activities. You know those little advertising banners on top of some pages? These banners may also include code to create and access cookies, therefore tracking your progress across unrelated Web pages. My point? Some people disable the cookie feature on their browser, so if your scripts rely on cookies, this property will let you know.

Java is another sore point for some people since its security is often in question. Many people disable Java support on their browsers. If you need to know if the browser has Java enabled or disabled, you can use the javaEnabled() method to find out. The method accepts no arguments and returns *true* if Java support is enabled or *false* if it isn't. Be careful because, for reasons unknown to me, javaEnabled() is a method and cookieEnabled is a property. Another "enabled" method is taintEnabled(), which will return *true* if data tainting is supported or *false* if it isn't. Data tainting isn't currently supported in Internet Explorer, so this method will always return *false*.

Speaking of things unsupported by Internet Explorer, the navigator object contains two collections "for compatibility with other browsers." The "mimeTypes" collection would normally contain a list of the MIME types supported by the browser, and the "plugins" collection should contain a list of plugins currently installed. But like I said, Internet Explorer doesn't support either of these features so these collections will always return empty.

The Screen Object

The physical properties of the user's screen can be obtained from the screen object. The screens height and width are found in the "height" and "width" properties, respectively. And no, you can't change them. The "color depth" of the screen can be found in the "colorDepth" property. A screen's color depth is how many bits-per-pixel are available for color information. For example, a 256-color display has a color depth of 8 bits-per-pixel. A 16-color display only has a color depth of 4 bits-per-pixel. This value is also read-only; however, you can affect it indirectly with the "bufferDepth" property.

The "bufferDepth" property controls what is known as the "buffer depth" of the browser. When the document is obscured by another window or is shuffled off the edge of the screen, this property will determine if the data is first buffered or if the data will need to be redrawn when it is uncovered. By changing this value, you can tell the browser how much buffering it should do. Since it would be silly to buffer less (or more) color information then colorDepth is currently set for, this property and colorDepth are very strongly linked. If bufferDepth is set for 0, buffering is disabled and colorDepth is set to the screen's actual color depth. If set for -1, buffering and colorDepth are done at the screen's color depth. If set for one of the following values, buffering is done at this depth and colorDepth is set the same: 1, 4, 8, 15, 16, 24 or 32. An invalid value will set bufferDepth to -1.

So what does all this bufferDepth stuff really mean? Well, if the user's colorDepth is set too high you can downgrade the number of colors the browser will use to draw your document. Though I might add that I've never heard of a user being able to display "too many" colors. Generally, the opposite is true. Setting the bufferDepth to a higher value than the screen's current color depth isn't going to buy you anything either. After all, if the user only has a 256-color display, setting this property to 32 bits isn't going to do much, except possibly cause the browser to use more memory than it has to. On the other hand, I'm sure if you send your users a nice 32-bit video card free of charge, you can get them to set whatever color depth you want. What I'm trying to say is, don't mess with bufferDepth.

While we're talking about things you shouldn't mess with, the final property of the screen object is "updateInterval," which is meant to give you a bit more control over buffering. When set to a value above 0, it will buffer and redraw the user's window at the interval specified in milliseconds. For example, if you have reason to suspect that your document has so much activity that the browser may have a tough time keeping up, as may be the case if you have a lot of animations, you can set the updateInterval to let the browser know how long it should wait before redrawing. Leave this one alone too, please. If you set the value too low, you can compound the problem and the browser will drive itself, and the user's CPU, crazy trying to keep the display updated. If you set it too high, things may not update fast enough. If viewing the document on your browser suggests that you may need to play around with the updateInterval, what you may really need to do is reevaluate the document's design.

The Frames Collection

Just like the old object model, the new model has a frames collection that contains a list of all your frames. Each frame has its own window object, and you can access them by the frame's index number or with the item() method using the frame's name. Be careful when using the method item() method because if your frames' names are not unique, only the first matching frame will be returned. If the names are not unique, or you did not give your frames names, you should use the frame's index number instead. Once you've found the right frame, you need to keep in mind that it is represented by its very own window object, complete with its own document object.

A complete discussion of frames is a bit beyond the scope of this book. For more information, try a good JavaScript or VBScript text. If you've already used frames, then you should be completely at home here. All the same window properties—parent, top, and self—are available, and all the techniques are basically the same as in the old object model.

Opening New Windows and Modal Dialogs

You will be happy to hear that creating and manipulating new windows is the same in the new object model as it was in the old, with a few minor enhancements. There is also a new kind of window, called a modal dialog, that retains focus until closed, like alert() boxes.

Regular windows are still opened with the open() method and can be closed with the close() method. The arguments to open() are a little different, however, so don't skip this section quite yet! The open() method accepts one to four arguments. The first argument is the URL to load into your new window as before. After the URL, you can specify an optional window name. The next argument is a string that identifies which features should be enabled or disabled on your new window, for example, if the window should be opened in fullscreen mode or not, the width, height, and even position relative to the user's screen. Table 4–2 provides a list of possible options. To specify more than one option, put them all in the same string separated by commas. The final argument is a boolean value used to determine how the new URL should be entered in the history list. If set to *true,* the new URL will replace the current history entry. If *false,* a new history entry will be created for the URL.

Table 4–2   Various Features That Can Be Enabled on Your New Window with the open() method

Feature	Description
channelmode=	If yes or 1, enables "theater mode" with the channels bar. If no or 0, this mode is disabled.
directories=	If yes or 1, add directory buttons. If no or 0, don't add directory buttons.
fullscreen=	If yes or 1, window is set to fullscreen mode. If no or 0, window is not fullscreen. Don't forget to give the user some way to close the window!
height=	The height of the window in pixels.
left=	The x position, in pixels, of the left edge of the new window relative to the screen.
location=	If yes or 1, the URL entry field is left on the window so the user can enter a new URL. If no or 0, the user cannot enter a new URL.
menubar=	If yes or 1, the menu bar is displayed. If no or 0, no menu bar is displayed.
resizable=	If yes or 1, the user can resize the window. If no or 0, the window cannot be resized.
scrollbars=	If yes or 1, the window has scrollbars. If no or 0, no scrollbars are given.
status=	If yes or 1, the window has a status bar at the bottom. If no or 0, the status bar is omitted.
toolbar=	If yes or 1, the browser toolbar (Back, Home, Stop, etc.) is displayed. If no or 0, no toolbar is displayed.
top=	The y position, in pixels, of the top of the new window relative to the screen.
width=	The width of the window in pixels.

Most of the features listed in Table 4–2 are self-explanatory; however, a few are interesting enough to warrant a second look. The "fullscreen" feature makes the window occupy the entire screen. There are no toolbars, no directory buttons, no widgets—the entire screen is occupied by the document, with the exception of scrollbars if necessary. It is, therefore, very important that you provide the user with a custom button to close this window! A simple <INPUT TYPE=BUTTON> element with an onclick="self.close()" event handler bound to it should be sufficient, but remember that many users will panic without the precious window widgets to guide them! If you're curious yourself, ALT-F4 will close the window in Windows 95.

The "channelmode" feature is another fascinating one. When selected, the window enters this bizarre fullscreen mode with the "channel band" down the left side and some browser controls at the top. If you have never seen this mode, try it out sometime! This little snippet of JavaScript will open a blank window with channelmode enabled:

```
window.open("about:blank","MyWindow","channelmode=yes");
```

The open() method will return the window object for the new window. Just like the old object model, your new window has access to the "opener" property to determine its parent window. You also have access to one more property, the "closed" property, which can be used to determine if a window has been closed or not.

If these new window features aren't enough for you, there is also a new type of window called a modal dialog. Modal dialogs are special because, unlike regular windows, they will refuse to give up focus until the user closes them. This finally allows us to display a short form for user input that cannot be ignored, for example, a custom username and password entry dialog that will stay in front and retain focus until the user either enters the information or cancels the window. No more worries about important windows getting "lost" behind its parent!

You can open a new modal dialog with the showModalDialog() method. It takes one to three arguments, the first being the URL to load into your new dialog window. You can load any document into a modal dialog, but in general modal dialogs are used to display short forms for user input. For example, if users click a link to change their passwords, you could use a modal dialog to prompt for new passwords and confirm the change. Let's try doing this right now. The code below will be the initial document with a button. When the user clicks the button, the modal dialog will be created.

```
<HTML>
<HEAD>
<TITLE>Modal Dialog Example</TITLE>
<SCRIPT LANGUAGE="JavaScript">
function new_password()
{
    var newPass;
    newPass = window.showModalDialog("list4-1b.htm", null,
                         "dialogWidth:13em;dialogHeight:16em");
    if (newPass != null)
    {
    alert("New password is '" + newPass + "'");
    }
```

```
}
</SCRIPT>
</HEAD>
<BODY>

<FORM>
<INPUT TYPE="button" VALUE="Change Password"
onClick="new_password()">
</FORM>

</BODY>
</HTML>
```

All the action takes place in the new_password() function, triggered when the user clicks the "Change Password" button. The showModalDialog() function is called with three arguments. The first is the document that contains our new form. We'll look at the other two arguments shortly; however, you may have guessed that the third argument is used to specify additional parameters for our new window.

```
<HTML>
<HEAD>
<TITLE>Passwords</TITLE>
<SCRIPT LANGUAGE="JavaScript">
function doOK()
{
    var myForm = window.document.forms[0];

    if (myForm.NEW_PASS.value == myForm.AGAIN.value)
    {
        window.returnValue = myForm.NEW_PASS.value;
        window.close();
    }
    else
    {
        alert("Doesn't match—try again!");
    }
}
function doCancel()
{
    window.returnValue = null;
    window.close();
}
</SCRIPT>
</HEAD>
<BODY>
Enter your new password twice in the spaces provided below:
```

```
<FORM>
Passwd <INPUT TYPE="password" NAME="NEW_PASS" SIZE=10><BR>
Again <INPUT TYPE="password" NAME="AGAIN" SIZE=10><BR>
<P>
<INPUT TYPE="button" VALUE="Ok" onClick="doOK()">
<INPUT TYPE="button" VALUE="Cancel" onClick="doCancel()">
</FORM>

</BODY>
</HTML>
```

The second listing is the document that will be loaded in our new window. Nothing too outrageous here either. A form is created with two text entry fields. The first field is for the user to enter her password, and the second is for the user to retype it to confirm that there were no mistakes. Since the <INPUT TYPE="password"> element hides what the user types, this second field is very important. There's nothing quite like the feeling of changing your password but mistyping it and not being able to log back in. I know—I've managed to do it at least once, even after typing it a second time to confirm. The only thing worse is being the administrator who has to change the password back at 3 AM after a frantic phonecall. But I digress. There are also two buttons, one marked "OK" and one marked "Cancel." Both buttons have onclick event handlers.

Figure 4–3   The modal dialog window.

When the user finishes typing the new passwords and clicks the "OK" button, the doOK() event handler is called. The first thing it does is retrieve the form object and store it in the "myForm" variable for convenience. Then the values of each field are compared to ensure that the user didn't mistype the password. If they don't match, an alert() is sent to the user, explaining the situation and giving her an opportunity to correct. But if they do match, the following line of code is executed:

```
window.returnValue = myForm.NEW_PASS.value;
```

Like the event object, the window object also has a "returnValue" property. The modal dialog window can use this property to return information back to the original calling script, which is actually the whole point of modal dialog windows. In this case, I picked the first value of the first password field—since we've just confirmed both fields are identical, it doesn't matter which we choose—and assigned it to the returnValue property. Then the window is closed with the close() method, and control is back to the new_password() function on our first document.

```
function new_password()
{
    var newPass;

    newPass = window.showModalDialog("list4-1b.htm", null,
                        "dialogWidth:13em;dialogHeight:16em");
    if (newPass != null)
    {
        alert("New password is '" + newPass + "'");
    }
}
```

Looking back, you can see how the return value of the showModalDialog() method is assigned to the "newPass" variable. If the user didn't click the "Cancel" button, this variable will contain the actual text of the password, as returned in the returnValue property. The rest, as they say, is academic.

Now back to the showModalDialog() method's arguments. The second argument, which in our previous example is set to *null,* is one way the original script can pass a bit of extra information to the new modal dialog window's scripts. For example, I could have used this argument to tell the scripts in the new modal dialog how long it has been since our user last changed her password. If it has been too long, the script might send a warning if she decides to cancel the operation. The information given to the second argument can be anything: a number, string, even a boolean. When the new modal dialog is created, its window object is given the argument via the "dialogArguments" property. Rewriting the doCancel() function to perform this check is easy.

```
    function doCancel()
    {
        var myArg = window.dialogArguments;
```

```
    if (myArg >= 3)
    {
        alert("You must change your password!");
    }
    else
    {
        window.returnValue = null;
        window.close();
    }
}
```

To test our new function, all we need to do is change the second argument of the showModalDialog() method to the number of months, as shown below:

```
newPass = window.showModalDialog("list4-1b.htm",4,
                                 "dialogWidth:13em;
                                 dialogHeight:16em");
```

In this example, we told our function that the user hasn't changed her password in four months. Now, when the user clicks "Cancel," the script will issue a warning that the user must change her password.

Of course this brings up the question, how do you send multiple arguments? For example, maybe different users have different time constraints on their passwords; on many systems, administrative users must change their passwords more frequently then regular users. This, unfortunately, requires a bit of creativity. My preferred method is to jam all of the arguments into one long string, separated by an arbitrary delimiter, and then split the "real" arguments out of the string later. It's actually easier then it sounds, but a bit awkward.

```
function doCancel()
{
    var myArgs = window.dialogArguments.split(" ");
    var timeLimit = myArgs[0];
    var lastChange= myArgs[1];

    if (lastChange >= timeLimit)
    {
        alert("You must change your password!");
    }
    else
    {
        window.returnValue = null;
        window.close();
    }
}
```

In the code above, the myArgs variable has turned into an array. By applying the split() function directly to the dialogArguments property, each "real" argument, in this case separated by spaces, is stuffed into its own array cell. The first argument goes in myArgs[0], the second in myArgs[1], and so forth. To make the function a bit easier to understand, I immediately assign each array cell to a more descriptive variable. It makes it easier to understand your code later. To call our new function, all we need to do is change the second showModalDialog() argument to include both "real" arguments, separated by spaces. In the example below, we are passing "two" arguments. The first is the number of months the user is allowed before being forced to change her password, and the second is how many months it has been since her password was really changed.

```
newPass = window.showModalDialog("list4-1b.htm","2 3",
                    "dialogWidth:13em;dialogHeight:16em");
```

Passing multiple return values back to the calling script can be done in the same way. Just join the arguments into one long string, each separated by some sort of delimiter, and then split them apart later. You can choose whatever delimiter you want but try to keep your choice consistent.

The third argument to showModalDialog() is used to define additional properties for your new window. You can control the window's size, position, and even the default font. Unlike the open() method, the parameter names are separated from their values by a colon instead of an equals sign. Multiple parameters are separated by semicolons instead of commas. In the example we have been using throughout this chapter, our modal dialog window has been told set at a width of 13em and a height of 16em. The "em" designation is a unit of measure you may be familiar with if you do a lot of desktop publishing. It is the height of your font for that particular point size. In other words, a height of 1em would be roughly one line of text high. We'll go over font sizes and the like when we get into style sheets. For now, take a look at Table 4–3 for a list of the available showModalDialog() parameters.

Table 4–3 Parameters accepted by the showModalDialog() method's Third Argument

Feature	Description
border:	Accepts the arguments "thick" or "thin."
center:	If yes or 1, the window is centered. If no or 0, the window will use the dialog Top and dialogLeft arguments to determine positioning.
dialogHeight:	Height of window, defaults to pixels, but will accept a style sheet unit like "em."
dialogLeft:	Position of the left edge of the window.
dialogTop:	Position of the top edge of the window.
dialogWidth:	Width of window, defaults to pixels, but will accept a style sheet unit like "em."
font:	Sets the font using style sheet formatting.
font-family:	Sets the font family using style sheet formatting.
font-size:	Sets the font size, using style sheet formatting.
font-style:	Sets the font style, using style sheet formatting.
font-variant:	Sets the font variant, using style sheet formatting.

(continued)

Table 4–3 *Continued*

Feature	Description
font-weight:	Sets the font weight, using style sheet formatting.
help:	If yes or 1, will include the "help" button in the title bar. If no or 0, will not include the "help" button.
maximize:	If yes or 1, will include the "maximize" button in the title bar. If no or 0, will not include the "maximize" button.
minimize:	If yes or 1, will include the "minimize" button in the title bar. If no or 0, will not include the "minimize" button.

Most of the parameters in Table 4–3 are relatively straightforward; however, the "font" options require their arguments to be specified in style sheet format, but since I plan to go into great detail on this topic later, we'll defer this discussion until then.

If you need to know the size or position of your new modal dialog, you can learn these values from inside your new window. There are four window properties, each corresponding to one of the four parameters for size and position. The dialogLeft and dialogTop properties will report the window's position, and the dialogWidth and dialogHeight properties its size. These properties are only available on a modal dialog window. Oh, and did I mention you can change their values as well? Simply write the new value to the property of your choice and the window will automatically move or resize! Be sure to remember to specify the units, or your results may not be quite what you expected. Also, when making your window larger, I noticed that it sometimes doesn't redraw the status bar quite right. Keep an eye out for this problem, and hopefully it will be fixed in the next release.

Timeouts and Intervals

You can't always rely on user generated events to control your document. Sometimes you need to make sure a function is called at a specific time, not necessarily after any one event. For example, you may have an image, like a banner, that you would like to change every five seconds. But using events alone, this is not possible. The window object offers two solutions to this problem: timeouts and intervals.

The first solution, which was present in the old object model, is the timeout. A timeout is a set period of time after which a function is executed. In other words, you can use a timeout to execute your "changeImage()" function after a five-second delay. Setting a timeout is done using the setTimeout() method, found on our friend the window object. The first argument to setTimeout() is the function, or expression, to execute. The next argument is how many milliseconds to wait before executing the expression. If you would like, you can also include the language to use for your expression, as a third argument. For example, if you want to open an alert() box after a delay of five seconds, you would use the following code:

```
setTimeout("alert('Five seconds has passed!')",5000, "JavaScript");
```

Five seconds, or five-thousand milliseconds, after this setTimeout() method is called, your alert() box will be displayed. During these five seconds, your script will continue to execute as normal. The rest of your script won't wait for the five seconds to expire before continuing, but as soon as the time is up, your alert() box will immediately appear, interrupting any code currently running.

The setTimeout() method will return a "timeout identifier," which can be stored in a variable for later use. With this identifier, you can later cancel the timeout if you decide you don't want to perform the expression after all. This is done with the clearTimeout() method, which requires the timeout identifier as its only argument. The code fragment below will cancel the timeout before it gets a chance to open your alert() box.

```
var timeoutID = setTimeout("alert('Cancel me!')",5000);
clearTimeout(timeoutID);
```

The problem with timeouts is, once they have executed they won't repeat. So you can only change your image once, but you can't flip through them like a slideshow. The solution to this problem is to reset your timeout every time the function is executed, creating an infinite loop, with one timeout calling the next. Not bad, but not an optimal solution. Seeing this need, a new timing mechanism was added: the interval.

Intervals are like timeouts, except intervals will execute your code repeatedly while timeouts will do it only once. You define intervals using the setInterval() method, which is called just like setTimeout(). The first argument is the code to execute, the second is the time interval in milliseconds. You can also have an optional third "language" argument. The setInterval() method also returns an "interval identifier," which can be used to cancel your interval at any time with the clearInterval() method.

```
<HTML>
<HEAD>
<TITLE>Countdown</TITLE>
<SCRIPT LANGUAGE="JavaScript">
var intervalID;

function start_counter()
{
    intervalID = setInterval("countdown()",1000,"JavaScript");
}

function countdown()
{
    var count_element = document.all.Count;
    count_element.innerText-;

    if (count_element.innerText == 0)
    {
        clearInterval(intervalID);
        count_element.innerText = "LIFTOFF!";
    }
}
```

```
</SCRIPT>
</HEAD>
<BODY onLoad="start_counter()">

<H1>Countdown: <SPAN ID="Count">3</SPAN></H1>

</BODY>
</HTML>
```

The example above does a countdown starting at three, and announces "LIFTOFF!" when the counter reaches zero. The whole process is started when the document finishes loading. The onload event handler, start_counter(), is called, which initializes the setInterval() method. The interval identifier is saved to a global variable, "intervalID," so we can stop the counter later. As each second passes, the count_down() function is called. Here we find the <SPAN> element that contains our little counter, and then using the decrement operator, we subtract one. When the counter reaches zero, we use clearInterval() to stop the countdown and then replace the number zero with the word "LIFTOFF!"

There's not much else to timeouts and intervals. You give them some code to execute and a time to execute it in, and they do their thing. But one word of caution: these timers aren't 100 percent accurate. For applications that only require a precision of a second or so, you will find things will generally go off on time. But trying to time things to a fraction of a second can be futile. This is because if the browser is a bit busy, it may not be able to get to your timer at exactly the time you requested. If you're executing some heavy duty scripts, and the browser is struggling to keep up, your timers may "jitter" a little. This means you may see a split second slowdown here or there, and maybe a sudden burst as it tries to catch up. Generally not a problem, but don't expect "mission critical" results either.

A Few More Window Features

There are, of course, a few more window properties and methods I haven't yet covered. Most of these aren't new to the object model, and I'm sure you'll recognize most of them if you've done much scripting in the past.

For properties, the window object also offers "status," which is the message displayed in the status bar. I'm sure everyone remembers the infamous "scrolling status bar" messages when JavaScript was first introduced. You can write to the status property to change the message in the status bar, or you can read from it if you want to know what is currently being displayed. With status you will also find a new property, "defaultStatus." The defaultStatus property, if applied, will always reappear after something has occurred to change the status bar, for example, if the user moved her mouse over a link or another status property was set. The "status" property should be used for transient messages and the "defaultStatus" property if you want something more permanent.

Moving on, you will find all your old friends. The alert(), confirm(), and prompt() methods are all still there. There is also a blur() method for removing the focus from the window and a focus() method to grab it back. Be careful about blur-focus-blur tug-of-war, because these methods will trigger their respective events. Also, anytime you blur a window, any element in that window that had focus will be blurred as well, possibly triggering an extra onblur event you didn't expect.

One neat new method is scroll(), which if even X and Y coordinates, will scroll the window to that position relative to the document. For example, if you wanted to scroll to a specific element and you know its coordinates, you would use the scroll() method to do it. The example below will scroll the document in the current window to an X position of 0 and a Y position of 800.

```
window.scroll(0,800);
```

Another new one is showHelp(), which as the name implies, brings up a help file at the URL you specify in a separate "help" window. It takes two arguments, the first being the URL of the help file. The second is an optional argument to send to the window, much like the second argument in the showModalDialog() method.

The final method, another new one, is execScript(), which executes an arbitrary chunk of code. What is so special about this is, you can use execScript() to execute code stuffed inside a variable.

```
var exec_me = "var msg='Hello!'; alert(msg);";
window.execScript(exec_me, "JavaScript");
```

In the example above, some JavaScript has been written to the string "exec_me," and that string was then passed to execScript() for execution. The execScript() method accepts two arguments. The first is a string with the code to execute, and the second is the language to use. According to the documentation, the second argument is optional and should default to "JScript," but unfortunately if you leave out the second "optional" argument, you will get an error.

Be very careful about executing a user supplied argument! You should even be careful when mixing user supplied arguments with your own code because a clever user could turn a relatively benign code fragment into something you didn't intend. Perhaps I'm being a bit melodramatic since the user shouldn't be able to do anything harmful using any of the currently available scripting languages. Just keep in mind that if you use a value supplied by the user in execScript(), your script's code may be accidentally (or intentionally) modified.

THE DOCUMENT OBJECT

The window object offers a wide variety of useful objects, but the most important of these I have saved for last: the document object. Of course, we have been using the document object all along, but until now we have only taken a cursory look. The document object has a lot more uses than just a container for your element objects, and it's time we explored this wealth of properties, methods, and collections in further detail.

Document Object Properties

The document object offers over a dozen properties, and I've arbitrarily split these into two groups: color related and others. The color-related properties allow you to change the background, text, and link colors of your document. Other properties give you access to additional information, for example, the date your document was last modified or the referrering document.

The bgColor and fgColor represent the background and default text color of your document, respectively. Both properties can be read from, to determine the current settings, or written to, modifying the current colors. You can assign any valid color code to these properties to change their values. For example, if you prefer using hexadecimal triples, you can change the background color to blue with the following code:

```
document.bgColor = "#0000FF";
```

If for some unknown reason you prefer using the color's name instead of its hexadecimal value, you would use the following code instead:

```
document.bgColor = "blue";
```

The fgColor property works the same way. As soon as the new values are assigned, the colors will instantly change except if the default color has been manually overridden with the <FONT> element or some other method.

When reading the values of these properties, the browser will always return the hexadecimal triple, including the leading hash sign, and not the color name. For example, if the background color is set to green, reading the value of the bgColor property will return the value "#00FF00," not the name "green." This was done to ensure that you have a firm grasp of obscure topics, such as hexadecimal, and is used as a way to preserve the jobs of highly paid consultants. If when picking out the color for your new bathroom tile, you ask the salesperson if they have anything in "#00FFCC," you know you can start demanding the big bucks at work. Or you need a vacation. In any event, regardless of how the colors were initially set, these properties will always return the hexadecimal triple.

The three other color-related properties are alinkColor, linkColor, and vlinkColor. As the names imply, these properties represent the default active, unvisited, and visited link colors respectively. They are set the same way as fgColor and bgColor and reading them produces the same hexadecimal triples as well. Most browsers default linkColor to a nice bright blue and vlinkColor to a cool purple. A link is called "active" when it has been selected, but the browser hasn't begun loading the new page yet. For Internet Explorer, this color defaults to the same blue as linkColor. Netscape's browser defaults to a bright red.

Before changing any of these link colors, please decide whether the change is really necessary first. Most users expect unvisited links to be blue and visited links to be purple. Serious deviations from this norm can end up in confusion. For example, making visited links blue and unvisited links purple is a sure formula for chaos. Whatever you do, please don't use the color properties for "color cycling" tricks. Personally, nothing is more annoying then links, text, or background cycling through all the colors of the rainbow.

There is also a nice selection of other noncolor-related properties on the document object. We've already looked at a few of those in previous chapters: the selection object, readyState, and the body object. The rest of the properties are described in the following paragraphs in alphabetical order.

If you need a quick way to determine which element currently has the focus in your document, you can use the "activeElement" property. The property is automatically set when an element receives focus and cannot be written to directly. If you want to change the value of activeElement to a specific element, you will need to use that element's focus() method to assign focus.

The "cookie" property contains the value of any cookies for this document. This gives you a convenient method of writing and reading cookies. A full discussion of cookies is best left for another day; however, I would like to point out some concerns users have expressed. Cookies are a way of storing a short string of information on the user's machine, which you can retrieve later. It is a great way to "keep state" between user sessions since cookies can persist even after the user has shutdown the browser. What was the user doing the last time she visited your page? What color scheme does she prefer? What was her last search string? All these things are excellent things to store in cookies. But the very thing that makes cookies so special, the fact that they persist between sessions, is what users object to most.

Another problem with cookies is that they can be very easily abused. I like revisiting a Web site and seeing all my previous settings still in place. It's convenient to have search forms set the way you last left them. That's not the problem. The problem is when cookies are used as a market research tool. I don't like advertising sites being able to track my Web exploits using cookies, and I don't like people I don't know storing *any* information I don't know about on *my* harddrive. Many other users feel the same way. What this all boils down to is that many users disable the cookie feature on their browser, if possible, so you shouldn't rely on cookies being available for your application to work.

The "domain" property can be used in cases where you have two or more documents being displayed in frames, and you need to communicate between them. Normally, for security reasons, unless the documents are in the same domain, they aren't allowed to communicate. But sometimes your documents may be on two or more different servers that you control. For example, you may have most of your documents on a machine named "www.prenhall.com" but some additional documents on your sales department's server, "sales.prenhall.com." In cases like these, you can use the domain property to change the domain both documents report they are from to just "prenhall.com." This causes the domain names to match and allows the frames to communicate with each other without raising a security exception.

Of course, if you could just change your domain arbitrarily, that would defeat the whole purpose of restricting communication between frames by domain. After all, if I wanted access to a document on a server I did not control, I could simply change my domain and bypass security completely. So, as you might guess, there are some serious restrictions on what you can assign to this property. Essentially, the new domain must be a subset of the old domain. For example, if one of your servers is named "www.prenhall.com" and the other is named "sales.prenhall.com," you can only change the domain to "prenhall.com." Anything else would trigger an error.

Another useful property is "lastModified," which records the date and time the current document was last modified. The format the date is returned in is "MM/DD/YY HH:MM:SS," which is unfortunately rather nonstandard. For one thing, most non-US countries record their dates with the day before the month. Also, there are already standards that specify how dates should be represented, and this definitely isn't one of those standards. Nice to see they are looking ahead toward the "Year 2000" problem as well. But if you can look past this minor shortcoming, the "lastModified" property can be quite useful. One excellent, if not somewhat trivial, use is for inserting the last modified date at the bottom of your document, particularly when server side includes aren't available to do the job for you. The following code will insert a line with the document's modified date straight into your document:

```
<SCRIPT>document.writeln("Modified "+document.lastModified);
</SCRIPT>
```

Anywhere this line is inserted in your document, the output "Modified 09/27/97 22:05:47" will appear, with the date of course replaced with the correct value. Before getting your hopes up, you can *not* change the value in the lastModified property.

·If you need a quick and easy way to find the full URL of the current document, you can use the "location" property. This is an actual property and is in no way related to the "location" object. It contains the full URL of the current document and is a read-only property. If you want to change the document's URL, you should use the "location" object instead, located on the window object.

The "parentWindow" property can be used to retrieve the current window object in which this document is contained. Like the location property, which is just another way to retrieve a document's location, the parentWindow property is just another way to retrieve the current window. You can also use the "window" keyword, which is synonymous with the document's current window, or even the "self" object, which is yet another alias for the current window. On the other hand, using parentWindow may be a little clearer then "window" or "self." Well, maybe not "self"—I don't see how you can be clearer then that—but at least with parentWindow, there is no doubt which window you're talking about.

If you need to know what URL the user just came from, you have access to the document's "referrer" property. Some great information can be obtained from this property. For example, did the user get to this document from another document on your site, or did she use a bookmark? If she came from a document on another site, was it from a site you know of, like a partner's, or did someone you don't know create a link to your pages? If the user came from another site, would it be best to send her to an introductory page, or would a short set of instructions somewhere at the top of your document be appropriate? Do you have a special arrangement with a partner to display a welcome message or special options for users arriving from her site? With the referrer property, your script can find out where the user just came from and model the page appropriately.

You also have access to your document's current title, as set by the <TITLE> element, via the "title" property. This property can be read from as well as written to, so you can change the document's title at any time, simply by modifying this property. Not that modifying a document's title is necessarily a good thing to do. Generally speaking, your users probably won't notice your document's title unless they just bookmarked your page, so using this feature for status message is inappropriate. But if you have the need to do so, the "title" property is there for your use.

If the location property frustrated you with its read-only nature, and you don't want to use the location object to change the current URL, then the "URL" property is your solution. The URL property is actually an alias for "window.location.href" and can be read from, to retrieve the current full URL, or written to, if you want to change the current document. You can use the document's URL property just as you would the location object's href property. It's exactly the same thing.

Document Object Methods

Most of the methods available on the document object are for execCommand() and its support methods, as we discussed in previous chapters, and for the "old way" of manipulating documents with open(), write(), writeln(), and close(). There are also a couple of miscellaneous methods. We've already covered the execCommand() methods, but it would be advantageous to review the remaining methods.

If you've been scripting long, you probably have some experience with write() or writeln(), and maybe open(), close(), and clear() as well. These functions allow your script to insert text into the document *as the document is being written.* We actually did this once already with the "lastModified" example. There, the writeln() method was used to insert some text and the contents of the lastModified property. The writeln() method inserts a text string into your document, as it is being written, and appends a newline to the end of the string. The write() method behaves identically as writeln(), with the exception that it does not insert a newline at the end of the line.

The trick with write() and writeln() is that the document must not be finished loading for them to work properly. One excellent use of these methods is to insert text into your document at load time. For example, you can use the referrer property to determine where the user is coming from and insert a special message if she is using a link from a friend's page to get to your pages.

```
<HTML>
<HEAD>
<TITLE>My Special Document</TITLE>
</HEAD>
<BODY>

<H1>This Is My Special Document</H1>

<SCRIPT LANGUAGE="JavaScript">

if (document.referrer == "http://www.prenhall.com/links.html")
{
    document.writeln("<CENTER>Ah, you're a friend of Prentice-
Hall!</CENTER>");
}
```

```
</SCRIPT>

<P>Please enjoy your stay!</P>
</BODY>
</HTML>
```

In the example above, if the user reached this document from a specific URL, a special message is inserted in the document. Otherwise, the special message isn't displayed. If the document has finished loading and you attempt to use one of these methods to add some more text, you will receive an error. Instead, use the dynamic content techniques described earlier.

You can also use write() and writeln() to create an entire document using JavaScript. For example, after opening a new window, you may want to use your script to create the new document instead of loading one. In these cases, you would need the services of the document open() and close() methods.

The *document* open() and close() methods are very different from the *window* methods of the same name. The window methods open and close new windows, but the document methods open and close new documents in an already existing window. Or more specifically, the document open() method resets the current document and prepares the browser to receive information for a new document, and document close() closes the document for input and sends it to the browser.

```
<HTML>
<HEAD>
<TITLE>Using open() and close()</TITLE>
<SCRIPT LANGUAGE="JavaScript">
function new_doc()
{
    document.open();
    document.writeln("<H1>A New Document</H1>");
    document.close();
}
</SCRIPT>
</HEAD>
<BODY>

<H1 onClick="new_doc()">Click Here</H1>

</BODY>
</HTML>
```

In the example above, when the user clicks the <H1> element, the function new_doc() is called. In new_doc(), a document open() method "resets" the document to accept new information. A writeln() is then used to send some simple output to our new document, and finally document close() tells the browser it should display the document to the user.

When the document open() method is applied to an already existing document, the current document is cleared from the browser to make way for the new information. However, there is a method specifically for this purpose: the clear() method. Right now, as far as I can tell, clear() and open() do exactly the same thing. You can start writing to your document right after using the clear() method with no ill effects. So what is it used for, really? At this point, my guess is backwards compatibility with older browsers.

There are two more, unrelated methods at your disposal. The elementFromPoint() method accepts two arguments, an X and Y coordinate relative to the browser window. The closest element object to that point is then returned. The last method, createElement(), is a little more complicated.

Using the createElement() method, you can create new <IMG> and <OPTION> elements to be added to your documents. This method accepts one argument, the name of the tag you are attempting to create, and it returns the element object of the newly created element. Right now, these are the only elements you can create, and therefore the only valid argument values are "img" and "option." Once you have your new element object, you need to manually "install" them.

Creating and installing a new <OPTION> element is relatively easy, as illustrated in the code sample below. Here, the createElement() method is called with the "OPTION" argument to create a new <OPTION> element. The resulting new element is stored in the variable "myElement," which is then used to assign a text value to our new option. Finally, the option is added to a <SELECT> element named "MySelect" in one of the forms in our fictitious document.

```
function add_new_option()
{
    var myElement = document.createElement("OPTION");
    myElement.text = "Testing";
    document.forms[0].MySelect.add(myElement);
}
```

The add() method is a special method found on <SELECT> elements. In the example above, the one argument is our new element object. The add() method adds this new <OPTION> element to the end of our <SELECT> element's list of options. If you supplied add() with a second argument, an index number, this index number is used as the position for the new option instead of the end.

For images, createElement() works in much the same way as using "new Image()" to create a new image. Instead of creating an entirely new and separate image for your document, your new image object will be used to replace an existing image in your document. In the example below, a new image is created and the resulting object is assigned to the "myElement" variable. The images URL is then assigned to its "src" property. Your new image is now ready, but you still need to place it on the document. An existing

<IMG> element name "MyImage" is used for this purpose, and its contents are replaced with the new image we just created.

```
function add_new_image()
{
    var myElement = document.createElement("IMG");
    myElement.src = "new_image.gif";
    document.all.MyImage.src = myElement.src;
}
```

In the future, I'm sure createElement() will be able to create other types of elements for your document. Right now, it is simply a convenient replacement for the JavaScript "new" operator. All of these "replacements" for already existing features may seem rather silly at first, but actually this type of method paves the way for compatibility with other scripting languages that may not support some of the built-in operators and functions currently found in JavaScript or VBScript.

Document Object Collections

You're already familiar with at least one collection on the document object: the "all" collection. Collections contain pointers to all objects in a specific category. In the case of the "all" collection, the category is "everything," but there are other more specialized collections at your disposal. For example, the "forms" collection contains pointers to all of the forms in the current document.

Collections are all accessed in basically the same way. You can specify the index number of the object you're interested in directly as an argument to the collection, or you can use the unique identifier instead. You also have access to the special item() method, to retrieve a specific object, and the length property to determine how many objects are in the collection. The "all" collection also gives you access to the tags() method, for retrieving another collection of element objects with that specific tag.

There are currently eleven collections on the document object, including "all." These are: all, anchors and links, applets, embeds and plugins, forms, frames, images, scripts, and stylesheets. Some of these collections, like anchors and links, are very closely related or contain the same information but with a different name. These are all briefly described in the following paragraphs.

The "all" collection contains a list of every element object in your current document. This is, in my opinion, one of the most important collections because with it, you can easily retrieve any element object in your document. We've been using this collection extensively until now, and if you only learn one of these collections, make it this one.

The anchors and links collections are very closely related. Both contain lists of <A> element objects but also subcategorized by the type of <A> element object. In the anchors collection, you will find all <A> element objects that contain the "NAME=" or "ID=" attributes. The links collection, on the other hand, contains all <A> element objects that contain the "HREF=" attribute, as well as any <AREA> elements. In other words, things that act as hyperlinks. Some element objects can be in both collections at the same time, for example, an <A> element that contains both "NAME=" and "HREF=" attributes will appear in both collections.

The applets collection contains a list of all <APPLET> element objects in your document.

The embeds and plugins collections are actually different names for the same collection, or more specifically, the plugins collection is an alias for the embeds collection. In this context, "plugins" does not refer to third-party plugins used to give extra functionality to your browser. Instead, you will find a list of all <EMBED> element objects in the current document. Either collection name can be used; however, it is recommended that you use "embeds" in favor of "plugins."

The forms collection is a list of all <FORM> elements in your document, just like in the old object model. You have probably already seen me use forms collection in some of our examples. In these cases, I used the older square-bracket method of retrieving a specific form: document.forms[0] instead of document.forms(0). The square-bracket method is perfectly valid, at least for JavaScript, but strictly speaking using regular parentheses is probably a bit more proper. My only defense is, old habits die hard. Incidentally, the square-bracket method will work on all the other collections, including the "all" collection. Not that I am encouraging this technique, but if you do use square brackets instead of parentheses, I'm certain the world will continue turning.

The frames collection, on the document object, is essentially the same frames collection as is found on the window object. It contains a list of all frames, or <IFRAME> elements if appropriate, currently in use by your document.

The images collection contains a list of all <IMG> element objects in the current document. This is the same collection that was available in the old object model.

The scripts collection contains a list of all <SCRIPT> element objects in the current document, regardless of where they appear. This not only includes any scripts in the <HEAD> element but also scripts that appear inline in your document and any for-event event handlers as well.

The stylesheets collection contains a list of all stylesheets applied to your document, including those defined with the <STYLE> element, external stylesheets included with the <LINK> element, and imported stylesheets. If none of this makes sense right now, don't worry! In the following chapters, we will be aggressively covering stylesheets and their relationship to the Dynamic HTML Object Model.

MORE ON ELEMENT OBJECTS

In the first few chapters, we learned all about the dynamic content features of element objects. By using special properties and methods, like innerText and insertAdjacentHTML(), element objects can be modified by your script after the document has been loaded. But there are still a few features of element objects we haven't covered. For example, is there an easy way to access and modify an element's attributes? You bet there is!

Getting Element Attributes

Almost all HTML elements accept at least one attribute, to modify its default behavior. Some elements actually require one or more attributes to be set for the element to perform some useful function. For example, the <A> element is not too useful without attributes set, but with its HREF= attribute, it becomes a hyperlink. The <IMG> element is rather useless without its SRC= attribute set, but with it you get an image. These attributes, and many more, can all be accessed using special properties or methods on the element object.

Most element attributes have corresponding properties by the same, or a very similar, name. For example, to access an <A> element's HREF= attribute, you would use the element object's "href" property. An <IMG> element's SRC= attribute is accessed with the "src" property, and its ALIGN= property by the "align" attribute. If it is an "official" element attribute, there is probably a property you can use to access it.

```
document.all.MyAnchor.href = "http://www.prenhall.com/";
document.all.MyImage.align = "center";
```

Most of these "attribute properties" can be read from, to determine the current value, or written to. Writing to one of these properties instantly changes the value of the attribute, causing your document to redraw itself when appropriate. If you change an image's alignment to "center," that image will instantly center itself in the document. There are, of course, a few properties that are read-only. The one that first comes to mind is the "id" property, which corresponds to the ID= attribute. Changing an element object's identifier mid-script can have bizarre and often disastrous results, so the id property is read-only, but this is only one of very few exceptions.

Some attributes have names that, if referenced directly as a property, may cause some conflicts or ambiguities with the scripting language itself. In these cases, the corresponding property name may be slightly different then the attribute name. For example, the CLASS= attribute, which we'll cover a bit later, is accessed using the "className" property, not the "class" property. In general, however, this is rare and the property name is the same as the attribute name.

Occasionally we make mistakes and accidentally set an attribute with an invalid value. For example, the ALIGN= attribute accepts "center" as a valid argument, but "middle" is meaningless to the browser. If you make this mistake in your HTML, the browser will ignore the attribute and use whatever is the default value. But if you attempt to retrieve this invalid "middle" value with the align property, you will read a blank instead of the keyword "middle." In any case when the attribute has an invalid value, the corresponding value returns nothing. Trying to write an invalid value to an attribute property is even worse. Instead of ignoring the invalid value, the script will return an error message.

Invalid attribute values are bad news, any way you look at it, but if you want to see what the value actually is, there are ways to do it. In other cases, there may be certain attributes that technically aren't valid but that you've put into your HTML for reasons of your own devising. For example, you may offer a service that weather maps of the user's local area updates once an hour and you would like to record some additional information with each image, like its age and satellite. To do this, you decided to create your own special attributes AGE= and SATELLITE= for the <IMG> element. These attributes are invalid, so they will be ignored by the browser, but it may be useful if your scripts could access this data.

```
<IMG SRC="weather.gif" AGE=54 SATELLITE="WeatherSat 1">
```

Since the attributes aren't "real," there are no properties you can use to retrieve their values. But you still have access to them with three special methods: getAttribute(), setAttribute(), and removeAttribute(). If you need to work with "fictitious" attributes, or invalid values on "real" attributes, these three methods will do the trick.

The getAttribute() method is used to retrieve the value of any attribute, real or not, from the current element. The first argument is the name of the attribute as it appears in the HTML source. By default, this method is case insensitive, so the attribute "ABC" is identical to "AbC." Either will retrieve the same attribute. If case is important to you, getAttribute() also accepts an optional second argument: case sensitivity. If set to *true,* getAttribte() will attempt to retrieve an exact match. If *false,* which is the default, case will be ignored.

```
<HTML>
<HEAD>
<TITLE>Weather Maps</TITLE>
<SCRIPT LANGUAGE="JavaScript">
function view_info()
{
    var myImage = document.all.SatImage;

    var imageAge = myImage.getAttribute("AGE");
    var imageSat = myImage.getAttribute("SATELLITE");

    alert("This map is " + imageAge + " minutes old " +
        "and was retrieved from " + imageSat + ".");
}
</SCRIPT>
</HEAD>
<BODY>

<IMG ID="SatImage" SRC="sat1234.gif" AGE=53 SATELLITE="WeatherSat 1"
    onClick="view_info()">

</BODY>
</HTML>
```

The previous listing shows how you would use getAttribute() to retrieve "fake" attributes using our weather map as the example. When the user clicks on the image, the

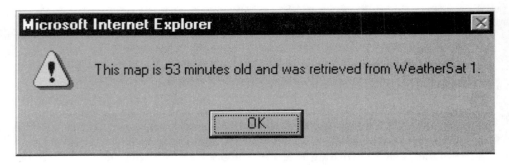

Figure 4–4   The results of getAttribute() on our "fake" attributes.

view_info() function will attempt to retrieve the two fake attributes AGE= and SATEL-LITE=. It will then display the information in an alert() box, as illustrated in Figure 4–4.

The getAttribute() method can also be used to retrieve the values of "real" attributes. Unlike retrieving an attribute using its property, getAttribute() will return the exact value, even if it is invalid. For example, if an ALIGN= attribute was accidentally set to "middle," the property would return nothing but the getAttribute() method would return the actual value, "middle."

If the attribute doesn't exist, the method will return "null." If it is a "real" attribute, however, and you simply forgot to set it, getAttribute() will return a blank instead. In other words, if you try to retrieve the fake attribute "ABC=," and it doesn't exist, getAttribute() returns "null." But if you try to retrieve the ALIGN= attribute, and you didn't explicitly set it, getAttribute() will return a blank instead.

The setAttribute() method can be used to modify the values of any attribute, including fake ones, or to create a new attribute if it doesn't already exist. The method requires two arguments, with an optional third. The first argument is the name of the attribute you would like to set. The second argument is its value. Unlike getAttribute(), the default for this method is for case sensitivity to be turned on. If you would like the method to ignore case, you can set the optional third attribute to *false*.

If you set an attribute with its property, the browser does a bit of error checking first and sends an error message if the value is invalid, for example, trying to set the align property to "middle." But setAttribute() has no such restrictions, and any value you attempt to use will be faithfully set by this method. If the value is invalid, the browser will simply ignore it, but it can still be retrieved with the getAttribute() method. In the example below, the value for this attribute is invalid, but the browser does not send an error message to warn you of the mistake.

```
document.all.myElement.setAttribute("align","middle");
```

One quirk I noticed is when using this method to set "real" attributes. By default, case sensitivity is set to *true,* so using "ALIGN" as the attribute name is very different from "align." The correct case for the ALIGN= attribute is the lower case version, "align." This is particularly frustrating to me, since by habit, I always consider attributes to be in the upper case. I believe this makes my HTML a little easier to read, and the attributes a bit easier to spot. But since case sensitivity is true by default, the code below will actually create a second ALIGN= attribute that is ignored by the browser.

```
document.all.myElement.setAttribute("ALIGN","center");
```

If you are attempting to work with "real" attributes, always use the attribute name in all lower case, or turn of case sensitivity. With the third argument set to *false*, the browser no longer cares about case and modifies the first matching attribute, in this case the real ALIGN= attribute.

```
document.all.myElement.setAttribute("ALIGN","center",false);
```

You can set the value of any attribute, even attributes that, if accessed via properties, would be read-only. If the attribute should be read-only, you won't get any errors but you also won't see quite the behavior as expected, either. What appears to happen is that a "second" attribute with the same name as the read-only attribute is created, but the real value of the attribute isn't affected at all. For example, using setAttribute() to change the value of the ID= attribute, which should be illegal, will appear to work. Checking the value of the attribute with getAttribute() would seem to support that assumption because it will return your new value. But checking the attribute with its property, "id," will return the original value, unchanged. Avoid using setAttribute() to modify read-only attributes because I'm honestly not certain if this behavior is a feature or a bug.

In addition to getting and setting attributes you can also remove them from the element with the removeAttribute() method. This method requires one argument, the name of the attribute to remove, with an optional second argument specifying case sensitivity. Like setAttribute(), the default is to be case sensitive, so the same warnings for setAttribute() go for removeAttribute() as well.

You can remove any attribute, even real ones like ALIGN= or HREF=. If a real attribute is removed, the element will instantly behave as if the attribute was really set to its default value. For example, if you center an <H1> element with its ALIGN= attribute but then remove the attribute, the <H1> element will instantly snap to the left, which is it's default alignment. Be careful when removing attributes like ID= because this can dramatically alter the behavior of the rest of your script. You could find yourself in a situation in which all of a sudden your element object no longer has an identifier! You should not be able to remove read-only attributes, and even though you can, I would recommend against it. It is probably a bug instead of a feature.

Other Properties and Methods

Element objects do contain a few other properties and methods not related to their attributes. These range from the obscure, for example, the "parentTextEdit" property, to the very useful, for example, the "parentElement" property. Some element objects have properties others don't. For example, there is the "tabIndex" property that is only available on elements that can be "tabbed" through, like form elements. There are even a few extra collections you can access. Since things are still changing, here and there, it would be very difficult or even impossible to list everything available, but I've endeavored to provide a list of at least some of the more promising properties and methods currently available on your element objects.

We've already seen the tagName property in a few of our examples. The tagName property returns the name of the current element's tag. For example, the <B> element's tagName is "B." Another useful property is sourceIndex. This returns the position of the element object in the "all" collection. These two properties are available in all element objects.

Two more properties available on all element objects are parentTextEdit and isTextEdit. These are used primarily in the creation of text ranges. The isTextEdit property tells you if the current element object can be used to create a text range, directly, with the createTextRange() method. If the createTextRange() method is available on this element object, the isTextEdit property will return *true,* otherwise it returns *false.* Since only <BODY>, <BUTTON>, <TEXTAREA>, and <INPUT TYPE="text"> elements can be used to create ranges, you probably won't see much use for this one. You will probably get even less use out of the parentTextEdit property, which returns the closest parent element object that you can use the createTextRange() method on. I'm still trying to figure out when this property will return anything other than the <BODY> element object. But these properties are there if you need them.

If you need to know what document object the current element object is in, you can use the "document" property, which is also found on every element. This is just an alias to the current document object, and a rather roundabout way of getting at the document object if you ask me. But once again, the property is there if you need it.

Every element object either contains, or is contained by, another element object. The parentElement property and contains() method allow you to step through this hierarchy and see where in the scheme of things the current element is located. The parentElement property, as you may have guessed, returns a pointer to the current element object's parent. In other words, which element object the current element is currently inside. If you would like to check in the other direction, the contains() method can tell you if a specific element object is contained in the current one. The contains() method accepts one argument, the element object to check, and returns *true* if that element object is inside the current one or *false* if it isn't. Using the parentElement property and the contains() method, you can easily step through the element hierarchy.

One of my favorite methods is scrollIntoView(), which is available on any element object that can be scrolled into view. It accepts one argument, whether the element should be scrolled to the top of the browser window or the bottom. If set to *true,* which is the default, the element will be scrolled to the top of the browser window. If it is *false,* the element will be scrolled to the bottom. Of course, if your document is very short or the element is very large, the browser may not be able to get it exactly on the top or bottom, but it will do its best to place it as close to the requested position as possible.

There are also a handful of properties and at least one collection, "filters," that are related to style sheets. I will cover these in the style sheet chapters.

CONCLUSION

In this chapter, we attempted to fill in some of the details we neglected in previous chapters. We took a closer look at the object hierarchy, starting at the window object. We then worked our way down, looking at the location, history, navigator, and screen objects in turn. We also had a quick refresher on creating new windows and learned about the new modal dialog window.

The window object has the ability to keep track of user-defined "timed events." We discussed the two types of timed events, timeouts and intervals, and learned how to set and clear them. We then rounded out our knowledge of the window object by looking at a few of its special properties and methods.

The document object was also largely neglected in previous chapters, so we took a closer look at some additional properties and methods. While we were at it, we also reviewed the various collections available in addition to "all."

Finally, we took a quick look at element objects, noting how to access attributes with properties as well as the three attribute methods: getAttribute(), setAttribute(), and removeAttribute(). We then took a quick peek at some additional methods and properties you may find useful.

CHAPTER 5

Introduction to Style Sheets

A *style sheet* is a way to specify precisely how your document should be displayed. With style sheets, you have control over fonts, colors, backgrounds, borders, margins, layout, and positioning. There are even advanced style sheet features, called *filters,* for fades, swipes, and other special effects. The addition of style sheets to HTML brings the Web one step closer to a professional publishing platform. Even more important, style sheets can act as templates for your Web pages, providing consistency of feel and design to your entire Web site with very little additional effort.

To fully realize the power of style sheets, the concept of *cascading* style sheets, or CSS, was developed. Cascading style sheets allow us to apply several style sheets to the same document in such a way that each complements the other. For example, you can create a basic *master* style sheet and several more specific ones for different sections of your Web site. When applied on the same document, the master style sheet provides some general rules, and the other style sheets refine the look and feel of your document.

When style sheets are combined with the new document object model and your favorite scripting language, you have *dynamic* style sheets. With just a few lines of script, your style sheets can be instantly changed and modified, creating many stunning and powerful effects! This is the direction we have been taking, and very soon we will achieve our ultimate goal: full control over our document and the ability to instantly change and morph it any way we want!

GETTING STARTED: STYLE SHEET BASICS

A style sheet is a set of "rules" that define the behavior of your document. A rule might define a font or the color of its text. It can specify the background for a specific element, or even a margin. Every aspect of your document's style is controlled by various rules.

For example, the rule below states that all <SPAN> elements will render their text in the color green.

```
SPAN { color: green }
```

A rule is split into several parts. The first part, in this case "SPAN," is called the *selector.* As you may have guessed, the selector determines what the rule should be applied to. After the selector is the *declaration,* which is always enclosed in curly braces. Where the selector determines what the rule applies to, the declaration determines what the rule actually does. The declaration itself is split in two. The first part of the declaration is the *property,* and the second part is the *value.* The property and value are always separated by a colon.

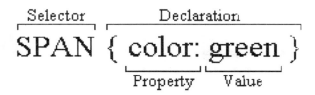

Figure 5–1   A style sheet rule and its components.

The *color* style sheet property controls the color of text for the element it is applied to. There are, of course, dozens of other properties available, all of which I plan on discussing in the following pages. Right now, let's see how we get the rules into your document.

EMBEDDED STYLE SHEETS: THE <STYLE> ELEMENT

There are several ways to incorporate style sheet rules into your document. The primary technique is called *embedding* and is accomplished with the <STYLE> element. The <STYLE> element is inserted in your document, usually before the <HEAD> element, and can contain all your style sheet rules. The listing below shows an HTML document with a style sheet defined in a <STYLE> element.

```
<HTML>
<STYLE TYPE="text/css">
    SPAN { color: green }
    H1 { text-align: center }
    H2 { font-style: italic }
</STYLE>
<HEAD>
<TITLE>Style Sheets</TITLE>
</HEAD>
<BODY>
```

```
<H1>I Am Centered</H1>
<H2>And I Am Italic</H2>

<P>And this word is: <SPAN>green</SPAN></P>
</BODY>
</HTML>
```

This style defines three rules. The first is our friend, the <SPAN> element, which has been asked to display itself in green. The next two rules request the <H1> and <H2> elements to center and to print in italics, respectively. The <SPAN> element is easy to understand, since by itself it has no default behavior. Without giving it a style rule, it does

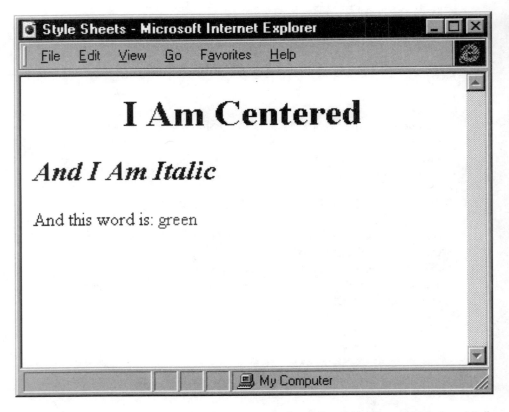

Figure 5–2   The <H1> element has been centered and the <H2> element has been italicized using style sheet rules. The <SPAN> element has also been defined as "green," but you'll have to take my word on that one!

absolutely nothing to your text. But the <H1> and <H2> elements already do something: appear in larger fonts then the rest of the text. How does giving additional rules affect them? Figure 5–2 shows you what happens.

When an element already has a *default behavior,* and that would be almost all of them, assigning new style sheet rules to them will add the new behavior and not delete the old. Unless the rules directly conflict with the element's already defined rules, such as telling the <I> element to use non-italic text, the new rules will simply be added to the list. This means you can continue to define additional rules for the same element until you have achieved the desired affect.

```
<STYLE TYPE="text/css">
    H1 { text-align: center }
    H1 { font-style: italic }
    H1 { color: red }
</STYLE>
```

The code above is perfectly valid and will result in an <H1> element that is centered, in italics, and red. As the style sheet is parsed by the browser, each new rule will be applied in turn to the <H1> element. There is, of course, a better way to do this. But before we refine our techniques, what in the world is the purpose of that "TYPE=" attribute in the <STYLE> element?

Like every other type of document, style sheets have their own MIME type that the browser uses to determine what kind of data it is dealing with. In the case of cascading style sheets, that MIME type is *text/css.* In the future, as different methods of defining styles are developed, they may also have their own MIME types. By specifying "TYPE= text/css" for our current style sheets, we ensure that our documents will be processed correctly by future browsers, which may be aware of more then one type of style sheet. For example, work is currently being done on a version of style sheets for the visually impaired, which will hopefully make our Web pages "sound" as good as they look. The browser will need a way to differentiate between regular cascading style sheets and the new "aural" style sheets. The "TYPE=" attribute will give us this ability. Without it, the browser will surely get confused.

Speaking of confused browsers, some older browsers may not understand style sheets at all. Browsers that don't know about style sheets will not only ignore your styles, but also mangle the top of your document as they try to include the text of your rules with the rest of your document. Very bad stuff. While many webmasters have the attitude that those unlucky users should just upgrade, you may feel compelled to be slightly more accommodating. By simply enclosing your rules inside an HTML comment, you can tell older browsers to completely ignore the text between the <STYLE> tags. We have the same situation with the <SCRIPT> element: Browsers that don't know about scripts try to include the script text with the rest of the document, creating an unreadable mess. The solution is the same, as illustrated by the following code.

```
<STYLE TYPE="text/css">
<!--
    SPAN { color: green }
-->
</STYLE>
```

The HTML comments prevent older browsers from confusing your style rules with regular text. Just be sure to put the comments *inside* the <STYLE> tags, and not *around* them, or even modern browsers will ignore your styles! For the code examples in this book, I will be omitting the comments to save on space and typing. Including them in your own code is up to you; however, I would recommend that you do. It's bad enough that the user won't be able to see the full of effect of your carefully crafted styles, and there is no sense in making it worse.

Grouping Declarations and Selectors

Before getting into MIME types and comments, I suggested that an easier way to define multiple rules on the same element existed. This is called *grouping,* and is an easy way to make your style sheets a bit more readable and prevented extraneous typing on your part. Multiple declarations can be grouped inside the curly braces for the same selector.

```
<HTML>
<STYLE TYPE="text/css">
    H1 { text-align: center;
         font-style: italic;
         color: red }
</STYLE>
<HEAD>
<TITLE>Style Sheets</TITLE>
</HEAD>
<BODY>
<H1>Centered, In Italics, and Red</H1>
</BODY>
</HTML>
```

The listing above shows how the previous "center, italic, red" example looks with the declarations grouped for the one "H1" selector. Each declaration is on its own line and separated by a semicolon. Actually, there are no compelling reasons, besides readability, for the declarations to even be on their own lines. You could stuff the entire rule onto a single line if you want to. The key is that the declarations are separated by those semicolons. You can group as many declarations in this manner as you need.

Multiple selectors can also be grouped for a single set of declarations. This can be a great time saver when you want several selectors to share similar styles. For example, if

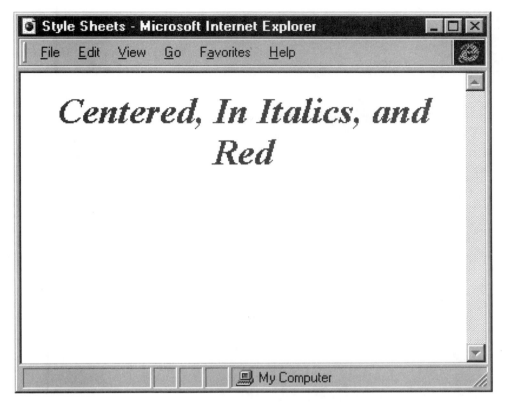

Figure 5–3 The <H1> element centered, in italics, and red. Once again, you'll have to take my word on the "red" bit.

you want <H1> and <H2> elements to all appear centered, in italics, and red, all you need to do is group the selectors and you only need half as much code.

```
<STYLE TYPE="text/css">
    H1,H2     { text-align: center;
                font-style: italic;
                color: red }
    H3,H4,H5 { text-align: center;
                color: green }
    H6        { text-align: center }
</STYLE>
```

The listing above takes this one step further and redefines all the header elements. The <H1> and <H2> elements are the familiar centered, italic, and red style. Elements <H3>, <H4>, and <H5> are also centered, but green and not italic. Finally, the <H6>

element is simply centered. To group our selectors, we put them all just before the declaration group, separated by commas.

Inheritance

Inheritance will be easier to understand if we forget about style sheets and look at a more mundane example first. I'm sure that at least once you have used the <I> element with the <B> element to create bold-italic text. If you haven't, all you need to do is put the <I> element inside the <B> element, or vice versa, as demonstrated below. The resulting text is bold as well as italic.

```
<I><B>I am bold and italic!</B></I>
```

This behavior is called inheritance. In this case, the <B> element has inherited the "italic" style of the <I> element. Without inheritance, the browser would be forced to pick one or the other—bold or italic—but with inheritance, both styles can be applied at the same time to create a sort of "compound" style.

This technique can also be extended to style sheets. When an element is inside another element, that element inherits its parent's style. This inheritance continues all the way up to the <BODY> element and even to the <HTML> element itself! This means that you can apply a style to the <BODY> element, and all elements inside your document will inherit those style rules as well. The style sheet, listed below, was embedded in a short document to test this theory, and the results can be seen in Figure 5–4.

```
<STYLE TYPE="text/css">
    BODY { color: red }
    P    { font-weight: bold }
    SPAN { font-style: italic;
           color: black }
</STYLE>
```

In Figure 5–4, the top <H1> element, though it has no style rules specifically set, has inherited the <BODY> element's red color. Next is the <P> element, which is bold from its style rule, but has also inherited the <BODY> element's red color. Inside the paragraph is also found a <SPAN> element. Bold, from the <P> element's rules, it is also italic from its own, but it isn't red! This is because it has its own color—black—defined, which overrides the <BODY> element's red color. When inherited rules conflict, the child element always receives precedence. Finally, after the paragraph is a <DIV> element. Since it has no specific rules applied, it only inherits the <BODY> element's red color.

External Style Sheets

You don't have to embed all your style sheets inside your documents. Style sheets can also be kept as separate files and referenced by your documents externally. As a matter of

Figure 5–4   Inheritance in action.

fact, cascading style sheets were designed with these "external" style sheets directly in mind. The procedure is simple. Put all your frequently used style sheets in separate documents, then link to them from your HTML documents with the <LINK> element.

Let's say I have a set of Web pages where all level one headings should be centered and all level two headings should be centered and italic. Those are the basic rules. Some pages may have more rules applied to them, but at the very least all the pages will have those previous two rules. I could embed a style sheet with those two rules in all my documents, but that is too much typing and there is an easier way. Let's put those rules in a separate cascading style sheet document.

First, create a new document to hold the "generic" style sheet. I'll call it "generic.css" and put it in the same folder as my HTML document. The ".css" extension tells the browser that this document will contain cascading style sheet rules. The entire contents of the document appear below. Notice that there are no HTML tags! This document will only contain your style sheet rules.

```
H1 { text-align: center }
H2 { text-align: center;
     font-style: italic }
```

Now all I need to do is create a new HTML document to test the style sheet. The new HTML document appears below. Even though there are no embedded style sheets in this HTML document, the <H1> and <H2> elements both have redefined styles! The trick is in the <LINK> element, located in the document's <HEAD> element.

```
<HTML>
<HEAD>
<TITLE>External Style Sheets</TITLE>
<LINK REL="stylesheet" HREF="generic.css" TYPE="text/css">
</HEAD>
<BODY>
<H1>Level One Heading</H1>
<H2>Level Two Heading</H2>
</BODY>
</HTML>
```

The <LINK> element doesn't create one of those blue-underlined hyperlinks we are so familiar with. Instead, it is used to "associate" an external stylesheet with the current document. The first attribute, "REL=," tells the browser that the "relationship" of the <LINK> is a style sheet. So there is no confusion about what type of style sheet we mean, the "TYPE=" attribute is set to the style sheet's MIME type. As we have already discussed, the MIME type for cascading style sheets is "text/css." These two attributes will always be the same for the style sheets described in this book. The final attribute is the familiar "HREF=," which contains the URL to our external style sheet. The URL can be any valid URL, including one pointing to an entirely different server!

You can put as many <LINK> elements in your document as you need; however, there is yet another way to include new style sheets. The special "@import" style sheet rule allows you to insert one style sheet inside another. This is useful when you want your generic style sheet to include other style sheets as well. For example, you can use @import rules in your generic style sheet to include three additional style sheets with only one <LINK> element.

```
H1 { text-align: center }
H2 { text-align: center;
     font-style: italic }
@import url(style_1.css);
@import url(style_2.css);
@import url(style_3.css);
```

The example above includes our original two rules, plus three more imported style sheets. The @import, actually called a style sheet command, is always followed by the

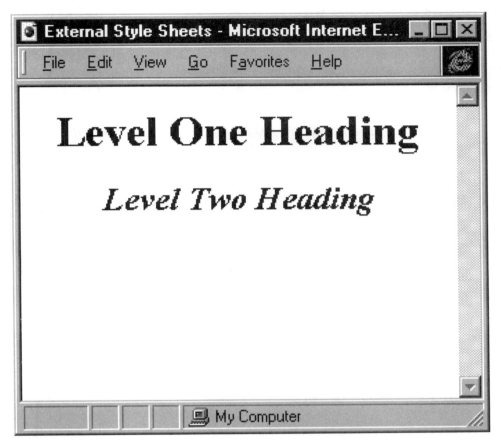

Figure 5–5   The results of our external style sheet.

"url()" argument. Inside this argument is the actual URL of the imported style sheet. Like the "HREF=" attribute of the <LINK> element, this can be any valid URL. Don't forget the semicolon after the @import command, or the style sheet won't be imported properly!

You can use the @import command in any style sheet, including embedded style sheets with the <STYLE> element or even other imported style sheets. Just be careful not to create a style sheet "loop," where style sheets accidentally import each other! The browser should be smart enough to cope with this situation and only include each style sheet once, but it is best to be safe and avoid a potentially dangerous situation.

It is hoped that some day, there will be large archives of style sheets for you to @import and <LINK> to, much as there are now archives of icons and graphics. Already a few of these archives are being formed, most notably one at Microsoft's Web site. You can visit this archive at the address listed below. There aren't many to choose from right now, but Microsoft claims that it intends to update this site frequently.

```
http://www.microsoft.com/gallery/files/styles/
```

Generally, it is a bad idea to print URLs in books, because they have a habit of changing right after print time. However, I feel strangely confident that this URL will stick around for a while. If it isn't there when you look, try visiting Microsoft's home page and search for "style sheets" or "styles." Even if you're not interested in the style sheets stored here, this URL has pointers to other "galleries," with some neat examples of Java, fonts, dynamic HTML, data binding, and a bunch of other stuff.

Inline Styles

Inline styles are used when you want to apply a style to a single element, but not affect other elements of the same type in your document. For example, if you want only one of your <H1> elements to been centered and in italics, you would apply an inline style to only that element.

The "STYLE=" attribute is used to apply an inline style to a single element. For example, in the listing below, the first of two <H1> elements has been centered and is in italics, while the second doesn't have a style applied to it.

```
<HTML>
<HEAD>
<TITLE>Inline Styles</TITLE>
</HEAD>
<BODY>

<H1 STYLE="text-align: center; font-style: italic">Inline
Styles</H1>

<H1>No Style Applied</H1>

</BODY>
</HTML>
```

You can apply any style rules using the "STYLE=" attribute. For multiple rules, simply separate them with a semicolon, as shown above. What you can't include is an actual style sheet; only the rules for the style are allowed. For example, you can't use inline styles to define one style sheet for the top half of your document and another for the bottom half. Rules defined using inline styles only apply to that specific element. Of course, elements *inside* that element will inherit the appropriate rules.

I'm sure you can see the connection forming between style sheets and dynamic HTML. Since you can apply a style to a single element with the "STYLE=" attribute, you should be able to set this attribute using the various properties and methods defined in the new document object model. This is true, but there are some interesting twists. I'll tell you all about it once we've covered a few more style sheet details.

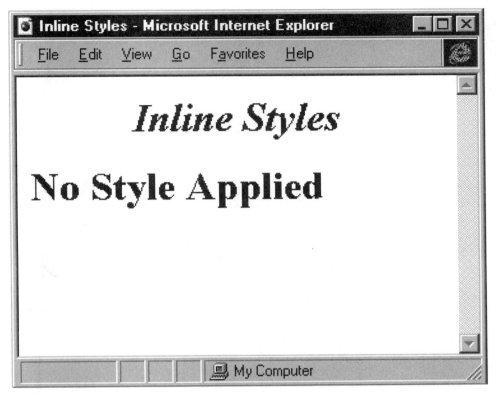

Figure 5–6 The first <H1> element has had an inline style defined with its STYLE= attribute, but the second is unaffected.

FONT AND TEXT PROPERTIES WITH STYLE SHEETS

Now that you have the very basics, let's take a look at some interesting style sheet properties. In particular, we are going to look at some of the font-and text-related properties. At first it will appear as if you can already do most of this stuff with the HTML <FONT> element, but we will quickly discover a bunch of abilities unique to style sheets. The topic of fonts is actually rather more complicated then you would think, and I will only be covering the essentials here. In a later chapter, I will revisit fonts once again, armed with a bit more experience and a few new features.

`font-family`: Property

Specifying the font in a style rule is as easy as telling the font-family property which font you want. Almost. Setting the font-family property is easy, but getting the font you *really* want is a bit more difficult. I'll explain in a moment. Let's take a look at a few examples of the syntax first.

The font-family property can accept one or more values, separated by commas. The values are, of course, the names of the fonts you want, and in general should appear in all lowercase. The first name in the list is your preferred font. If that font isn't available on the user's system, a situation likely to occur more then I would like to think about, the browser will attempt to use the next font in your list. If that one isn't available either, the browser will go down the list of fonts until it finds one that matches or runs out of names. If the browser can't find a match, it will use the browser's default font.

```
P { font-family: arial, sans-serif }
```

In the example above, the <P> element has requested the Arial font. If that isn't available, the rule states that sans-serif will do. Since only two options are given, if sans-

Figure 5–7   The top line is a <P> element using Arial font. The second line is a <DIV> element with the browser's default font.

serif isn't available, the browser can use whatever it thinks is necessary. Actually, if you're familiar with desktop publishing, you may have noticed that sans-serif isn't really a font, but what is known as a "generic font family." A generic font family is a group of fonts that share similar traits. The Arial font just happens to be a member of the sans-serif family, so if Arial isn't available, I've asked the browser to pick a font with an appearance at least similar to Arial. It's an important trick, and one I'll talk about in more detail later.

Other font options are available. In theory, you can use any font you want. The problem is that not all fonts are available on all systems. Mac users have some fonts that Windows users don't have, and vice versa. Font options will even differ from Mac to Mac or Windows to Windows! Even worse, the same font on the Mac sometimes is named a little differently on Windows. What a nightmare! The situation is usually a bit better when using generic font families, but even that can be somewhat touch and go at times. The solution? Once again, I would like to defer this conversation for later. Until then, you must be aware that the font you ask for has a good chance of not being on the user's machine.

`font-size`: Property

Font sizes with the <FONT> element are specified in a very simplistic manner. A font size of "1" is the smallest size, and a size of "7" is the largest. In theory, the numbers in between should smoothly change the font size from "really small" to "very large." In general, it gets the job done. The font-size property, on the other hand, gives you quite a bit more freedom. You can ask for almost any size font, from the barely readable to incredibly vast, and usually get what you're looking for. The price of this flexibility is a slightly more complex syntax.

The font-size property takes only one value, the size of the font, but there are several different ways of saying what you want. For example, you can ask for an exact point size or use a cruder keyword. There are actually five ways to specify the size:

- **Points**, which a is unit of measure familiar to those in the publishing field.
- **Absolutely**, using keywords directly related to the old method of number sizes from one through seven.
- **Relatively**, by asking for sizes either "smaller" or "larger" then the current size.
- By **percentage**, giving a percent relative to the current size.
- By **other units**, "em" and "ex." Also includes "in," "cm," "mm," "pc," or "px." You probably won't use these very often, but "em" and "px" can be useful.

If you have ever used a desktop publishing package or a professional publishing system, you have been exposed to the concept of *points*. A point is a unit indicating the maximum potential size of font measured from the top of the font's ascender line to the bottom of its descender line. Figure 5–8 illustrates the concept.

In the publishing world, a 1-point font will be about .0139 inches (.353 mm) from top to bottom. A typical 12-point font would be .1668 inches (4.236 mm) tall. Unfortunately,

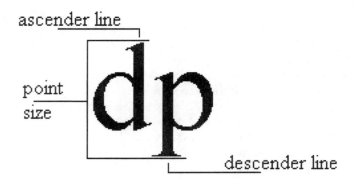

Figure 5–8   Point size is measured from the top of the tallest ascender line to the bottom of the lowest descender line. This is demonstrated with the letters "d" and "p."

this is the Web world, and things aren't quite as clean cut. For example, depending on your monitor's resolution, your desktop settings, and the phase of the moon, a 12- point font may be significantly smaller or larger than what the point size would suggest. If you can, turn the resolution of your screen up to its highest setting and then its lowest setting, comparing the sizes of the characters on the screen. See what I mean? Even worse, some browsers have unusual opinions on what certain font sizes should look like in the browser. The difference in font sizes between Netscape browsers and Microsoft browsers can be rather alarming.

Enough problems. Let's take a look at some code and examples. To specify a font size in points, append the letters "pt" after the number. For example, use "12pt" for a 12-point font. Point sizes must be whole numbers, and decimals will be truncated. The values "14pt" and "14.5pt" will be treated as identical. Also, negative point sizes are bad.

```
P { font-family: arial;
    font-size: 24pt }
```

The example above requests that <P> elements use 24-point Arial. A list of sizes and how they appear on Microsoft Internet Explorer 4.0 appears in Figure 5–9. The smallest point size I could coax out of the browser was 2pt. At that size, it looked like a mere squiggle on my laptop screen!

Sizing your fonts with absolute keywords is a tad easier then all this point stuff, but is even more inaccurate. You can use seven keywords, listed below, to specify the size of your fonts. These keywords are modeled directly after the one through seven numbering system of the <FONT> element.

1. **xx-small**
2. **x-small**
3. **small**

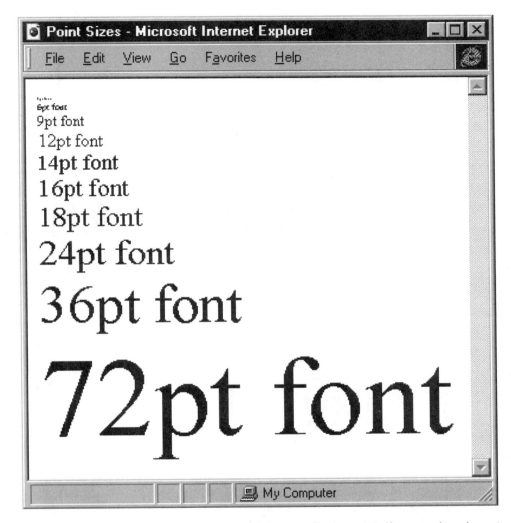

Figure 5–9 Various point sizes in Microsoft Internet Explorer 4.0. If you can't make out the top two sizes, they are 2pt and 6pt fonts. Smaller then 9pt and your users are likely to sue you for eye strain!

4. **medium**
5. **large**
6. **x-large**
7. **xx-large**

To use this system, simply apply the appropriate keyword to the font-size property. For example, to set the font size to "x-large," you can use the code below. For variety, I applied the rule to the <SPAN> element instead of <P>. Anything in <SPAN> elements will be an "x-large" font. A screen shot illustrating the sizes appears in Figure 5–10.

```
SPAN { font-size: x-large }
```

The relative keywords "smaller" and "larger" can also be used to change font sizes. These keywords work to increase or decrease the size of the parent element's font. In other words, they make the font "a little" larger or "a little" smaller. The term "a little" means slightly different things depending on the context. If the parent's font size was set using one of the absolute keywords, "a little" will mean "step up to the next absolute key-

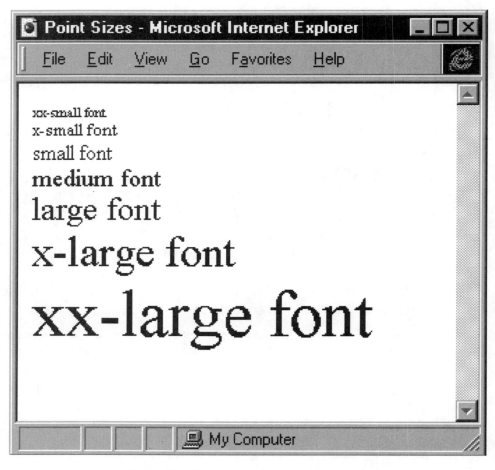

Figure 5–10   Specifying font sizes with absolute keywords.

word." For example, if the font is "large," then "smaller" will make the font "medium" and "larger" will make it "x-large."

On the other hand, the parent's font size was set using a specific point size and not one of the absolute keywords, the browser will increase or decrease the size by 50%. For example, if the font size was set to 20pt, the "larger" keyword will create a 30pt font and the "smaller" keyword will create a 10pt font. That is what the style sheet specification says, at least. In reality, the size difference is closed to a 20% increase or decrease. I wouldn't suggest relying on "smaller" or "larger" in any case where you *must* have a certain size. Calculate the size by hand instead.

```
<HTML>
<STYLE>
    H1 { font-size: large }
    H2 { font-size: 20pt }
</STYLE>
<HEAD>
<TITLE>Larger and Smaller Sizes</TITLE>
</HEAD>
<BODY>

<H1><SPAN STYLE="font-size: smaller">Smaller</SPAN>
    Large
    <SPAN STYLE="font-size: larger">Larger</SPAN></H1>
<H2><SPAN STYLE="font-size: smaller">Smaller (18pt)</SPAN>
    20pt
    <SPAN STYLE="font-size: larger">Larger (24pt)</SPAN></H2>

</BODY>
</HTML>
```

The above example attempts to shed a little light on this subject, and the results are illustrated in Figure 5–11. A style sheet with two rules has been embedded at the top of the document, defining the font size of the <H1> element to "large" and the <H2> element to "20pt." Then, using <SPAN> and inline styles, the font size is made "smaller" and "larger." The key here is that the new font size for the <SPAN> element is being based on the font size of its parent element.

If "larger" and "smaller" are too vague for you, it is also possible to specify font sizes as exact percentages. Once again, the new size is based on the parent element's font size. For example, if <P> is the parent element and its size is 20pt, and there is a <SPAN> element inside the parent requesting a 200% font size, the size inside the <SPAN> will be 40pt. Percentage values can be any whole number, but be careful not to create a font that is too large to be easily read or too small to be visible!

If you want to make the size smaller, don't use negative values. The percentage is calculated as percentage of the current size, not as the percentage to increase. A size of 100% will

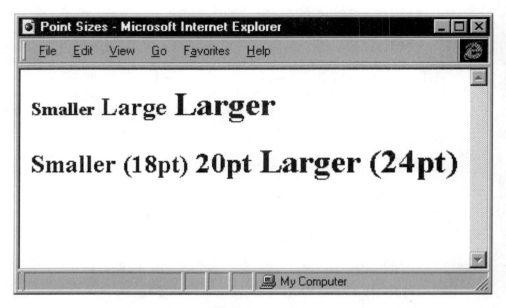

Figure 5–11   The effects of "smaller" and "larger" on font sizes.

not change the size of the font. To halve the size of the font, use a size of 50%. To double it, you should use 200%. In the example below, a <P> element has been given a font size of 20pt. The paragraph is then filled with several <SPAN> elements, each requesting a different size. The accompanying screen shot in Figure 5.12 shows the results of this experiment.

```
<HTML>
<STYLE>
    P { font-size: 20pt }
</STYLE>
<HEAD>
<TITLE>Percent Sizes</TITLE>
</HEAD>
<BODY>

<P>This is the base 20pt font.<BR>
   <SPAN STYLE="font-size: 50%">50% size</SPAN><BR>
   <SPAN STYLE="font-size: 100%">100% size</SPAN><BR>
   <SPAN STYLE="font-size: 150%">150% size</SPAN><BR>
   <SPAN STYLE="font-size: 200%">200% size</SPAN><BR>
</P>

</BODY>
</HTML>
```

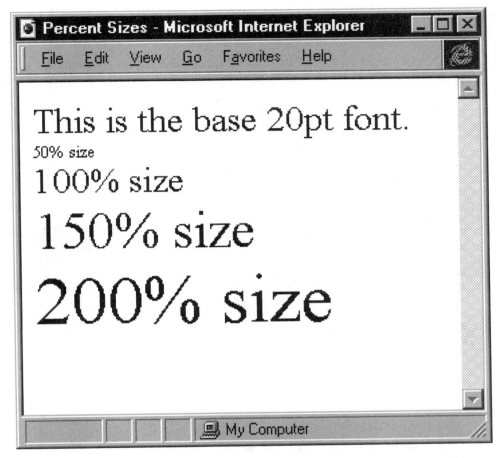

Figure 5–12 Various percentages applied to a 20pt base font. The point sizes of the resulting fonts are: 10pt for 50%, 20pt for 100%, 30pt for 150%, and 40pt for 200%.

There are a handful of other units you can use to specify font size, though most of them are more useful for setting margins then sizing your fonts. For example, if you don't like using "points," you do have the option of using "inches" instead. But inches aren't very well suited for specifying font sizes, unless you're designing billboards. A nice readable font for the Web is around 12pt. In inches you would have to specify this as 0.1668in. Not very convenient, in my opinion. Points were designed specifically for font sizes, and you will probably be better off to use them instead of inches.

Other units you may run into are centimeters, millimeters, and picas. You can use these units instead of points by appending "cm," "mm," and "pc" to your value, respectively. Of these, only picas can be considered a true alternative to points. One pica equals 12 points, which is a nice and convenient number to work with. But even so, I would still recommend using points for your font sizing needs. Points are the acceptable standard for specifying font sizes, and using anything else will make your pages more difficult for other webmasters to maintain.

You can also specify your font sizes using "pixels" by appending "px" to your value. At first glance, using pixels might look like a good idea, but, honestly, it will just compound many of the font size problems we already talked about. Your 28px font might look fabulous on your monitor, but be so small on mine as to be completely unreadable. The best use I can think of for pixels is matching your font size exactly with an image's height for a banner or logo. Even then, I think desktop publishing purists would likely cringe at the thought of using pixels to specify font size.

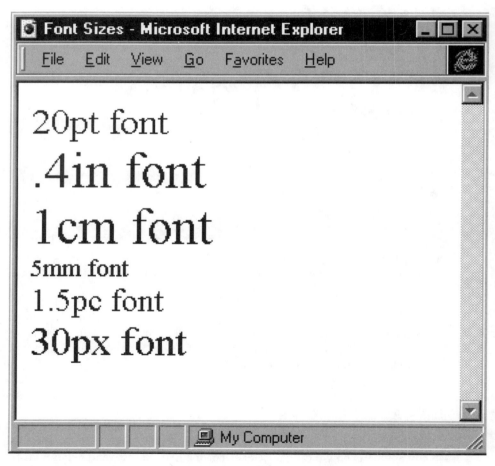

Figure 5–13   A sampling of the different font size units.

Fonts size can also be specified relative to a parent font size. We already saw two examples of relative font sizes with the "percentage" and "larger/smaller" techniques. Two new examples are "em" and "X-height" units. These units use the size of the parent element's font as the basis for the new size.

An "em" is unit of size that equals the point size of the parent font. To use ems, append "em" to the value. For example, if the point size of the parent element is 12pt, then 1em is equal to 12pt. In this case, if you want your new font to be 18pt, you would use a value of 1.5em.

"X-height" units are a little more obscure. A font's X-height is the maximum size of its lower-case letters, minus the ascender and descender lines. A perfect example is the lowercase "o" character, which is exactly one X-height tall. To use X-height, append an "ex" to your value.

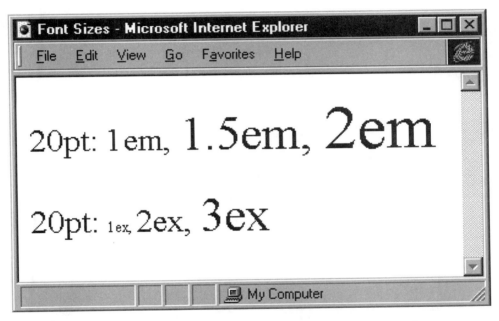

Figure 5–14   How "em" and "ex" stack up against a 20pt parent font.

Figure 5–14 shows how em and ex units stack up against a 20pt parent font. The first line begins with a 20pt sample font size, for reference. It is then followed by samples of 1em, 1.5em, and 2em sizes. Notice how the 1em size is the same as the original 20pt font. The second line also begins with a 20pt reference font, but instead is followed by 1ex, 2ex, and 3ex samples. These look a little off in size to me. If the first sample really was 1ex, the "1" should be just about as tall as the top of the "p" in the reference font. It looks about .75ex instead. Actually, the 1ex font appears to be about 10pt. This, combined with the observation that the 2ex and 3ex samples appear to be 20pt and 30pt, respectively, makes me think Microsoft cheated a bit and made 1ex equal to .5em, or half the point size of the font. Oh well, you probably won't use X-height very often, anyway.

`font-style:` **Property**

The font-style property determines if the font should be "normal," "italic," or "oblique." It accepts one of the following three values: normal, italic, or oblique. The "normal" value, sometimes called "roman" or "upright" in publishing circles, should be obvious enough, but the differences between "italic" and "oblique" are rather vague. Essentially, both are "slanted" to the right. If you ask for "italic," and the font doesn't have an italic version, the browser will attempt to display the "oblique" version. Figure 5–15 shows how a 24pt Arial font behaves when displayed normal, italic, and oblique.

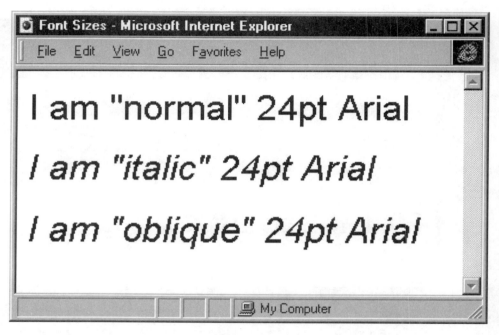

Figure 5–15   A 24pt Arial font displayed as normal, italic, and oblique. In this case, italic and oblique look identical.

```
<HTML>
<STYLE>
    P { font-family: arial;
        font-size: 24pt }
</STYLE>
<HEAD>
<TITLE>Font Sizes</TITLE>
```

```
</HEAD>
<BODY>

<P>I am "normal" 24pt Arial</P>
<P STYLE="font-style: italic">I am "italic" 24pt Arial</P>
<P STYLE="font-style: oblique">I am "oblique" 24pt Arial</P>

</BODY>
</HTML>
```

`font-variant:` Property

The font-variant property has only one purpose right now—selecting a "normal" or "small-caps" variant for your font—and it only accepts one of the two values, normal or small-caps. A font is called "small-caps" when the lowercase letters look like the font's uppercase letters, but smaller. THIS SENTENCE IS IN A SMALL-CAPS FONT. A relatively simple concept, with a code sample found below, and a screen shot of the results is shown in Figure 5–16.

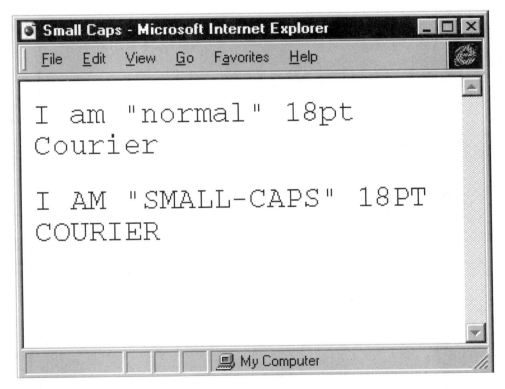

Figure 5–16 A 18pt small-cap Courier variant. Oops! This doesn't look quite right . . .

```
<HTML>
<STYLE>
    P { font-family: "courier";
        font-size: 18pt }
    SPAN { font-variant: small-caps }
</STYLE>
<HEAD>
<TITLE>Font Sizes</TITLE>
</HEAD>
<BODY>

<P>I am "normal" 18pt Courier</P>
<P><SPAN>I am "small-caps" 18pt Courier</SPAN></P>

</BODY>
</HTML>
```

Of course, there is a problem. Microsoft Internet Explorer 4.0 doesn't do small-caps quite right. Instead of making lowercase letters look like slightly smaller uppercase letters, it makes every letter uppercase. Hopefully this will be fixed sometime in the near future.

`font-weight:` Property

The font-weight property controls the boldness of your font. By now you're probably thinking that the logical values for this property should be "normal" and "bold." If so, you're correct—partly. The font-weight property will accept "normal" and "bold" as values, and personally I would be happy to just leave things at that and move on. But font weight is a bit more complicated then that. You also have two "relative" values of "lighter"—which makes the font "less bold"—and "bolder"—which makes it more bold. These work just like the "smaller" and "larger" font-size values. In addition to that, you can also specify a specific weights of: 100, 200, 300, 400, 500, 600, 700, 800, or 900. This allows you to "fine tune" the boldness of the font. A value of "400" usually equates to "normal" and "700" is roughly equivalent to "bold."

As neat as this "fine tuning" sounds, the world of fonts is a weird one and things probably won't work as you would hope. For example, it sounds like for any font you can specify up to nine different bold settings. The reality is, fonts simply don't work that way. Most fonts probably support only two levels of bold—"normal" and "bold"—so most of those numbers will end up being "rounded" to the nearest applicable weight. Figure 5–17 shows what happens when you apply weights from 100 through 900 to an Arial font. Arial happens to have four bold levels. Values from 100 to 500 are treated as "normal," at 600 we get "demi-bold," 700 to 800 is "bold," and 900 is "ultra bold." The same experiment with Courier, however, produces only two levels: "normal" from 100 to 500 and "bold" from 600 to 900. You're just going to have to do a little experimentation, since your results depend largely on the font you're working with.

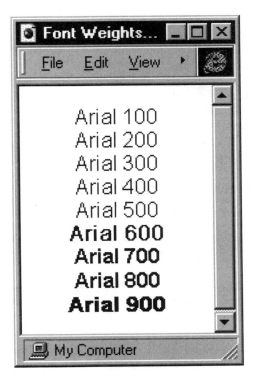

Figure 5–17   Font weights from 100 through 900 on the Arial font. Notice how there are only four true bold levels.

font: Property

The previous five font-related properties allow you to tailor your document's fonts in a variety of ways. You can set the font-family to a specific font, then set its size with the font-size property. You can make it bold or italic with font-weight and font-style, respectively, and can even request the small-caps variant with the font-variant property. So, for example, if you want your <P> element to use a 24pt italic Arial font, you would use the style sheet code below.

```
P { font-family: arial;
    font-size: 24pt;
    font-style: italic
  }
```

It's simple and effective, but a bit too much typing for me. Imagine setting these properties on six or seven elements! Your style sheet could end up being almost the same size as the rest of the document. And besides that, when setting up your fonts, you will probably end up setting font-family and font-size at the same the time anyway. It sure would be nice if you could set all these options in one fell swoop, and not have to mess around with three or four different properties . . .

The "font" property alleviates the "too much typing" problem by allowing you to combine several properties into one. Instead of needing three separate properties, as in the previous example, you can combine them into one, as shown below. The "font" property combines the function of the previous five properties into one.

```
P { font: italic 24pt arial }
```

The "font" property can accept a variety of values, depending on the effect you're trying to achieve. In the example above, the first value is the font-style, the second is the font-size, and the third is the font-family. Valid values are anything the "original" property accepts. Each value should be separated by a space.

The order of the values should always follow these rules:

1. Zero or more of font-style, font-variant, or font-weight
2. font-size
3. font-family

The font-size and font-family values are required, but you don't have to set the font-style, font-variant, or font-weight values. It doesn't matter which order the font-style, font-variant, or font-weight properties are in, but they all must appear before font-size. For example, "italic bold" is the same as "bold italic." It sounds complicated at first, but after looking at a few examples it should become clear. Various configurations and their effects can be found in Table 5–1.

Table 5–1   Combinations of "font" Property Values and Their Effects

Values	Effect
font: 16pt helvetica	A 16pt Helvetica font.
font: large courier, monospace	Large Courier font, or alternatively any large font in the "monospace" generic family.
font: bold italic 18pt arial	An 18pt bold, italic Arial font.
font: italic bold 18pt arial	Same as above: An 18pt bold, italic Arial font.
font: bold small-caps italic xx-large sans-serif	An xx-large bold, italic sans-serif font in small-caps.

text-decoration: Property

The "text-decoration" property adds or removes the various embellishments we like to use to make our text more interesting. "Decoration" keywords include underline, overline,

line-through, and blink. To eliminate all decorations, you can also use the keyword "none." Figure 5–18 shows all four decoration types in action. The "overline" option, unfortunately, doesn't work. Sometimes it doesn't draw a line at all, and when it does, the line can appear anywhere *except* over your text. The "blink" option is also broken, though I can't say that I'm disappointed.

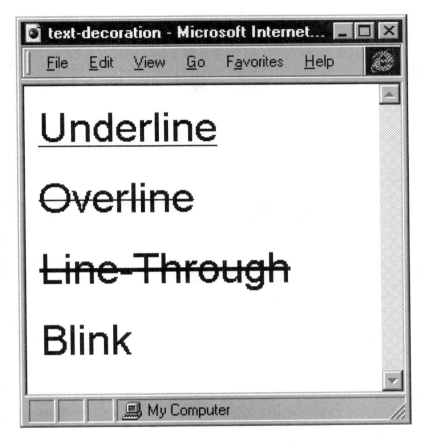

Figure 5–18   The four text decorations. Yes, overline isn't quite over-the-line and "blink" is blinking just as rapidly on the page in front of you as it is on my screen. I'm sure overline will be fixed at some point, but I'm not disappointed with the lack of blinking!

Decoration options can also be combined to apply multiple effects on the same text. Simply specify each option on the same line, separated by a space. Of course, "none" should never be combined with the other options. The style sheet below adds an underline and line-through effect to a 24pt courier font.

```
P { font: 24pt courier;
   text-decoration: underline line-through
}
```

text-transform: Property

The "text-transform" property also causes your text to be altered. When applied, text affected by this property can be converted to uppercase or lowercase. The four valid values are: uppercase, lowercase, capitalize, and none.

- **uppercase** converts all characters to their uppercase equivalent.
- **lowercase** converts all characters to their lowercase equivalent.
- **capitalize** converts only the first letter of each word to uppercase.
- **none** eliminates the inherited value.

An example of each option can be found in Figure 5–19. The document that created this output is listed below. The last option in the <DIV> element demonstrates how applying "none" to the <SPAN> can override the parent element's "capitalize" rule.

Figure 5–19   The effects of text-transform on your text.

```
<HTML>
<STYLE>
    DIV { text-transform: uppercase }
</STYLE>
<HEAD>
<TITLE>text-transform</TITLE>
</HEAD>
<BODY>

<P STYLE="text-transform: uppercase">I am all uppercase.</P>
<P STYLE="text-transform: lowercase">CONVERTED TO LOWER
  CASE.</P>
<P STYLE="text-transform: capitalize">Just capitalize the
  first letter.</P>
<DIV>Uppercase <SPAN STYLE="text-transform: none">except
  me.</SPAN></DIV>

</BODY>
</HTML>
```

text-align: Property

The "text-align" property alters the alignment of its text. It accepts one of four values: left, right, center, or justify. This property should be self-explanatory; however, there are a few subtleties. First, you can only align block elements. For example, attempting to align an <I> element will result in no action being taken. The code below, while no error is produced, will fail to "center" any of the text.

```
<P>You can only <I STYLE="text-align: center">center</I>
  blocks.</P>
```

The "justify" value also requires a little explanation. For many languages, left justification is the most natural. English, for example, is most naturally read left justified. Some languages, on the other hand, are easier read when justified to the right. Hebrew jumps to mind, as a language that is right justified. If you use the "justify" value, instead of "left" or "right," the browser will justify the text in whatever direction makes the most sense for the current language.

vertical-align: Property

With the "vertical-align" property you can also align your elements vertically, in addition to horizontally. The property is supposed to accept one of nine options, explained below. Unfortunately, this property hasn't been completely implemented yet, so don't expect dramatic results at this time.

- **baseline** aligns the baseline of this element with that of the element's parent. If the element doesn't have a baseline, alignment is to the element's bottom.

- **bottom** aligns the bottom of this element with the lowest element on the current line.
- **middle** aligns the middle of the current element with the middle of the parent element.
- **sub** subscripts the element.
- **super** superscripts the element.
- **text-bottom** aligns the bottom of the current element with the bottom of the parent element's text.
- **text-top** aligns the top of the current element with the top of the parent element's text.
- **top** aligns the top of the element with the tallest element on the current line.
- A percentage value raises the baseline of the element that percentage of the element's height. A negative value will lower the baseline instead.

Internet Explorer 4.0 only supports the "sub" and "super" values and ignores everything else. In time, I'm sure the other options will be supported as well. Until then, we can only create subscripts and superscripts.

`text-indent:` Property

Tired of indenting text with non-breaking spaces or other creative hacks? The "text-indent" property lets you set up real indented text. The value can be either a length value or a percentage. Length values can be in any of the "font size" units; however, inches, centimeters, and ems are the most popular. The first line of text in a block will be indented by this value.

```
<HTML>
<HEAD>
<TITLE>text-indent</TITLE>
</HEAD>
<BODY>

<P>I am not indented.</P>
<P STYLE="text-indent: 1in">I am indented by one inch.</P>
<P STYLE="text-indent: 2em">My indent is 2em.</P>
<P STYLE="text-indent: 25%">I've been indented by 25%.</P>
<P STYLE="text-indent: -0.10in">Negative indenting!</P>
<P STYLE="text-indent: 1cm">Indented by 3cm. Notice how only
   the first line is indented in a block.</P>
</BODY>
</HTML>
```

Indenting has one really neat feature: negative indenting! By giving a negative value, the text will be indented to the left—all the way off the left edge of the screen and

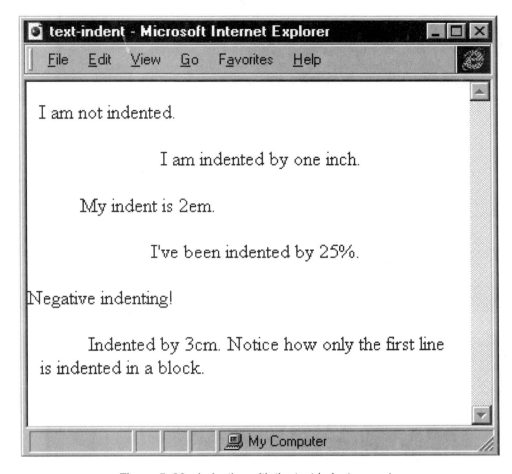

Figure 5–20 Indenting with the text-indent property.

into oblivion, if you let it. Another important feature is the ability to indent by percentage. Instead of a length value, use a percentage and the text will be indented that much across the browser window. For example, indenting by 50% will start your text at the window's halfway point.

Actually, this isn't 100% true. The official ruling is that the percentage is of the element's actual width. In other words, if your text is in a table cell, a 50% indent would be in the middle of the cell, not in the middle of the browser window.

`word-spacing`: Property

The "word-spacing" property will give you the opportunity to add a bit more space between the words in your text. One of two values are accepted: "normal" or a length. The length can be any unit. You can set the spacing to whatever you want, but very large spacing can make your text unreadable. If you want to shrink the space between words, give the property a negative value. Take care, because you *can* end up overlapping words! Length values are actually *added* to the "default" word spacing, so a value of 0in should do absolutely nothing to the word spacing.

Unfortunately, word-spacing isn't supported yet. All this stuff is still rather new, however, so given time I'm sure we will see this function implemented. Right now, any values for word-spacing are ignored.

`letter-spacing`: Property

The spacing between the letters of your text can be adjusted with the "letter-spacing" property. In the publishing world, this is also called *kerning*. The syntax of the property is the same as word-spacing, except this one actually works! A value of "normal" resets kerning to its default, or you can specify any length value, including a negative one. Be careful, because adjusting kerning too far in either direction can make your text difficult to read.

```
<HTML>
<STYLE>
    P { font-size: 18pt }
</STYLE>
<HEAD>
<TITLE>letter-spacing</TITLE>
</HEAD>
<BODY>

<P>This line has the "normal" letter spacing.</P>
<P STYLE="letter-spacing: 1em">Set to 1em.</P>
<P STYLE="letter-spacing: .25in">Set to .25in.</P>
<P STYLE="letter-spacing: -2mm">Set to -2mm.</P>
<P STYLE="letter-spacing: -1mm">Set to -1mm.</P>

</BODY>
</HTML>
```

The screen shot for the code above can be found in Figure 5–21. Remember, you are not setting the spacing to the value, but adding that value to the current level of spacing. If you want to shrink the spacing between letters, use a negative value.

`line-height`: Property

After you've managed to get your text's kerning just right, you can then move on and adjust the spacing between entire lines of text. The "line-height" property accepts one of

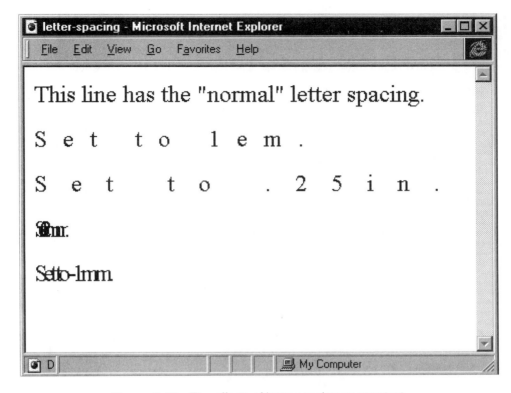

Figure 5–21   The effects of letter-spacing on your text.

four values: "normal," a number to be used as a multiplier, a length value, or a percentage. Each value affects the *leading,* or extra vertical space above and below the line, of the text in that element.

The best way to visualize line height is to pretend that your fonts have two sizes. The first size is the actual height of the font itself, and the second size is the height of an imaginary box surrounding the font. For example, the font is 16pt and is centered inside a box 18pt high. That 2pt difference is used as padding to separate the lines of text. Changing the line height of your text is essentially changing the size of the "box" the text is inside. A 16pt font with a line height of 16pt would have no vertical space separating it from the lines above and below it. A 16pt font with a line height of 32pt would, in effect, become double-spaced text.

You can directly change the line height of your text by specifying an exact length value. For example, if you want double-spaced text and your font is 12pt, you can request a line height of 24pt. You can use any units you want, but points and ems are the most convenient. A 2em line height would also be double-spaced, because an em is equal to the point size of the font. If you want to *shrink* the space between your lines, you can use a size that is *smaller* then the size of your font. A 8pt line height on a 16pt font would overlap each line over the next! Setting the line height to .5em would have the exact same effect. You can't, however, specify a negative value. The smallest value, zero, will overlap each line directly on top of the other.

You can also specify a number as a multiplier by omitting the unit. For a 16pt font, a line height of 1 would create a line height of 16pt. A multiplier of 2 would increase the line height to 32pt. A multiplier of .5 would reduce the line height to 8pt. Once again, negative numbers are not allowed. If you think in terms of percentages easier then multipliers, you can also request your line height as a percentage of the current font size. For example, a line height of 150% is the same as 1.5 multiplier.

A few examples can be found in the code below. To see how they appear in the browser, take a look at Figure 5–22.

```
<HTML>
<STYLE>
    P { font-size: 18pt }
</STYLE>
<HEAD>
<TITLE>line-height</TITLE>
</HEAD>
<BODY>

<P>These lines of text have the default line height.</P>
<P STYLE="line-height: 1.5">These lines of text have a line
   height with a multiplier of one and a half.</P>
<P STYLE="line-height: .25">These lines of text have a line
   height with a multiplier of one quarter.</P>
<P STYLE="line-height: .5em">These lines of text have a line
   height of 1em and are close together.</P>
<P STYLE="line-height: 150%">These lines of text have a line
   height of 150% and is the same as the 1.5 multiplier.</P>
</BODY>
</HTML>
```

While we're on the topic, I should mention that you can set the line-height using the "font" property as well. To give the font property a line height, put the required line-height value right after the font size, separated by a slash. For example, for a 16pt Arial font with a 32pt line height, you would say:

```
P { font: 16pt/32pt arial }
```

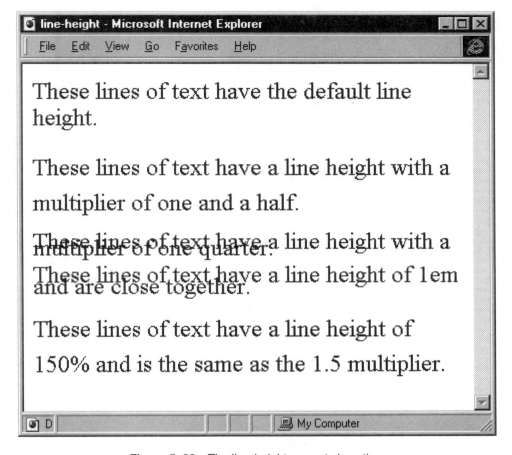

Figure 5–22   The line-height property in action.

Any valid line height value can be used with this syntax. To get the same effect, you could have used 2em instead of 32pt, a multiplier of 2, or 200%. It's a great little shortcut, if you need it.

SETTING COLORS AND BACKGROUNDS

There are seven style sheet properties for changing colors and backgrounds. The great thing about style sheets is that you have a lot more control over how your backgrounds are rendered. You can control how your background image is tiled, how the image is positioned, and even whether it should scroll with the document or remain fixed.

`color:` Property

The "color" property allows you to change the color of your text. You may have remembered seeing this property used in previous chapters. It only accepts one value, the new text color, but you have several options to describe the color. The easiest is to use one of the descriptive color names. For example, for red text, you would use the value "red." The rule below sets the color of text in the <SPAN> element to red.

```
SPAN { color: red }
```

You can also use hexadecimal triples to describe your colors. A hexadecimal triple is a set of three hexadecimal numbers that represent the "amount" of red, green, and blue which are combined to make the required color. The hexadecimal triple for red is #FF0000. The typical hexadecimal triple is six "digits" long and is preceded by a hash sign. Each group of two digits represents one of three colors: The first two digits represent red, the second two represent green, and the last two represent blue. There is also an abbreviated three-digit version of the hexadecimal triple. The abbreviated version of red is #F00. In this case, only one digit is used to represent each color. A list of color names and hexadecimal triples can be found in Table 5–2. Don't worry if this whole hexadecimal thing is foreign to you. Most people use the color names nowadays because hexadecimals can be a little difficult to work with.

Yet another way to describe colors is with the rgb() function. The rgb() function accepts three arguments: the quantity of red, green, and blue respectively. This time, however, you can use regular "decimal" numbers instead of cryptic hexadecimal. A value of 0 means add none of that color, and a value of 255 means add the most of that color. The example below is, once again, red.

```
SPAN { color: rgb(255,0,0) }
```

Don't get too caught up in this hexadecimal and RGB business. I admit, you get more control over the final color when using these methods, but generally the color name is all you really need. As a matter of fact, many times you can get in trouble when using "strange" color values. That beautiful salmon pink color might look great on your screen, but can look awful on everyone else's. Remember: Not everyone has his or her browser set to display thousands of colors. My laptop can only show 256 colors. Someone else may only be able to display 16! Stick with the "basics" in Table 5–2, however, and you should be fine.

Table 5–2   The Recommended Style Sheet Color Table (watch the spelling of "gray")

Color Name	Hexadecimal Triple	Abbreviated Hex Triple	RGB Value
aqua	#00FFFF	#0FF	rgb(0,255,255)
black	#000000	#000	rgb(0,0,0)
blue	#0000FF	#00F	rgb(0,0,255)
fuchsia	#FF00FF	#F0F	rgb(255,0,255)

Table 5–2   *(Continued)*

Color Name	Hexadecimal Triple	Abbreviated Hex Triple	RGB Value
gray	#808080	#888	rgb(128,128,128)
green	#008000	#080	rgb(0,128,0)
lime	#00FF00	#0F0	rgb(0,255,0)
maroon	#800000	#800	rbg(128,0,0)
navy	#000080	#008	rgb(0,0,128)
olive	#808000	#880	rgb(128,128,0)
purple	#800080	#808	rgb(128,0,128)
red	#FF0000	#F00	rgb(255,0,0)
silver	#C0C0C0	#CCC	rgb(192,192,192)
teal	#008080	#088	rgb(0,128,128)
white	#FFFFFF	#FFF	rgb(255,255,255)
yellow	#FFFF00	#FF0	rgb(255,255,0)

Incidentally, to set the color for your entire document, you can apply the "color" property to the <BODY> element. But please, double check that your color combination is actually readable. If I see one more web document with yellow letters on a silver background, I'm going to scream!

background-color: Property

The "background-color" property works just like the "color" property, except that it changes the color of the background *for the element it is applied to*. With regular HTML, you can only change the background for the *entire* document. But with style sheets, only the background of the *element* is affected. Of course, if you apply this rule to the <BODY> element, the entire document's background will be affected.

In addition to setting actual colors, the background-color property can be set to "transparent." A transparent background will allow details under the element to show through. If a <SPAN> element is inside a <P> element with a gray background, the <SPAN> element doesn't actually inherit the parent element's "gray" color. Instead, its background color is set to "transparent," which allows the <P> element's gray to shine through. See Figure 5–23 for an example of transparent backgrounds. The listing below was used to generate this output.

```
<HTML>
<STYLE>
    BODY { background-color: gray }
    P { background-color: silver }
    SPAN { background-color: transparent }
</STYLE>
<HEAD>
<TITLE>background-color</TITLE>
</HEAD>
<BODY>
```

```
<P>The document's background is gray, except for paragraphs
like this one which is silver. The <SPAN>&lt;SPAN&gt; element
is also transparent</SPAN> which means it uses the paragraph's
background.</P>

</BODY>
</HTML>
```

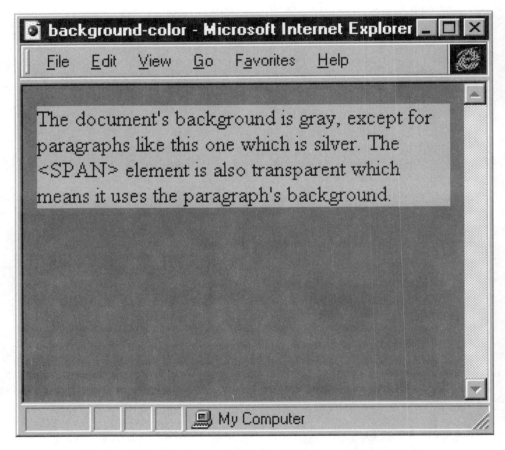

Figure 5–23   Background colors and transparent backgrounds.

background-image: Property

The "background-image" property sets the image to be used as the background for this element. The URL is specified using the special url() construct shown in the line below. You can also use the "none" keyword to request that no background image is used.

```
BODY { background-image: url(bground.gif) }
```

Background images can be set on the <BODY> element so they affect the entire document, or on individual elements. Like the background-color property, background images set on an element inside the document's body will have that background, but no other part of the document will be affected. The following listing puts a simple background image on the <BODY> element of a small document.

```
<HTML>
<STYLE>
    BODY { background-image: url(bground.gif);
           background-color: white }
    H1 { background-color: white }
    DIV { background-color: silver }
    SPAN { background-image: url(bground.gif) }
</STYLE>
<HEAD>
<TITLE>background-image</TITLE>
</HEAD>
<BODY>

<H1>I Don't Have A Background</H1>

<P>But the rest of the document does have a background.</P>

<DIV>This &lt;DIV&gt; element has been told to use a silver
background color, and not the image, but you can still tell
<SPAN>individual elements</SPAN> to use a background.</DIV>

</BODY>
</HTML>
```

One interesting twist here is that the <H1> element is has been given a white background color. This color overrides the background image, making it easier to read the text. No such precautions were taken for the <P> element, making that text very difficult to see. Further on, a <DIV> element with a silver background appears, once again overriding the background image. But inside the <DIV> element is a <SPAN> element that has been given a background image. This background is displayed instead of the silver.

It is always a good idea to give your background images a "backup" background color, in case the image can't be loaded. If the background image can be loaded, the color will be ignored. But if there is a problem loading the image, the color will be used instead. Speaking of background images not being loaded, when using relative URLs like we've done here, the URL is relative to the style sheet, not necessarily the document. If we had used <LINK> to load an external style sheet and that style sheet wasn't in the same directory as the image, the image would not load. Be careful!

Figure 5–24   Tiling vertically with background-repeat set to "repeat-y."

`background-repeat`: Property

One neat feature is the ability to control how your background image is tiled. With the "background-repeat" property, we can cause the background to tile normally, tile horizontally, tile vertically, or not tile at all. This is accomplished by giving the background-property one of the following four keywords: repeat, repeat-x, repeat-y, or no-repeat. The "repeat" keyword will tile your background normally. This is the default. If you want to tile horizontally only, you would use "repeat-x." Likewise, you can tile vertically using the "repeat-y" keyword. This is useful for those running-down-the-left-side-of-the-browser backgrounds that we see from time to time. The "no-repeat" property prevents tiling completely.

```
<HTML>
<STYLE>
    BODY { background-image: url(bground.gif);
           background-repeat: repeat-y }
</STYLE>
<HEAD>
<TITLE>background-repeat</TITLE>
```

```
</HEAD>
<BODY>

<H1>You control the tiling!</H1>

</BODY>
</HTML>
```

The simple example above, illustrated in Figure 5–24, has a background image that tiles only vertically. Tiling always begins in the upper-left corner of the browser window. If tiling is disabled with the "no-repeat" keyword, the single tile would be stuck up in that upper-left corner. If we tiled horizontally with "repeat-x," instead of vertically with "repeat-y," the background would extend across the top edge of the document.

`background-position:` Property

Since we can control tiling, we now need a way to position the background image. The "background-position" property allows us to tell our background where to start tiling. There are three ways to specify the position: by keyword, by length, or by percentage. We'll take each in turn.

Positioning by keyword is easy. Select one of "top," "center," or "bottom" to select the vertical position. Then select the horizontal position with "left," "center," or "right." For example, to start tiling from the bottom left corner of the browser window, you would use the following rule:

```
background-position: bottom left
```

It's that easy. Now, instead of tiling from the upper-left corner of the browser window, your background will begin tiling from the lower-left corner. In the example below, the background image begins tiling from the exact center of the document. A screen shot of the action can be found in Figure 5–25.

```
<HTML>
<STYLE>
    BODY { background-image: url(bground.gif);
           background-position: center center }
</STYLE>
<HEAD>
<TITLE>background-position</TITLE>
</HEAD>
<BODY>

<H1>You control the position too!</H1>

</BODY>
</HTML>
```

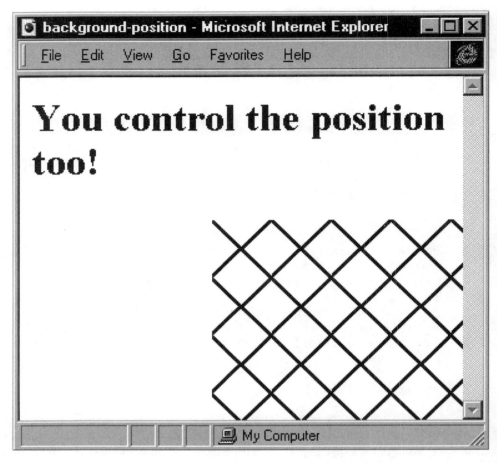

Figure 5–25 Background image with its starting position centered in the middle of the document.

The question is, what would happen if the document was too large to fit in the browser window and had to be scrolled? Would the background image remain centered in the browser window, or would it scroll with the document? Actually, neither and both. When you position your background image, the image is actually positioned *relative to the document*. If the document is larger than the window can handle, you may actually have to scroll the document just to see the background image! If you center the background image, it is centered in the document, which is not necessarily the center of the browser window. Or more specifically, background-position places the background relative to the *element* it is applied to.

You don't have to give both a vertical and horizontal position. If you only give one keyword, the browser will position the background as follows:

- **top** alone will position to the "top center"
- **center** alone will position at "center center"
- **bottom** alone will position to the "bottom center"
- **left** alone will position to the "left center"
- **right** alone will position to the "right center"

Positioning by percentage is just as easy as positioning by keyword, except you have a little finer control of exactly where the positioning begins. When using percentages instead of keywords, the first percentage is the horizontal position and the second percentage is the vertical. For example, "25% 75%" places the background at 25% of the element horizontally and 75% of the element vertically (see Figure 5–26).

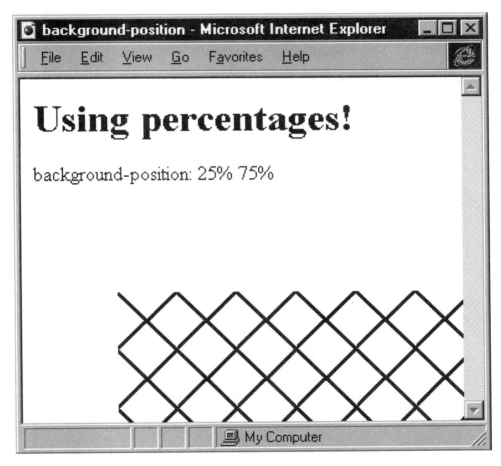

Figure 5–26 By replacing the keywords with percentages, you can fine tune where the background begins.

For even finer control, you can use length units instead of percentages. For example, "2in 5em" would position the background image 2in from the left edge of the document, and 5em from the top edge. Unfortunately, length units aren't supported yet. I know I'm beginning to sound like a broken record, but at some point in the near future I'm sure this will be fixed.

`background-attachment:` Property

Large documents in small windows tend to require a bit of scrolling to read. For most backgrounds, this isn't a problem. The background simply scrolls with the document. But sometimes you're aiming for a specific effect, and scrolling backgrounds can ruin everything. For example, suppose you're attempting to produce a "watermark" of your company's logo directly in the center of the browser window. You can use background-position to center your watermark directly in the center of the browser window, and background-repeat to eliminate strange tiling effects. But if your document is large, the user may have to scroll and your watermark effect is ruined. What you need is a way to keep your background image from scrolling with the document. The solution is the "background-attachment" property.

For a change of pace, this one is actually very simple. It accepts only one of two values: "scroll" and "fixed." The default, "scroll," tells your background image that it should scroll with the document. If you want the image to stay put, use the "fixed" value instead. Of course, this only has an effect on things that scroll, like the <BODY> element. Other than that, however, and there are no real caveats. Finally, something straightforward! Best of all, when background-attachment is set to "fixed," the background-position property works relative to the browser window and not the entire document. This allows you to center your watermark exactly in your browser window (Figure 5–27).

To create the effect in Figure 5–27, the following simple style sheet was used:

```
BODY { background-image: url(bground.gif);
       background-position: center;
       background-repeat: no-repeat;
       background-attachment: fixed }
```

`background:` Property

All five of the previous background properties can be combined using the handy "background" property. It's the same concept as the "font" property: Why use five properties when you can save some space and typing and use only one property?

The "background" property accepts one or more of the following values, in any order: background-color, background-image, background-repeat, background-position, and background-attachment. For example, to duplicate the style sheet in the "watermark" example, you would do the following:

```
BODY { background: url(bground.gif) center no-repeat fixed }
```

That's all there is to it!

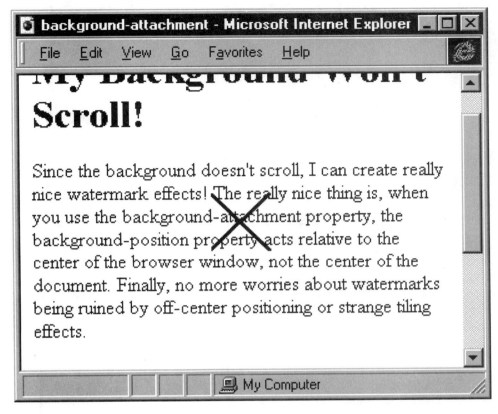

Figure 5–27 A beautifully centered "watermark." Scrolling the document doesn't scroll the background. Picture your company's logo in place of my ugly little "X" background.

CONCLUSION

We covered a lot in this chapter. Not only did we introduce the concept of style sheets, but we also got quite a bit into the details. You can now include basic style sheets into your documents with the <STYLE> and <LINK> elements, as well as with the @import command. We also covered grouping selectors and declarations, inheritance, and inline styles. We then dove straight into the font, text, color, and background properties, forming a solid foundation for experimentation. We covered more material in this one chapter then most style sheet books do in three or four, so treat yourself to a nice break and feel free to do a little bit of experimentation before going on to the next chapter! You already have enough knowledge to create useful, albeit somewhat simple, style sheets.

There's still a lot more to cover, so don't linger over that hot cup of coffee too long!

CHAPTER 6

Advanced Style Sheets

Now that you have the basics down, let's explore some more advanced style sheet concepts. There's still a lot more to cover, and we're going to jam quite a bit into this chapter. Some of the topics I intend to cover are classes, link effects and pseudo-classes, contextual selectors, and dynamic styles. We'll also review the cascading model, and then dive into a bunch more properties. So warm up the computer, grab a quick snack, and read on!

STYLE SHEET CLASSES

Style sheets allow us to redefine how each HTML element in our document behaves. For example, you can redefine the <P> element to use a green 18pt Arial font with 1in indenting, instead of the browser's default. This is a very powerful feature, but we're still missing a basic capability. What can you do if you want the <P> element to behave one way for most of your document, but a different way at other times? Right now, the only way to get an element to use two different styles is define them inline with the "STYLE=" attribute. This is rather clumsy and not entirely within the spirit of style sheets. With inline styles, you have to repeat the style for each occurrence of the element in your document. Not fun.

Fortunately, style sheets have a feature called "classes," which allows you to define several different rules for the same element. With classes, you can style the <P> element with a double-spaced 18pt Arial font some of the time, but easily switch to a single-spaced 14pt Courier font for a specific application. For example, suppose you have a page that contains an interview with a famous celebrity. For your questions, the <P> element should be a bold 14pt Courier, but for the celebrity's answers <P> should use an italic 16pt Arial. Don't use inline styles and redefine <P> each time. Instead, define each style once as separate class. Let's make this example a reality.

The first step is to create a style sheet with one rule for each class. We need two classes: one for the interviewer's questions and another for the celebrity's answers. We'll call these classes "question" and "answer," respectively. Our new style sheet is below.

```
P.question { font-family: courier;
            font-size: 14pt;
            font-weight: bold }
P.answer { font-family: arial;
           font-size: 16pt;
           font-style: italic }
P { font-size: 9pt }
```

Classes are identified by appending a class name to the selector with a period. For example, the <P> element's "question" class is identified as "P.question" in our style sheet. The <P> element now has two classes, but I also defined a "default." More on the default later. Right now, take a look at Figure 6–1 and its source, below.

```
<HTML>
<STYLE>
    P.question { font-family: courier;
                font-size: 14pt;
                font-weight: bold }
    P.answer { font-family: arial;
               font-size: 16pt;
               font-style: italic }
    P { font-size: 9pt }
</STYLE>
<HEAD>
<TITLE>Interview with Classes</TITLE>
</HEAD>
<BODY>
<H1>Interview with Classes</H1>

<P CLASS="question">So tell me, Classes, what are the benefits
  of using you over inline styles?</P>

<P CLASS="answer">Well, there are a few reasons. First, there
  is much less typing involved. Define your rules once as
  classes, and apply them as needed. Also, it makes your pages
  much easier to maintain.</P>

<P CLASS="question">That's just great! Well, thanks for your
time!</P>

<P CLASS="answer">Not a problem!</P>

<P>This interview is Copyright 1997 Robert Jon Mudry.</P>
```

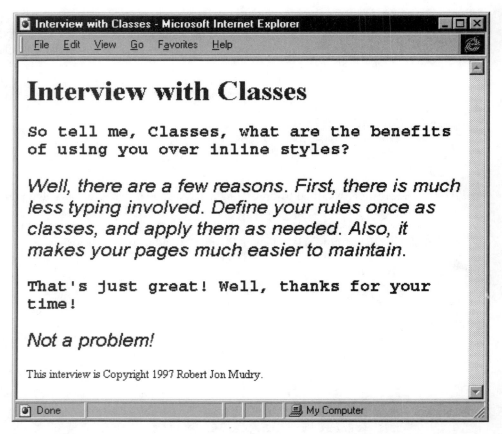

Figure 6–1   Classes in action. In this example, the <P> element uses its "question" class to display the interviewer's questions and its "answer" class for the celebrity's answers.

```
</BODY>
</HTML>
```

After your classes have been defined, you can access them using the element's "CLASS=" attribute. For example, to use the "question" class, you would assign the class name "question" to the element's "CLASS=" attribute.

```
<P CLASS="question">I will use the question class.</P>
```

Whenever you request that the <P> element use the "question" class, your text will be rendered in 14pt bold Courier. When it is time to display the celebrity's answer, you can ask the <P> element to use the "answer" class instead. This time, the text is rendered in 16pt italic Arial. But what happens if you don't specify a class name with the "CLASS=" attribute? In this case, the <P> element will use our "default" rules, defined without the class name. Here, it will be a 9pt font. If we hadn't created this "classless" definition, the browser would have simply used the paragraph's default font.

Classes are quite powerful, but there are a couple of things you can't do. First, you might be tempted to try to combine classes, perhaps by putting two or more names in the same "CLASS=" attribute. This won't work. You can only have one class on an element at a time. The other thing you can't do is use a class defined for one selector on another. For example, if you have a class defined as "P.question," you can't apply that class to a <SPAN> element. You will have to either define another class specifically for the <SPAN> element, or turn "question" into a "generic class."

A generic class is a class that wasn't defined for any specific selector. In the previous example, the "question" and "answer" classes were declared specifically for the <P> element, and they can only be applied to <P> elements in your document. A generic class, on the other hand, can be applied to any element. Let's rewrite the interview example, this time using generic classes. The new style sheet appears below.

```
.question { font-family: courier;
            font-size: 14pt;
            font-weight: bold }
.answer { font-family: arial;
          font-size: 16pt;
          font-style: italic }
P { font-size: 9pt; }
```

The only difference this time, is that instead of saying "P.question" or "P.answer" to declare the classes, they are declared without the selector. These classes can now be applied to *anything*, not just the <P> element. The "question" class is just as happy on <P> as it is on a <SPAN> or even a <B> element. If you omit the selector from the class declaration, the class can be applied to any element.

Classes follow selector grouping rules just like regular, classless selectors. In the example below, an <H1> element, the "B.uline" class, and the "myclass" generic class all share the same rule via selector grouping. All three will apply an underline to their text.

```
H1, B.uline, .myclass { text-decoration: underline }
```

Using ID's as Selectors

The "ID=" attribute has special meaning in dynamic HTML as one of the ways we use to identify elements in our documents. It also has a use in style sheets, but not quite the same one. Instead, the "ID=" attribute can be used in a way similar to the "CLASS=" attribute. The theory is, all the "ID=" attributes in your document should be unique; therefore, you can use the "ID=" attribute as a special class that can only be applied to one element. The "ID=" attribute behaves almost exactly like the "CLASS=" attribute, except you can only use an ID name once.

The syntax to declare an ID is the same as declaring a class, except the period is replaced with a hash sign. A sample document using "ID=" attributes appears below. Three unique IDs are created. The first is "H1#uline," which can only be used on an <H1> ele-

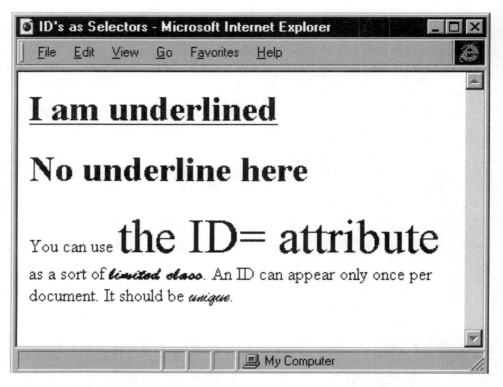

Figure 6–2   Using the "ID=" attribute as if it were a class.

ment. The second is "#myID," which can be applied to any element, but keeping in the spirit of the "ID=" attribute, it can only be used once. Finally, the last is "#unique," declared along with the <B> element. IDs can be declared using selector grouping rules just like regular classes. The results can be found in Figure 6–2.

```
<HTML>
<STYLE>
    H1#uline { text-decoration: underline }
    #myID { font-size: 32pt;
            font-color: red }
    B, #unique { font-family: "brush script" }
</STYLE>
<HEAD>
<TITLE>ID's as Selectors</TITLE>
</HEAD>
<BODY>
```

```
<H1 ID="uline">I am underlined</H1>
<H1>No underline here</H1>

<P>You can use <SPAN ID="myID">the ID= attribute</SPAN> as a
sort of <B>limited class</B>. An ID can appear only once per
document. It should be <SPAN ID="unique">unique</SPAN>.</P>

</BODY>
</HTML>
```

Of course, technically there is nothing to stop you from reusing ID names in the same document, effectively making the "ID=" attribute equivalent to the "CLASS=" attribute. Don't do this! It's poor form, bad style, and against the specifications. If you use this feature, make sure all your "ID=" attributes are completely unique in the document.

Pseudo-classes and Link Effects

In addition to your user-defined classes, the style sheet specification also provides a small handful of built in *pseudo-classes*. Currently, there are five pseudo-classes in the specifications; however, only three of these have been implemented: the link effects. Link effects determine how your links appear before they have been clicked, while they are being clicked, and after they are visited.

The three link effect pseudo-classes are "A:link," "A:visited," and "A:active." The "A:link" pseudo-class sets the style for unvisited links. Visited links are set with the "A:visited" pseudo-class, and "A:active" controls the appearance of links that the user just selected. Pseudo-classes are distinguished from regular classes by the colon separator. When the browser sees a colon before the class name, it knows you are accessing a pseudo-class. An example of the link effects is below, and a screen shot can be found in Figure 6–3.

```
<HTML>
<STYLE>
    A:link { font-size: larger;
             font-weight: bold }
    A:visited { font-style: italic;
                text-decoration: none }
    A:active { text-transform: uppercase }
</STYLE>
<HEAD>
<TITLE>Link Effect Pseudo-classes</TITLE>
</HEAD>
<BODY>

<P>This is an <A HREF="unvisited.html">unvisited</A> URL.</P>
<P>This URL has been <A
HREF="http://www.prenhall.com">visited</A>.</P>
```

```
<P>I just clicked this <A HREF="active.html">active</A>
URL.</P>

</BODY>
</HTML>
```

You can set any style you want using the link effect pseudo-classes. In this example, all unvisited links will appear bold and in a "larger" font. Links that have already been visited will be in the same size font as the rest of the text, but will appear in italics without the classic underlining. Active links, which the user has just clicked but the new page hasn't loaded yet, are transformed into all uppercase. Of course, you can also change the link colors, too.

Notice in the HTML that we don't need to use the "CLASS=" attribute on any of the anchors for the link effects to work. The browser automatically applies the proper pseudo-class depending on the state of the link. All you need to do is define the link effects in your style sheets and you're ready to go! But this does bring up an interesting question. What do you do if you only want some of your links to use the new link effects?

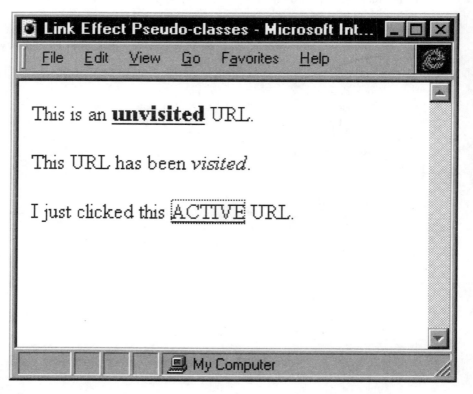

Figure 6–3 Link effects at work. The top link has never been visited, the middle has been visited, and the bottom link has just been clicked but hasn't loaded the new page yet.

Pseudo-classes can be combined with regular classes in your style sheets, by appending the pseudo-class name after the regular class name.

```
A.fancylinks:link { font-size: x-large;
                    font-style: italics }
```

In this example, the regular class "fancylinks" is used in combination with the pseudo-class "link" to apply an x-large italic font to unvisited links. To get one of your links to use this pseudo-class, you can use the "CLASS=" attribute with the "fancylinks" class name.

```
<A CLASS="fancylinks" HREF="http://www.prenhall.com/">Home</A>
```

Only links with the "fancylinks" class will use the new style. Other links will be unaffected.

While we're on the topic of link effects, I would like to reiterate my view on altering the appearance of your links. Unvisited links have historically been blue and underlined and visited links purple and underlined. When I see something blue or purple with an underline, I know at a glance that it is a link. By changing the colors of visited and unvisited links, it is easy to lose the sense of which links have been visited, or even if the text is a link at all. Removing the underline makes it even tougher to figure out which is what. Whenever you change link colors or remove the underlines, you introduce at least some level of initial confusion to your pages.

I hate to lecture, but please be very careful when changing link appearances. I've been to pages where the only way to tell the links from surrounding text was to put my pointer over it and see if a URL popped into the status bar or my pointer changed to indicate a link. It wasn't fun navigating those pages, and I ended up going somewhere else out of frustration. The page was beautiful, but the webmaster sacrificed utility for appearance. Don't make this same mistake!

If you are curious about the other two unsupported pseudo-classes, they are "first-letter" and "first-line." The first-letter pseudo-class is used to define a "drop cap." Ever read a magazine article where the first character of the first line of text in the article is in some giant, fancy font? That is a drop cap. The first-line pseudo-class takes this a bit further and affects the entire first line of text, not just the first character. Once again, flip through any magazine and you will probably spot at least one example of this.

```
P:first-letter { font-size: xx-large }
```

This example will, hopefully sometime in the near future, tell the browser to make the first letter of every paragraph xx-large.

There actually is another link pseudo-class I didn't mention earlier, called "hover." The hover pseudo-class isn't in the "official" style sheet specification, and Internet Explorer 4.0 doesn't support it yet, either. But it will probably become supported shortly, so I thought I should mention it. When the user "hovers" her mouse pointer over the link, but pauses for a moment before clicking, the hover style will be applied. It won't happen if the user just passes the pointer by quickly—she has to pause for a moment, first.

```
A:hover { color: red }
```

For example, if the user hesitates for a moment before clicking your link, you can change the link's color to red, nudging the user into action.

Contextual Selectors

Contextual selectors are a powerful feature that allows you to define rules that only apply in certain contexts; for example, a <B> element that acts "like normal" when in a <P> element, but turns green when found in a <BLOCKQUOTE> element. The <B> element will use different rules depending on its context.

To create a contextual selector, put each selector before the declaration of your rule as if you were grouping them, but use a space instead of a comma as the separator. For example, to create a contextual selector for the <B> element that only applies in the context of a <BLOCKQUOTE> element, you would use the following code.

```
BLOCKQUOTE B { color: green }
```

In these example, the <B> element will be green, but only if it is inserted in a <BLOCKQUOTE> element. If it appears anywhere else, it will behave as normal. The order of the selectors is very important! If the order was reversed, the rule would turn the <BLOCKQUOTE> green if it appeared inside a <B> element!

One of my favorite uses for contextual selectors is modifying the levels in lists, such as the <UL> and <OL> elements. For example, the first list level can be x-large, the second level can be large, the third average sized, and the forth small. It is easy with contextual selectors.

```
<HTML>
<STYLE>
    UL LI { font-size: x-large }
    UL UL LI { font-size: large }
    UL UL UL LI { font-size: medium }
    UL UL UL UL LI { font-size: small }
</STYLE>
<HEAD>
<TITLE>Contextual Selectors</TITLE>
</HEAD>
<BODY>

<UL>
<LI>Level One</LI>
    <UL>
    <LI>Level Two</LI>
```

```
         <UL>
         <LI>Level Three</LI>
            <UL>
            <LI>Level Four</LI>
            </UL>
         </UL>
      </UL>
   </UL>

   </BODY>
   </HTML>
```

The trick here is to convince the <LI> element to do different things depending on how deeply buried it is inside the <UL> elements. If it is the first level, it appears inside only one <UL> element, so "UL LI" is sufficient. At the second level, the <LI> element will be inside *two* <UL> elements, so we need to use "UL UL LI" as the contextual selector. This can be read as "apply this rule to the <LI> element that is inside a <UL> element that itself is inside a <UL> element." The output from this document is in Figure 6–4.

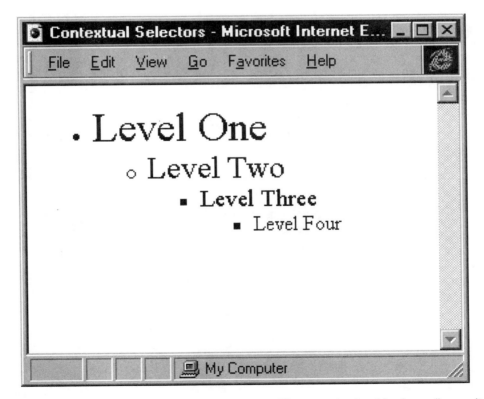

Figure 6–4   Using contextual selectors to apply different styles to <LI> depending on its depth.

As you can see, contextual selectors are powerful but can be a bit difficult to grasp at first. They get even more confusing when classes and pseudo-classes are tossed into the mix. The following example shows a few contextual selectors and what they do. The screen shot is in Figure 6–5.

```
<HTML>
<STYLE>
   P B I { font: large arial }
   P.class1 SPAN { font: large arial }
   .class2 B { font: large arial }
   BLOCKQUOTE.class3 A:link { font: large arial }
</STYLE>
<HEAD>
<TITLE>Contextual Selectors</TITLE>
</HEAD>
<BODY>

<P>Paragraph with <B>bold and <I>italics</I></B>.</P>
<P CLASS="class1">Paragraph (class1) with
<SPAN>span</SPAN>.</P>
<DIV CLASS="class2">Div (class2) with <B>bold</B>.</P>
<BLOCKQUOTE CLASS="class3">Blockquote (class3) with <A
HREF="new.html">link</A>.</BLOCKQUOTE>

</BODY>
</HTML>
```

Contextual selectors can be grouped just like other selectors. For example, these three rules:

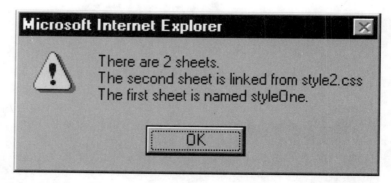

Figure 6–5   The styleSheets collection can be used to access embedded and linked style sheets.

```
P B { font-size: larger }
P I { font-size: larger }
SPAN EM { font-size: larger }
```

can be reduced to:

```
P B, P I, SPAN EM { font-size: larger }
```

The best way to master contextual selectors is through experimentation!

Comments

With grouping, classes, pseudo-classes, contextual selectors, and the plethora of properties, your style sheets can become rather complex. There are few things as frustrating as designing a style sheet, getting distracted by another project for a day or two, and then forgetting how your style sheet works when you get back to it. It is even worse when you've been asked to maintain someone else's style sheets. Programmers have learned that by "commenting" their code, maintenance becomes easier for themselves and for others after them. Style sheets also give you the ability to insert "comments."

Comments in style sheets are ignored by the browser. They are simply notes to remind yourself of your intentions and give others an idea what you did and why you did it. The code below has three comments.

```
/* These are my paragraphs */
P B { color: red } /* Bold elements are red when in paragraphs */
P I { color: blue } /* Italic elements are blue inside paragraphs */
```

These are called "C-style" comments, because they are the same kinds of comments used in the C programming language. Everything between the /* and */ characters is ignored by the browser. Comments can also be used to "comment out" a bit of your style sheet for testing.

```
/* These rules are commented out for now
  P { font-size: x-large }
  P B { font-color: green }
*/
```

As you can see, comments can be started on one line and "closed" on another. The rules inside the comment are ignored.

When should you use comments? I had one instructor in a C programming class who always insisted that everything be commented. Everything. Every command, every statement, every function. At times, I had more comments then actual code. Next semester I had another instructor who, upon seeing all my comments, thought I was a "little slow," if you catch my meaning. "Why comment code whose operation should be obvious to any programmer?" he would say.

There is no hard-and-fast rule for when to use comments and when not to use comments. I use comments whenever I do something weird or complex that I think needs a little explanation. For example, "Bold only inside a paragraph," or "This is to get around a browser bug." If I think I won't remember why I did something six month from now, or if other people need to maintain the style sheet, I'll use comments. If it is obvious what I'm doing, I won't. A good sign you are commenting too much is when you have more comments then style sheet rules!

MORE ON CASCADING

As your style sheets become more sophisticated and you begin to develop a small library of pre-made style sheets to <LINK> and embed, you are bound to create some conflicts. A linked style sheet might define a rule or two that is also defined in an embedded style sheet. You may also have an inline style or two in conflict with an @import'ed style sheet, and you will most assuredly create conflicts between styles and HTML elements. Take a look at the simple example below and you'll see what I mean. Conflicts are as common in style sheets as they are in real life.

```
<HTML>
<STYLE>
    P { font-family: courier;
        font-size: 18pt;
        color: blue }
</STYLE>
<HEAD>
<TITLE>Cascades and Conflicts</TITLE>
<LINK REL="stylesheet" HREF="sheet1.css" TYPE="text/css">
</HEAD>
<BODY>

<P><I STYLE="color: red">How do I look?</I></P>

</BODY>
</HTML>
```

The contents of the linked style sheet "sheet1.css" is below.

```
P { font-family: arial;
    font-size: 8pt;
    color: black }
I { color: yellow }
```

So how does the text "How do I look?" appear? The inline style says it should be red, but it is in a <P> element, which is blue. And don't forget about the linked style sheet that says the <P> element should really be black but the <I> element should be yellow. Yikes! Is it 18pt Courier, like the embedded style sheet says a <P> element should be, or is it 8pt Arial like the linked style sheet says? The embedded style sheet also says <P> element text is specifically *not* italic. So how *does* it look?

The answer is actually 8pt Arial in red, which the browser determines using the "cascading order" rules. The cascading order rules tell the browser exactly how to handle conflicts when several style sheets attempt to modify the same element.

Colliding Style Sheets

Conflicts come in two flavors: style sheets conflicting with other style sheets and rules conflicting with rules within the same style sheet. To unravel this mystery, the browser's first course of action is to pick the most important style sheet.

The official CSS specification says that style sheets should be given precedence in the following order, with the first being the most important and the last being the least important:

1. **Inline** style sheets, defined with the "STYLE=" attribute. Rules in inline style sheets are the most important.
2. **Embedded** style sheets, defined with the <STYLE> element.
3. **Linked** style sheets, loaded into the document with the <LINK> element.
4. **Imported** style sheets, imported into a style sheet with the @import command.
5. **Reader** style sheets, which are defined by the user. No browsers support reader styles at this time, but I'm sure we'll see them soon enough.
6. **Browser default** style sheets, defined by the browser itself. Every browser has one, though they are hidden from your view. The browser default style sheet determines how HTML will be rendered in the absence of other style info.

In our previous example, the text was red because the color rule was defined in an inline style. Inline styles have priority over all other styles. But why is it 8pt Arial, and not 18pt Courier, as the rules would imply? After all, the 18pt Courier was defined in an *embedded* style sheet, which should have beaten out the 8pt Arial defined in the linked style sheet. The reason for this is simple: *Our current browsers are all broken*. In an ideal world, the text would indeed by 18pt Courier, but unfortunately Internet Explorer 4.0 treats linked styles more important then embedded styles.

Keep in mind that when we say *rules* we really do mean *rules*. It is easy to fall into the trap of considering all rules that have been grouped into one large declaration as a single, giant compound rule. But this thinking is doomed to failure. In the style sheet below, the declaration contains *three separate rules*. Not one large rule.

```
P { font-family: arial;
    font-size: large;
    font-weight: bold }
```

Rules collide only when they are attempting to do mutually exclusive things; for example, one rule setting the font-family of the <P> element to Arial, and another setting the font-family of the <P> element to Courier. We only care about rules that are in direct conflict—other rules, even if they are on the "losing" style sheet, will apply just fine.

Rules Colliding with Rules in the Same Style Sheet

If the rules in conflict are in the same style sheet, the browser needs to work a little harder. For example, in the following example, which rule wins? Does the <P> element's blue color win, or is the <B> element's red color more important?

```
<HTML>
<STYLE>
    P { color: blue }
    B { color: red }
</STYLE>
<HEAD>
<TITLE>Cascades and Conflicts</TITLE>
</HEAD>
<BODY>

<P><B>Blue or Red? Red!</B></P>

</BODY>
</HTML>
```

The text will be red. Even though the <P> element says that it should contain blue text, there is a specific declaration for <B> that wants red. Specific declarations always win out over inherited values.

There are other rules, of course. The specifications state that if you put the keyword "! important" after a rule that rule should be more important then the others. Of course, this useful feature hasn't been implemented yet. There is also a complex system of "weighting," called "specificity," which involves counting ID attributes, class attributes, and selectors. Yet again, not implemented.

```
P { font-family: arial;
    color: red ! important } /* Color red is more important */
```

To make matters worse, what has been implemented hasn't been implemented to the specifications or consistently. For example, the specifications say embedded style sheets are more important then linked, but we discovered that isn't necessarily true. In time, all of this stuff will sort itself out. Until then, when you think you have a rule conflict, double check what the browser actually does—that's the only way to be sure right now.

DYNAMIC STYLE SHEETS

Finally, the moment you have all been waiting for—dynamic styles! Your style sheets are hooked directly into the document object model, making them fully accessible to your scripts. And I'm not talking about read-only access. Almost every aspect of your style sheets can be read, written, and otherwise mangled on the fly. Change an element's style or switch classes and the browser instantly redraws the document. Even better, once we get into the layout, positioning, and filters portions of style sheets, we're no longer looking at a regular web document but full-featured multimedia experience.

The "style" Property

Any element object that can accept an inline style has a "style" property. The style property is actually another object that represents that element's inline style sheet. Through it, you have full read and write access to every style sheet property available for that element. Add, delete, and modify style sheet rules on the fly!

```
<SPAN onClick="this.style.color = 'blue';">Click Me!</SPAN>
```

This is a simple example of changing the color property of a <SPAN> element. For "single word" style sheet properties like "color," you can use the style sheet property name directly with the style object. Most style sheet properties, however, are two words separated by a dash. Unfortunately, dashes are invalid in object property names, so an alternate naming convention has been devised to get around this problem. When a style sheet property name contains a dash, the dash is removed and the first character after the dash is capitalized. For example, the style sheet property "font-size" is replaced with the object property "fontSize" for use with the style object.

```
<SPAN onClick="this.style.fontSize = '24pt';">Click Me!</SPAN>
```

Let's try a complete example. The HTML document below uses the onmouseover and onmouseout events to change the style of our <H1> element. This type of code should remind you a lot of the dynamic content code we used to write.

```
<HTML>
<HEAD>
<TITLE>Dynamic Styles!</TITLE>
<SCRIPT LANGUAGE="JavaScript">
function do_over(myElement)
{
    myElement.style.fontSize = "xx-large";
    myElement.style.fontFamily = "arial";
    myElement.style.color = "green";
}
function do_out(myElement)
```

```
    {
        myElement.style.fontSize = "x-large";
        myElement.style.fontFamily = "times new roman";
        myElement.style.color = "black";
    }
</SCRIPT>
</HEAD>
<BODY>

<H1 onMouseOver="do_over(this)"
    onMouseOut="do_out(this)">Dynamic Styles Are Great!</H1>

</BODY>
</HTML>
```

The style object represents an element's *inline* style only. This is not normally a problem, because inline styles almost always have precedence over all your other style sheets. The biggest drawback is the inability to read style sheet properties on the element from other sources, like embedded or linked style sheets. We'll learn how to access embedded and linked styles shortly.

The other drawback with the style object is that you're constantly forced to redo your work. Every time you want to change a style, you have to rebuild it from the ground up. What would really be helpful is a way to change an element's class. As luck would have it, we have that capability! An element's class can be changed via the read-write element object property "className." Let's rewrite the previous example using classes instead of inline styles.

```
<HTML>
<STYLE>
    .over { font-family: arial;
            font-size: xx-large;
            color: green }
    .out { font-family: "times new roman";
           font-size: x-large;
           color: black }
</STYLE>
<HEAD>
<TITLE>Dynamic Styles!</TITLE>
<SCRIPT LANGUAGE="JavaScript">
function do_over(myElement)
{
    myElement.className = "over";
}
function do_out(myElement)
{
    myElement.className = "out";
}
```

```
</SCRIPT>
</HEAD>
<BODY>

<H1 onMouseOver="do_over(this)" onMouseOut="do_out(this)"
    CLASS="out">Dynamic Styles Are Great!</H1>

</BODY>
</HTML>
```

The first thing we do is create an embedded style sheet with two classes. The generic "over" class will handle onmouseover events, and the generic "out" class will handle onmouseout events. Now the scripts can be much simpler. When the onmouseover event is captured, the element's className property is changed to "over," and the style is instantly updated. When onmouseout is captured, the "out" class is used instead. Once again, the change is instantaneous. The className property is a direct reflection of the "CLASS=" attribute.

Actually, we could have made this document even shorter by eliminating the <SCRIPT> element and binding to the assignment directly:

```
<H1 onMouseOver="this.className = 'over';"
    onMouseOut="this.className = 'out';"
    CLASS="out">Dynamic Styles Are Great!</H1>
```

The possibilities are endless!

The styleSheets Collection: Accessing Embedded and Linked Styles

To get at your embedded and linked style sheets, we need to approach the problem from a slightly different angle. The className property opened this door a little bit, allowing us to at least use classes from embedded and link style sheets. The "styleSheets" collection, located on the document object, is our key.

All of the document's <STYLE> and <LINK> elements can be found on the styleSheets collection. Imported style sheets with the @import command are also available, however only indirectly. Imported style sheets are "rolled up" into their parent style sheets. For example, if the style sheet was imported into an embedded style sheet, the imported rules can be accessed as if they were a direct part of the embedded style sheet. The collection itself is just like any other. You can give the collection an index number, which corresponds to the style sheet's position in the document, or better yet, you can give it an identifier and reference the style sheet by name. There is even a "length" property that you can use to determine the number of style sheets in the current document.

```
<HTML>
<STYLE ID="styleOne">
    P { color: green }
```

```
      B { font-size: larger;
          color: red }
</STYLE>
<HEAD>
<LINK REL="stylesheet" HREF="style2.css" TYPE="text/css">
<TITLE>Dynamic Styles!</TITLE>
<SCRIPT LANGUAGE="JavaScript">
function what_styles()
{
    var numStyles = document.styleSheets.length;
    var styleLoc  = document.styleSheets[1].href;
    var styleID= document.styleSheets.styleOne.id;

    alert("There are " + numStyles + " sheets.\n" +
        "The second sheet is linked from " + styleLoc + "\n" +
          "The first sheet is named " + styleID + ".");
}
</SCRIPT>
</HEAD>
<BODY>

<H1 onClick="what_styles()">Click Me For Style Sheet Info</H1>

</BODY>
</HTML>
```

This document contains two style sheets. The first is an embedded style sheet with the identifier "styleOne." We can use this identifier later to access the style sheet directly, the same way identifiers are used in element objects. The second is a linked style sheet. When the user clicks on the <H1> element, the what_styles() function — which reports a little bit of information on the style sheets — is called. The results are shown in Figure 6–5.

The first thing the what_styles() function does is use the styleSheet collection's length property to count the number of style sheets in the current document. This value is assigned to a variable for later use. Next, the second style sheet is accessed and its href property is read. Remember, collections start with zero as the first object. Since the second style sheet is linked, the href property will contain the URL of the linked style sheet. This too is stored in a variable for later use. Finally, the "styleOne" style sheet is accessed, and its id property is read. All these values are then sent to an alert() box for examination. Not a very exciting example, but it covers most of the bases.

Adding Rules and Importing Style Sheets

The styleSheets collection contains styleSheet objects, which represent the style sheets in your document. These styleSheet objects expose two powerful new methods: addRule() and addImport(). The addRule() method lets you add new rules to your embedded style sheets, and the addImport() method imports additional style sheets. Here's how they work . . .

To add a new rule, the addRule() method requires two arguments. The first argument specifies the selectors, and the second argument contains the declaration. For example, if you wanted to add rule for the <SPAN> element, you would use:

```
document.styleSheets[0].addRule("SPAN","color: blue");
```

Instantly, the new rule is added to the bottom of the first style sheet and all <SPAN> elements will turn blue. The addRule() method isn't restricted to a single selector and single rule. You can also use grouping and contextual selectors:

```
document.styleSheets[0].addRule("B,I,SPAN","color: red");
document.styleSheets[0].addRule("DIV","font-size: 8pt; color:
  blue");
document.styleSheets[0].addRule("SPAN I","font-family: arial");
```

These three lines are all equally valid, and produce the expected results. The addRule() method will also accept an optional third argument, if you don't want the rule added to the end of the style sheet. Giving an index number will add the rule at that point in your style sheet. For example, if you want to add a rule to the beginning of the style sheet, you could use:

```
document.styleSheet[0].addRule("SPAN","color: green",0);
```

Unfortunately, the addRule() method will only work on embedded style sheets, with the <STYLE> element. If the style sheet is linked with the <LINK> element, addRule() will fail! Linked style sheets are read-only. At least, that is what the documentation says. In reality, I had no problem using addRule() on a linked style sheet. Go figure.

If you want to verify whether the style sheet is read-only or writable, you can check the styleSheet object's readOnly property. If the style sheet is read-only, like linked style sheets are supposed to be, the property will contain "true." If you can write to the style sheet, as you can with embedded style sheets, the property will contain "false." Not that it makes much of a difference now, but I would still recommend that you avoid assuming you can write to linked style sheets as this behavior may suddenly change.

```
if (document.styleSheets[0].readOnly == false)
{
    alert("You can write to this style sheet.");
}
else
{
    alert("You can only read this style sheet.");
}
```

If you want to add a whole bunch of rules at once, you can use the addImport() method to import a style sheet into the current one. The addImport() method requires one argument, the URL of the style sheet to import. Essentially, it adds an @import command to your style sheet.

```
document.styleSheets[0].addImport("newSheet.css");
```

When complete, the document is instantly updated to reflect the new imported styles. If you want to specify the position of the imported style sheet, relative to the other imported style sheets, you can provide an optional second argument with the new position. Otherwise, the style sheet will be imported last relative to the other imported style sheets.

Other styleSheet Object Properties

The styleSheet object has seven properties, which contain additional information about your style sheet. These are: disabled, href, id, owningElement, parentStyleSheet, read-Only, and type.

One really neat property is "disabled," which allows you to disable an entire style sheet! Instantly, your document will update to reflect the loss of these rules. To disable your style sheet, simply write "true" to this property. When you're ready to enable it again, write "false." The example below toggles the state of the style sheet whenever the button is pushed.

```
<HTML>
<STYLE ID="styleOne">
    H1 { color: green }
</STYLE>
<HEAD>
<TITLE>Dynamic Styles!</TITLE>
<SCRIPT LANGUAGE="JavaScript">
function toggle_styles()
{
    var myStyle = document.styleSheets.styleOne;

    if (myStyle.disabled == true)
    {
        myStyle.disabled = false;  // Enable stylesheet
    }
    else
    {
        myStyle.disabled = true;   // Disable stylesheet
    }
}
</SCRIPT>
</HEAD>
<BODY>
```

```
<H1>Style Sheets Can Be Disabled!</H1>

<FORM>
 <INPUT TYPE="button" VALUE="Toggle Styles"
onClick="toggle_styles()">
</FORM>

</BODY>
</HTML>
```

The "href" property returns the URL of the style sheet if it has been included with the <LINK> element. For embedded style sheets, this property will be empty. Yes, you *can* write to the href property, but only for linked style sheets. After the new style sheet is loaded, your document will instantly update using the new rules.

```
document.styleSheets[0].href = "new_style.css";
```

The "id" property is read-only and contains the identifier of this style sheet, as defined by the "ID=" attribute in the <STYLE> or <LINK> elements. If there is no identifier, then this property is empty.

One convenient way to ensure that you are indeed working with a linked style sheet, or instead have an embedded style sheet, is to read the value in the "owningElement" property. The owningElement property contains the element object where this style sheet was defined from. For example, if this is an embedded element, the owningElement property will return the <STYLE> element object. Let's rewrite the "href" property example with this new safety check.

```
if (document.styleSheets[0].owningElement.tagName == "LINK")
{
    document.styleSheets[0].href = "new_style.css";
}
```

Now, before the "href" property is accessed, your script will check if it really can write to the href property or if it is about to generate an error. If the owningElement's tagName is "LINK," we know it is safe. Otherwise, the assignment is skipped.

The "type" property will return the MIME type of the current style sheet. Since Internet Explorer 4.0 only supports "text/css" style sheets, this property is really just planning for the future. Right now, it won't actually return anything—just a empty string. In the future, it will return "text/css" for cascading style sheets.

The "imports" Collection

When a style sheet imports another style sheet with the @import command, those style sheets are all gathered into the "imports" collection on the parent styleSheet object. In the example below, the view_imports() function steps through the "styleOne" style sheet's imports collection and prints the URL of each imported style sheet and where it was imported to. Just for good measure, it calls the addImport() method to import yet another style sheet. The output can be found in Figure 6–6.

```
<HTML>
<STYLE ID="styleOne">
    @import url(import1.css);
    @import url(import2.css);
</STYLE>
<HEAD>
<TITLE>Dynamic Styles!</TITLE>
<SCRIPT LANGUAGE="JavaScript">
function view_imports()
{
    var mySpan  = document.all.importsHere;
    var mySheet = document.styleSheets.styleOne;
    var myText = "";

    mySheet.addImport("import3.css"); // Import another...

    for(var num=0;num < mySheet.imports.length;num++)
    {
```

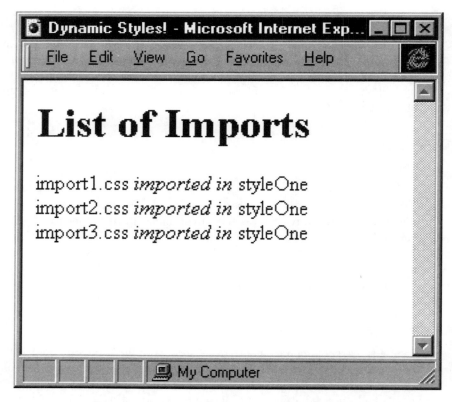

Figure 6–6   Stepping through the "rules" collection.

```
            myText += mySheet.imports[num].href + " <I>imported in</I> ";
            myText += mySheet.imports[num].parentStyleSheet.id + "<BR>";
        }
    mySpan.innerHTML = myText;
}
</SCRIPT>
</HEAD>
<BODY onLoad="view_imports()">

<H1>List of Imports</H1>

<SPAN ID="importsHere"></SPAN>

</BODY>
</HTML>
```

Each object in the imports collection is a full-fledged styleSheet object and can be accessed using the properties and methods, including an interesting new one called "parentStyleSheet." The parentStyleSheet property is a pointer to the style sheet object into which that style sheet was imported. The property is also available on embedded and linked style sheets, but since they don't have parents, it will always return "null."

In general, you really don't need to go through all this trouble to access imported style sheets, because all of their rules will automatically be available in the parent style sheet. For example, in the example above, all the rules from each of the three imported style sheets can be accessed directly from the "styleOne" style sheet.

The "rules" Collection

Every rule in your style sheet can be found in the "rules" collection. At least, that is the plan. Ironically, the less useful "imports" collection is fully implemented, but the "rules" collection doesn't work at all yet. Not a problem—I am sure it will be working soon. Until then, here is what the rules collection will do when it is done.

The rules collection will contain one property—length—that will be the number of rules in the current style sheet. To access an individual rule, you will use that rule's index number, which is its position in the style sheet. For example, the access the third rule in the first style sheet, you would use the following code.

```
var ruleObject = document.styleSheets[0].rules[2];
```

The third rule will be stored in the "ruleObject" variable. From here, you can examine or modify the rule object's two properties: selectorText and style.

The selectorText property will contain the rule's selectors. For example, in the following style sheet, the selector "H1" is the selectorText.

```
H1 { font-size: 24pt;
     color: red }
```

The style property behaves just like the element object style property. Using the same example, the following code can be used to read the size of the font for this rule. In this case, it will return "24pt."

```
alert( document.styleSheets[0].rules[0].style.fontSize );
```

In theory, you will be able to read the selectorText and style properties for any style sheet, including embedded, linked, and imported. However, you will only be able to write to the properties if they are from an embedded style.

Moving On

Tying style sheets with the document object model was a big step, but with a little experimentation I'm sure you will find a million neat things you can do already. For the rest of this chapter we will go over some more new style sheet features, including layout and classification properties. There are also a few neat "other" properties tossed in for good measure. After that, it is on to "positioning"—a new style sheet feature that allows you to precisely control where your elements go at the pixel level—and the even newer "filter" properties.

BOX (LAYOUT) PROPERTIES

The "box" properties control the margins, border, padding, and "floating" of every element in your document. As style sheets have become more widely accepted, the box properties have earned the nick-name "layout" properties, because of the way they affect the layout of your document.

Formatting Model: The Box

Every element—for example, the <P> and <BLOCKQUOTE> elements—is inside an imaginary box. At the center of each box is the element's content, surrounded by a layer of padding, the border, and finally the margin. Take a look at Figure 6–7 and you will see what I mean.

- **Content box** is the actual text or image inside the element.
- **Padding box** is a little bit of extra room between the context box and the border.
- **Border box** is the element's border. Most elements don't have borders, but some do. For example, tables can have borders as well as images. In theory, however, *any* element can have a border.
- **Margin box** is the space after the border that separates this from other elements. The margin is always transparent, so anything underneath will always show through.

Each layer of the box has four sides. For example, the padding layer consists of the top-padding side, the bottom-padding side, the left-padding side, and the right-padding side. The content-box itself has four sides called inner-top, inner-bottom, left-inner-edge, and right-inner-edge. The outside edges of the entire box are labeled top, bottom, left-outer-edge, and right-outer-edge. Finally, the element width is the width of the content box, measured from the left-inner-edge to the right-inner-edge, and the element height is, as you would suspect, the height of the content box measured from the inner-bottom to the inner-top. The box width is the width of the entire box from the left-outer-edge to the right-outer-edge. Likewise, the box height is the height of the entire box from the bottom to the top. Whew!

We didn't name every piece of the box just for the sake of confusion! The box properties actually have control over every aspect of the box, all the way down to the width of every little part. For example, the border-left property controls the width of only the left side of the border box. Don't worry, because it will all become clear after we've had a few real examples. But first, let's add one more level of confusion . . .

Boxes Inside Boxes Inside Boxes Inside . . .

If your document contained only a single element, all of this would be relatively simple. But presumably your documents are a tad more complex than that! A typical document might contain a few headings, a paragraph or two, an unordered list, and maybe even a blockquote or two. All of these elements are happily nested in their own little boxes, and each of these boxes is forced to interact with the others. Take a look at the HTML below.

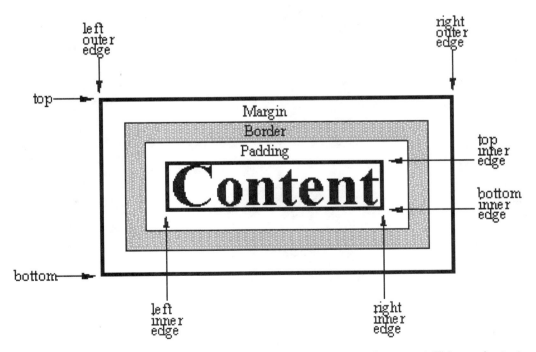

Figure 6–7 The imaginary box. At the center is the element's content. This can be text, an image, or anything else you can jam inside an element.

```
<P>Some paragraph text.</P>
<UL>
<LI>Item One Text</LI>
<LI>Item Two Text</LI>
</UL>
```

This simple document contains a <P> element and a <UL> element. Inside the <UL> element there are also two <LI> elements. Each one has its own box. Until now, the browser had complete and sole control over how these boxes interacted, and you really didn't have to think too much about it. Now, however, you have control as well, so

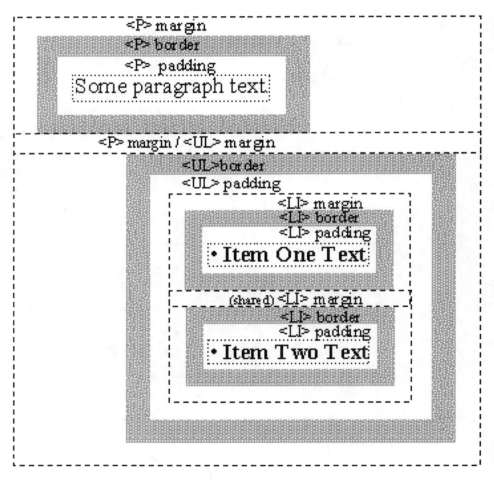

Figure 6–8   It looks simple on the page, but underneath it all is a rather complex system of boxes. Notice how adjacent elements actually share margins.

it's important to understand how the browser handles a situation like this. Figure 6–8 shows all of the boxes, as the browser sees them.

That's quite a little layout, isn't it? Each <LI> element has its own box; these in turn are inside the <UL> element's box. See how the <UL> element's left margin extents all the way to the left? The <UL> element is also adjacent to the <P> element, which has a box of its own. Wherever boxes meet, they share that border. In this example, the top <LI> element shares its bottom margin with the second <LI> element's top margin. Where the <P> and <UL> elements meet, they share their bottom and top margins as well. Margins are shared where elements meet, not added to each other! The larger margin always wins over the smaller margin. We'll hear more on this later.

You may also have noticed that in Figure 6–8, every element has a nice, large gray border. Surely these elements don't *really* have borders, right? Well, no, they normally don't. Or more precisely, they do but the borders are zero width so you don't see them. But in theory, any element *can* have a border.

margin Properties

Margins control how much space is between elements. The margin properties allow you to change all four margin sizes of an element: margin-left, margin-top, margin-bottom, and margin-right. Of all the box properties, the margin properties are arguably the most important, or at the very least the most useful.

You can use any valid unit to set the size of your margins. I prefer using ems, because that makes the margins proportional to the fonts. If you want something more precise, you can use inches, centimeters, or even pixels. Just keep in mind that one inch on my laptop monitor has quite a different effect than one inch on the 21" monitor at work.

```
P { margin-left: 0.5in }
```

As you can guess, the example above sets the left margin of the <P> element to a half an inch. See the listing below and Figure 6–9 for more examples.

```
<HTML>
<STYLE>
    P.a { margin-left: 0.5in }
    P.b { margin-left: 4em }
    P.c { margin-top: 1in;
          margin-left: 1in;
          margin-right: 1in }
</STYLE>
<HEAD>
<TITLE>Box Properties: margins</TITLE>
</HEAD>
<BODY>
<P>Normal paragraph with no extra margins set.</P>
<P CLASS="a">Paragraph with a 0.5in left margin.</P>
```

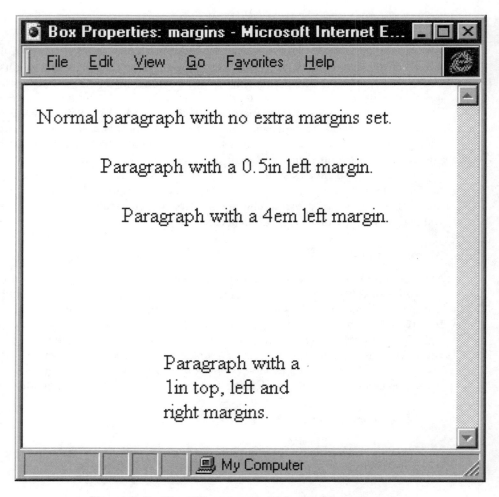

Figure 6–9   Four different paragraph with different margins.

```
<P CLASS="b">Paragraph with a 4em left margin.</P>
<P CLASS="c">Paragraph with a 1in top, left and right mar-
gins.</P>
</BODY>
</HTML>
```

Margins can also be set with a percentage value. The percentage is taken from the size of the parent element's box. In the example below, the parent element is <BODY>, so the heights and widths are relative to the size of the browser window.

```
<HTML>
<STYLE>
   P.a { margin-top: 10% }
   P.b { margin-left: 25% }
   P.c { margin-left: 50%;
         margin-right: 25% }
</STYLE>
<HEAD>
<TITLE>Box Properties: margins</TITLE>
</HEAD>
<BODY>
<P CLASS="a">Paragraph with a 10% top margin.</P>
<P CLASS="b">Paragraph with a 25% left margin.</P>
<P CLASS="c">Paragraph with a 50% left and 25% right margin.</P>
</BODY>
</HTML>
```

The first paragraph has a 10% top margin, which means its margin will be equal to 10% the height of the <BODY> element. The second paragraph's left margin has the paragraph starting 25% across the width of the browser window. The last paragraph has both left and right margins set, confining it to a thin strip. Take a look at Figure 6–10.

Finally, margins can be set to "auto," which tells the browser to figure it out for you.

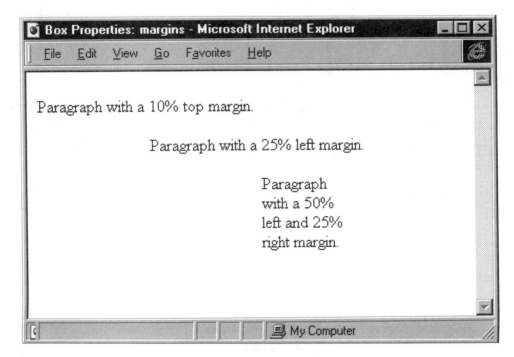

Figure 6–10   Margins set by percentage.

Just in case you were wondering, margins can be set negative. Check out the example below and Figure 6–11. Overlap elements to your heart's content!

```
<HTML>
<STYLE>
    P.a { font-size: 24pt;
          margin-left: -1cm }
    P.b { font-size: 24pt;
          margin-top: -0.5in }
</STYLE>
<HEAD>
<TITLE>Box Properties: margins</TITLE>
</HEAD>
<BODY>
<P CLASS="a">Paragraph with -1cm left margin.</P>
<P CLASS="b">Paragraph with -0.5in top margin.</P>
</BODY>
</HTML>
```

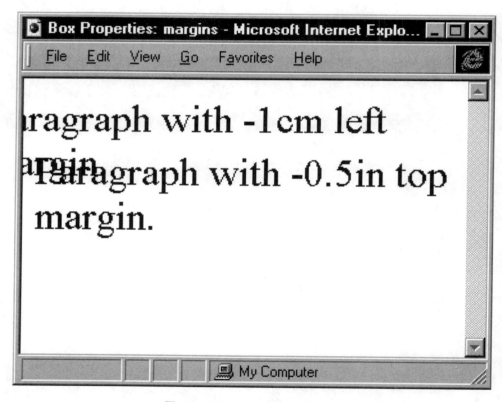

Figure 6–11   Negative margins!

The special "margin" property can be used in a shorthand way that combines all four properties into one. To use it, simply list each margin, separated by a space, in the following order: margin-top, margin-bottom, margin-right, and margin-left. For example, to give your <P> elements a top margin of 3em, a bottom margin of 3em, a right margin of 2em, and a left margin of 4em:

```
P { margin: 3em 3em 2em 4em }
```

You don't have to list all four values here, either. If you give the margin property less then four, it will interpret the values in the following order:

- One value: Will be used for every margin.
- Two values: First value is top and bottom margins, second is right and left margins
- Three values: First value is top margin, second is right and left margins, third is bottom margin

padding Properties

Padding is the space between an element's content and its border. Refer back to Figure 6–7 if you need a quick reminder of how padding relates to the other boxes. Really, the only reason to change an element's padding is when your element has a border. Unfortunately, Internet Explorer 4.0 doesn't support borders on elements other then tables or images, and ironically the padding properties don't work on these at all. But there is support for padding, regardless, and I assume border properties will be supported very soon.

The padding properties use the same syntax as the margin properties, but unlike margins, you can't use negative values. There are five padding properties, each mirroring the margin properties: padding-left, padding-top, padding-bottom, padding-right, and padding. For example, the following style sheet sets the <DIV> element's top padding to 0.25 inches, its left padding to one inch, and its right padding to one centimeter.

```
DIV { padding-top: 0.25in;
      padding-left: 1in;
      padding-right: 1cm }
```

Since borders aren't yet supported, the screen shot in Figure 6–12 uses a "simulated" border. I simply stuck the <DIV> element into a table with a border. It's not exactly right, but shows what I mean.

border Properties

As I mentioned earlier, the border properties aren't supported in Internet Explorer 4.0 yet, but I assume they will be shortly. Since the border properties are listed in the documentation, and they are a fairly important part of style sheets, I decided to cover them anyway.

Figure 6–12   Padding with "simulated" borders.

Keep in mind, however, that these may or may not work by the time you read this, and I have no way to confirm that things will work exactly as I describe them here. With that said, let's take a look at the border properties, and hopefully you'll be able to actually use them real soon now.

There are three varieties of border properties: width-related, color-related, and style-related. The width-related properties deal with, logically enough, the width of your borders. Color-related properties let you define the colors of your borders, and style-related properties determine how your borders will look.

The five width-related properties are: border-top-width, border-right-width, border-bottom-width, border-left-width, and border-width. Each property accepts one of four arguments: thin, medium, thick, or an exact width. The border-width property lets you control the width of all four borders at once. Honestly, I can't think of too many occasions where it makes sense to have borders of varying widths, so you will probably end up using the border-width property most of the time.

```
DIV { border-width: thin }
LI { border-width: 1px }
P.change { border-left-width: medium }
```

This style sheet defines a thin border on the <DIV> element and a one pixel border on the <LI> element. These borders will surround the element on all sides, because when given only one argument, the border-width property sets all the border sides equally. There is also a class, "change," defined on the <P> element, that sets a medium left border. The border will only appear on the left side—the other sides of the element will not have any borders.

After you've set up your border widths, you may want to give them a specific color. The five color-related properties let you set the color on each border side individually, or all at the same time. Following the established naming convention, these properties are: border-top-color, border-right-color, border-bottom-color, border-left-color, and border-color.

```
P { border-width: 4px;
    border-color: black blue }
DIV { border-width: thick thin;
    border-left-color: red }
```

This time, we have a <P> element with a four-pixel border. The top and bottom borders are black, and the left and right borders are blue. Remember, when you give only two values to one of the shortcut properties, like border-color, the first value will affect the top and bottom, and the second value will affect the left and right. Next is a <DIV> element with thick top and bottom borders and thin left and right borders. The left border has been set to the color red.

So you now have your border widths set and their colors just the way you want them. The next step is to set the border style, using the five style-related properties: border-top-style, border-right-style, border-bottom-style, border-left-style, and border-style. Each side of your border can be set individually, or you can set them all at once with the border-style property. If there is rarely a reason to have different border widths, I can't imagine ever needing to set different border styles on the same element, but you can do it if you want.

The style properties accept one of nine values, representing the style of border: none, dotted, dashed, solid, double, groove, ridge, inset, or outset. Ideally, all of these will be supported, but in the browser world, nothing is ever ideal. Don't be too disappointed if all of these aren't supported when borders are finally implemented.

```
DIV.a { border-style: solid double;
        border-color: red;
        border-width: thick }
DIV.b { border-top-style: ridge;
        border-bottom-style: ridge }
```

The <DIV> element's "a" class has a solid (single line) top and bottom border and a double-line left and right border. The "b" class has a ridge top and bottom border, but no borders on the left or right.

The remaining five border properties are all shortcuts: border-top, border-right, border-bottom, border-left, and border. These allow you to set the width, style, and color of your borders all at the same time. They each accept one to three values: the width, the style, and the color.

```
DIV.a { border-top: medium solid blue;
        border-bottom: medium double red }
DIV.b { border-left: thin red }
DIV.c { border: thick double green }
```

Class "a" sets a medium solid blue top border and a medium double red bottom border. There are no left or right borders. Class "b" only has a thin red left border. Finally, class "c" has thick double green borders on all sides. The "border" attribute sets all border sides to the same values.

width and height Properties

The width and height properties attempt to force an element to a specific size. They are analogous to the "WIDTH=" and "HEIGHT=" attributes on the <IMG> element, except they can apply to any element, including text.

The width property accepts either a length value, a percentage, or auto. When applied to an image, it is automatically scaled, proportionally, to the new width. In other words, the image's height will be scaled along with its width to preserve the image's appearance. Elements with text, on the other hand, behave a bit differently. Instead of scaling the font size so the text fits in the allocated space, the text will "break" and continue on the next line, within the width bounds of the box. Take a look at Figure 6–13 to see what I mean.

```
<HTML>
<STYLE>
    SPAN { font-size: 16pt;
           width: 2in;
           background-color: gray;
           color: white
         }
</STYLE>
<HEAD>
<TITLE>Box Properties: width and height</TITLE>
</HEAD>
<BODY>
<P>My span <SPAN>This element's width will be two
inches.</SPAN> with width.</P>

<IMG SRC="bground.gif">
<IMG SRC="bground.gif" STYLE="width: 1in">
<IMG SRC="bground.gif" STYLE="width: 10%">
</BODY>
</HTML>
```

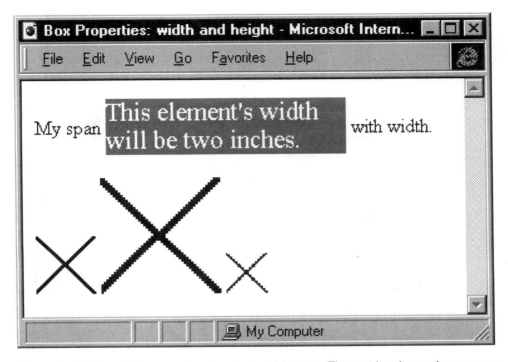

Figure 6–13 The width property set on text and images. The text has been given a gray background so it is easier to see the bounds of its box.

Length values can be in any valid unit. In the example above, the <SPAN> element's width has been set in inches. You can also use a percentage value, as is the case with the last <IMG> element. Percentages are figured based on the parent element's width, in this case the <BODY> element. A width of 100% would stretch completely across the browser window.

The auto setting is reserved for use with the height property. When set, the browser should automatically size the width, based on the height setting, to keep the width in proportion to the new height. What really happens, at least now, is that the element completely vanishes. Since the default behavior is auto, this bug shouldn't present too much of a problem.

The height property is used to force an element's height to a specified value, and it can be used as a companion to width. It accepts the same values as width; however, it behaves a bit differently for text elements. If the text "overflows" its set height, the browser simply stretches the element to fit. It should be the other way around, in my opinion, and the text's font size should scale to fit the element. Using height on text is generally futile. On images, however, it works flawlessly, as can be seen in Figure 6–14.

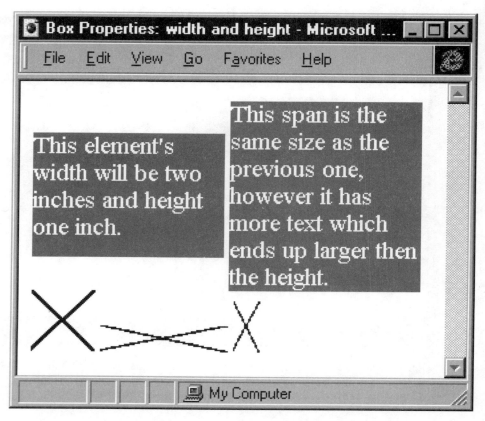

Figure 6–14   The height property works well on images, but for text it leaves a bit to be desired.

```
<HTML>
<STYLE>
    SPAN { font-size: 14pt;
           width: 1.5in;
           height: 1in;
           background-color: gray;
           color: white
         }
</STYLE>
<HEAD>
<TITLE>Box Properties: width and height</TITLE>
</HEAD>
<BODY>
<P><SPAN>This element's width will be two inches and
height one inch.</SPAN> <SPAN>This span is the same
```

```
size as the previous one, however it has more text
which ends up larger then the height.</SPAN></P>

<IMG SRC="bground.gif">
<IMG SRC="bground.gif" STYLE="width: 1in; height: 20px">
<IMG SRC="bground.gif" STYLE="width: 20px; height: 20%">

</BODY>
</HTML>
```

As you can see, height also accepts length values or percentages, as well as auto. Auto doesn't work on height either, but if it did, it would adjust itself with the element's width to keep the element in proportion. Oh, and before you're tempted to try, width and height do not accept negative values.

float and clear Properties

I remember how excited I was when browsers gave you the ability to "float" an image to the left or right of the document. Watching my text flow around floating images was pure joy, compared to the old ways, when you could only have one line of text next to your images. Style sheets give you the ability to float images, just like the "ALIGN=" attribute does, but takes it to the next level: floating text. Now, instead of just images floating, you can set aside chunks of text to float, like an <H1> element, and have the rest of your text flow around it.

The float property accepts one of three values: none, left, or right. If given a value of "none," no floating will occur. This is the default. But give a value of "left," and the element will "float" to the left of the document, and everything else will "float" around it, to the right. A value of "right," does the same thing, but in reverse. See Figure 6–15 for an example of floating images and text.

```
<HTML>
<STYLE>
    DIV { font: 16pt arial;
          float: left;
          width: 1.5in;
          margin: 5px }
    IMG { float: right }
</STYLE>
<HEAD>
<TITLE>Box Properties: float and clear</TITLE>
</HEAD>
<BODY>

<P><IMG SRC="bground.gif">It's easy to float images to either
the left, or in this case, the right side of your document.
```

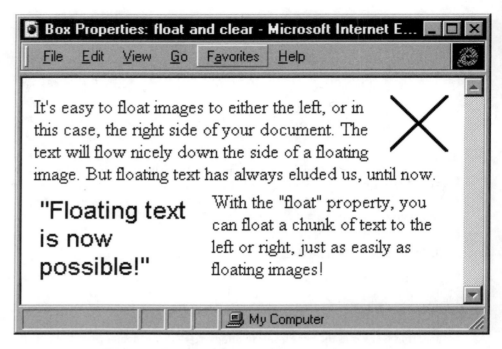

Figure 6–15   Now you can float text as well as images.

```
The text will flow nicely down the side of a floating image.
But floating text has always eluded us, until now.
<DIV>"Floating text is now possible!"</DIV> With the "float"
property, you can float a chunk of text to the left or right,
just as easily as floating images!</P>

</BODY>
</HTML>
```

The <DIV> element will contain the floating text. I increased the float size, so our floating text stands out, and set the element's margin at 5px, to give it a little breathing room. In order to prevent the text from turning into one long line, its width was set for 1.5in.

When working with floating images in "regular" HTML, you have to access the "CLEAR=" attribute of the <BR> property to stop floating. The equivalent style sheet property is "clear." By setting the clear property, you can stop unwanted text from floating.

The clear property accepts one of four arguments: none, left, right, or both. When set to "none," floating is not disturbed. Setting it to "left" stops elements floating to the left, and setting it to "right" stops elements floating to the right. To stop floating on either side, use "both." For an example, take a look at Figure 6–16.

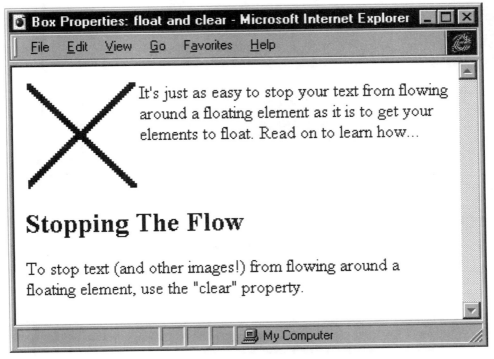

Figure 6–16 Use the "clear" property to stop text from floating.

```
<HTML>
<STYLE>
    IMG { float: left;
          width: 1in }
</STYLE>
<HEAD>
<TITLE>Box Properties: float and clear</TITLE>
</HEAD>
<BODY>

<P><IMG SRC="bground.gif">It's just as easy to stop your text
from flowing around a floating element as it is to get your
elements to float. Read on to learn how...</P>

<H2 STYLE="clear: both">Stopping the Flow</H2>

<P>To stop text (and other images!) from flowing around a
floating element, use the "clear" property.</P>

</BODY>
</HTML>
```

Check out the <H2> element. If the clear property wasn't set, the text "Stopping the Flow" would appear next to the image. Since we set clear to "both," the <H2> element ends up underneath the image, instead.

CLASSIFICATION AND OTHER PROPERTIES

The "classification" properties control how the browser classifies elements. For example, is a <P> element inline or block? Normally, <P> is a block element, but the classification properties allow us to change it to inline, or even a "list" item. The classification properties also handle the various aspects of list items, including how bullets appear and how items are formatted. This section will cover the classification properties, as well as an "other" property that doesn't fit anywhere else. Take note, however, that most of these properties aren't implemented yet, so your mileage may vary. I'll let you know what is and isn't implemented as we get to them.

display: Property

The display property tells the browser in what context it should treat an element. For example, the <DIV> element is normally a "block" element, so it inserts its own line breaks and acts as a container for other elements. The <SPAN> element, on the other hand, is an "inline" element and doesn't insert line breaks or disrupt the flow of your text. With the display property, we can tell a <DIV> element to behave as if it were inline, or a <SPAN> element to act like it is a block element. In reality, the display property isn't fully implemented. What it currently *does* do, however, more then makes up for this.

The display property accepts one of four values: block, inline, list-item, or none. If it were fully implemented, you would be able to cause a <P> element to behave inline, or an <I> element to act like a block and insert its own line breaks. You would even be able to cause <DIV> elements to act like list items. But right now, none of this is possible. What you can do—and this is the exciting part—is tell an element that it is "none" and *shouldn't display at all*. The element still exists, it just isn't displayed and doesn't take up any room in your document. No big deal? Normally, it wouldn't be. But we have a powerful tool on our side: dynamic styles! Remember that "collapsing outline" example I said we would rewrite back in Chapter 2? Let's rewrite it right now, using the display property and "none."

Remember all the trouble we went through to create the collapsing outline? We had to worry about keeping track of which section was currently being displayed and completely reconstruct each section using various dynamic content properties and methods whenever it needed to be displayed. It was a rather messy document and would become complete chaos if it were any larger. But now we have style sheets, and with the "display" property, we can temporarily hide each section until it is needed. Then, when it is time to display it, simply change the display property and you're all set. We only need one simple function. The complete listing is below, and a screen shot of our new outline can be found in Figure 6–17.

```
<HTML>
<HEAD>
<SCRIPT LANGUAGE="JavaScript">
function toggle_Section(section)
{
    if (section.style.display == "none")
    {
        section.style.display = "block";
    }
    else
    {
        section.style.display = "none";
    }
}
</SCRIPT>
<TITLE>The NEW Collapsing Outline</TITLE>
</HEAD>
<BODY>

<UL>
<LI onClick="toggle_Section(document.all.Section_1)">Introduc-
  tion</LI>
    <UL ID="Section_1" STYLE="display: none">
    <LI>Who I am</LI>
    <LI>What I do</LI>
    <LI>Where I live</LI>
    </UL>
<LI onClick="toggle_Section(document.all.Section_2)">My Life</LI>
    <UL ID="Section_2" STYLE="display: none">
    <LI>I was born</LI>
    <LI>I got married</LI>
    <LI>I paid taxes</LI>
    <LI>I wrote a book</LI>
    <LI>More tax joy</LI>
    </UL>
<LI onClick="toggle_Section(document.all.Section_3)">Conclusion
  </LI>
    <UL ID="Section_3" STYLE="display: none">
    <LI>Not done here yet!</LI>
    </UL>
</UL>

</BODY>
</HTML>
```

It's not pretty, but it serves its purpose. The key is that each section that should not be initially displayed has its display property set to "none." The elements are still there,

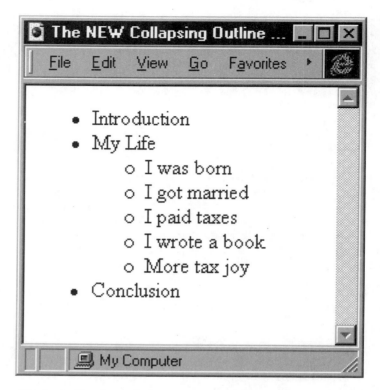

Figure 6–17   Our collapsing outline using the display property.

but the browser ignores them. When the user clicks on one of the section headings, the toggle_Section() function is called, and given the section that needs to be toggled. The toggle_Section() function is very simple. First, it checks to see if the element's display property is set to "none." If it is, the display property is changed to "block," and the section is instantly displayed! The browser sees that the section is no longer "none" and rearranges the document to squeeze the element in. If, on the other hand, the display property is set to something other than "none," our function sets the display property to "none" and the browser instantly "undisplays" the element, shuffling the document around again.

Adding new sections is a snap, and you can even nest sections inside other sections easily. All we need to do now is "pretty it up," and we will have a really nice collapsing outline. We'll clean things up a bit in a moment. First, I want to finish covering the classification properties. There is one more property that will be useful to us in our outline, but we'll get to that.

white-space: Property

The white-space property lets you change how an element handles white space. Normally, when you have several spaces together or a few new lines, the browser collapses them all into a single space. The only way to get around this was to use non-breaking spaces with " " or stick everything into a <PRE> element. With the white-space property, you can tell other elements to display your white space just as it appears in the document.

The white-space property accepts one of three values: normal, pre, or nowrap. When set to "normal," white space is collapsed like normal. But when set to "pre," the element doesn't collapse your white space and displays it just as it appears in your HTML source. In other words, you can set white-space to "pre" on the <P> element and your text will be displayed as if it were in a <PRE> element instead. Unlike the <PRE> element, however, your text *will* wrap to the next line when it reaches the edge of the browser window. If you don't want the text to wrap, you can specify "nowrap" instead of "pre." Now your text will keep going, even off the edge of the browser window. The user will have to scroll sideways to see the rest of your text.

That is the way it is supposed to work. In reality, the white-space property isn't supported in Internet Explorer 4.0 yet. Maybe it will someday, which is why I mention it here, but for now it isn't supported and since it is listed in the "official" documentation as unsupported, I am under the impression it won't be for a while.

The list-style Properties

The final set of classification properties are the four list-styles: list-style-type, list-style-image, list-style-position, and list-style. As you can imagine, these properties allow you to change how list items are rendered.

The list-style-type property changes the bullets or numbering of your list items. It accepts one of the following nine values: disc, circle, square, decimal, lower-roman, upper-roman, lower-alpha, upper-alpha, or none. It's pretty straightforward. The inline style below will use a square bullet for the list-item.

```
<LI STYLE="list-style-type: square">I have a square bullet!
</LI>
```

An example of each bullet type can be found in Figure 6–18, which was generated by the following source. Of particular note is the last list item, which makes use of the list-style-image property.

```
<HTML>
<HEAD>
<TITLE>list-style-type</TITLE>
</HEAD>
<BODY>
<UL>
<LI STYLE="list-style-type: disc">Disc</LI>
```

```
<LI STYLE="list-style-type: circle">Circle</LI>
<LI STYLE="list-style-type: square">Square</LI>
<LI STYLE="list-style-type: decimal">Decimal</LI>
<LI STYLE="list-style-type: lower-roman">Lower-Roman</LI>
<LI STYLE="list-style-type: upper-roman">Upper-Roman</LI>
<LI STYLE="list-style-type: lower-alpha">Lower-Alpha</LI>
<LI STYLE="list-style-type: upper-alpha">Upper-Alpha</LI>
<LI STYLE="list-style-type: none">None</LI>
<LI STYLE="list-style-image: url(bullet.gif)">Image!</LI>
</UL>
</BODY>
</HTML>
```

If the preset bullet choices aren't to your liking, the list-style-image property allows you to use your own. To use your own bullet, give this property a URL to the image and you're all set!

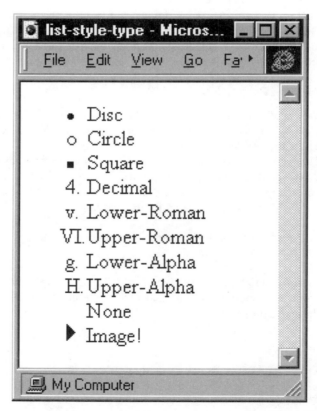

Figure 6–18 The list-style properties at work. Notice how the last example is a custom image. We're not limited to two or three preset bullet graphics anymore!

```
<LI STYLE="list-style-image: url(bullet.gif)">My bullet!</LI>
```

You can't set the width or height of your image, so make sure it is the size you want. Bullets that are too large for the size of your fonts look quite goofy. Also, if your image fails to load properly, the browser will pick a built-in bullet for you. In general, this will be whatever the default bullet would have been if you didn't try to set the image. If you want to get rid of your new bullet, the list-style-image property also accepts the value "none."

The benefit of using this property—instead of mocking up a bullet with the good old "fake list with <IMG> elements" trick—is that when the list item wraps, it will wrap to the "inside" of the bullet, not the "outside." For example, if I inserted the image by hand with a <P> or <DIV> element, it would look like the first "fake" list item in Figure 6–19. With the list-style-image property, however, it looks like the nicer second "real" list item. I artificially changed the <DIV> element's left margin to .25in so that it lines up with the real list.

```
<HTML>
<HEAD>
<TITLE>list-style</TITLE>
</HEAD>
<BODY>

<DIV STYLE="margin-left: .25in"><IMG SRC="bullet.gif"> I am a
"fake" list item with the bullet inserted with an &lt;IMG&gt;
element. See how this line wraps to the "outside" of the
bullet?</DIV>

<UL>
<LI STYLE="list-style-image: url(bullet.gif)">I am using the
list-style-image property to insert my custom bullet. Notice
how this line wraps to the "inside" of the bullet
instead?</LI>
</UL>

</BODY>
</HTML>
```

Of course, you very well could *like* the outside effect instead of the inside effect. If that is the case, the list-style-position property can help. It accepts one of two values: inside or outside. If set for "inside," wrapped lines line up inside the bullet, as it does in the second item in Figure 6–19. If set for "outside," wrapped lines line up outside the bullet, as it does in the first item. Unfortunately, the list-style-position property isn't supported yet, but when it is, you will have the option to change how wrapped text lines up with its bullets.

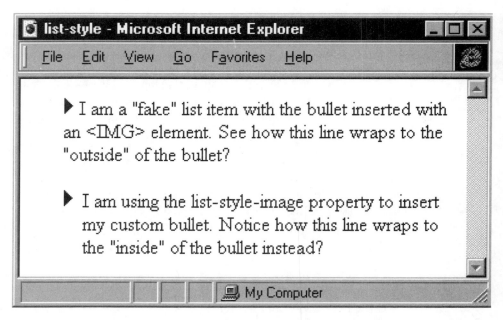

Figure 6–19   A "fake" and a "real" list item and the perils of using custom images as bullets with the list-style-position property.

You can set all three of these properties at once with the list-style shortcut. Just give this property the list-style-type, list-style-position, and the list-style-image and you're set. The real beauty of the list-style property is that if an image fails to load properly, you can specify your preferred bullet type. For example, the following line will use a custom image for the list item bullet, but if the image fails to load, it will use the built-in square bullet instead.

```
<LI STYLE="list-style: square url(bullet.gif)">My list item
</LI>
```

Well, that's it for the classification properties. The last property I would like to cover, before moving onto "positioning," is the one "other" property: cursor.

cursor: Property

Going back to our collapsing outline example again, the problem is that it is difficult for the user to know where she should click to get something to happen. The fact that the headings don't have any special style doesn't help much, but even worse is that the cursor doesn't change to that cute pointing hand like it does as it moves over a link. The solution is to use the "cursor" property.

The cursor property allows you to change the appearance of the mouse pointer as it moves over an element. When the user's cursor moves over a link, it changes to a pointing hand, but when it moves over another element that can handle the onclick event, there are usually no visual clues to alert the user to the fact that the element is clickable. But if we change the mouse pointer with the cursor property, the user will have the visual clue she needs.

There are no less then sixteen possible values for the cursor property. They are listed in Table 6–1 below, along with descriptions of what each does. Be sure that whichever cursor style you choose, it is appropriate for the action that is about to occur. For example, don't use the "move" style when you really want the user to click something. Use the "hand" style instead.

Keep in mind that this is all rather platform dependent. Also, users can and sometimes do change their pointer graphics. You can't assume that the "wait" pointer is an hourglass, but you can at least assume that the user will recognize whatever is displayed as the "wait" pointer. In other words, don't tell your users to expect their pointer to have any particular appearance.

Anyway, let's see what is involved in making the clickable headings in our collapsing list actually appear clickable. It's really very simple:

```
<LI onClick="alert('Clicked!') STYLE="cursor: hand">Click me!</LI>
```

In the line above, when the user moves her pointer over the "Click me!" text, her cursor will change to the familiar "pointing hand" cursor, indicating that something can be clicked. Go ahead and play around with the different cursor types. Your users will appreciate the extra visual clues this useful property can provide.

Table 6–1   The Types of Cursors and Their Descriptions

Value	Description
auto	Let the browser decide the cursor style for you.
crosshair	A cross hair. On Windows 95 it is essentially a thin plus-sign.
default	The default cursor. Usually an arrow, but it depends on the platform.
hand	A pointing hand, usually associated with clicking a link.
move	Something can be moved. On Windows 95, it is like a cross hair but with arrows at each corner.
e-resize	Resize east. Usually an arrow pointing to the right.
ne-resize	Resize north-east. Usually an arrow pointing up and to the right.
nw-resize	Resize north-west. Usually an arrow pointing up and to the left.
n-resize	Resize north. Usually an arrow pointing up.
se-resize	Resize south-east. Usually an arrow pointing down and to the right.
sw-resize	Resize south-west. Usually an arrow pointing down and to the left.
s-resize	Resize south. Usually an arrow pointing down.
w-resize	Resize west. Usually an arrow pointing to the left.
text	That hideous "text underneath" cursor you're probably trying to get rid of.
wait	A "busy" cursor. Usually an hourglass (Win95) or watch (Mac).
help	Help is available here, usually a question mark with an arrow.

CONCLUSION

Let's review what was in this chapter before moving on. First, we discussed classes, IDs, link effects, and other pseudo-classes. We then jumped to contextual selectors, which allow you to specify the context where a style rule should apply. For example, turn red only when inside a blockquote, otherwise turn green. Next, we took a brief look at comments in style sheets, which allow you to make notes to yourself or other webmasters that aren't displayed to your users. After that brief diversion, it was on to a discussion of the "cascading" part of "cascading style sheets." To tie everything together, we then looked at how to use dynamic styles to change style sheets on the fly. Exciting stuff!

Finally, we reviewed a bunch of new properties, starting with box/layout properties and finishing with the classification and "other" properties. You now have enough style sheet knowledge to create some pretty neat effects, but if you think that this is the end of style sheets, get ready to discover positioning and filters!

CHAPTER 7

Positioning and Filters with Style Sheets

Style sheets are incredibly powerful, but in the original specification there were no provisions for precise placement of your elements. For example, you could shuffle elements around and get things roughly where you wanted with some creative tweaking to margins, padding, and the other box properties, but there was no way to say "put this element exactly at this point." It was frustrating to have so much power, yet not quite enough to do exactly what you wanted. The "positioning" extensions to style sheets were created to fill in this obvious gap in style sheets.

Positioning is a new extension to style sheets developed jointly by Microsoft, Netscape, and Hewlett-Packard. I actually get a bit nervous whenever Microsoft and Netscape decide to cooperate on any project. Hopeful, but nervous. In this case, however, things may have turned out for the best. Positioning gives your style sheets the power to place elements *exactly* where you want, with a minimum of fuss and hassle. When it works, that is. Where the original style sheet specification is a relatively mature standard, positioning is brand new and not 100% fleshed out yet, so things are bound to change at least a little. Be sure to test everything here thoroughly, and don't be frustrated if things don't work *exactly* as they're described here. It's the price you have to pay to play with new technology.

Speaking of new technology, Microsoft decided to add yet another feature to style sheets: filters and transitions. There are currently dozens of these experimental filters, which give you the tools needed to create some stunning visual effects. For example, you can automatically create drop shadows, blurs, chroma effects, lighting effects, swipes, fades, wipes, dissolves, and a plethora of other advanced effects that you would expect to see in a full-featured multimedia presentation package. Very neat stuff, but still in the experimental stage.

This chapter will cover positioning, as it currently stands, and the new filter and transition features.

ABSOLUTE POSITIONING

There are three flavors of positioning: absolute, relative, and static. We'll take a look at each in turn, starting with absolute positioning.

When an element is positioned absolutely, its coordinates are set using the upper-left corner of the nearest positioned parent, or the document's <BODY> element if there are no other positioned elements. For example, if you position a <DIV> element absolutely, its coordinates are specified using the <BODY> element's upper-left corner as its origin, unless it is inside another positioned element. The easiest way to describe this is with an illustration, so take a look at Figure 7–1.

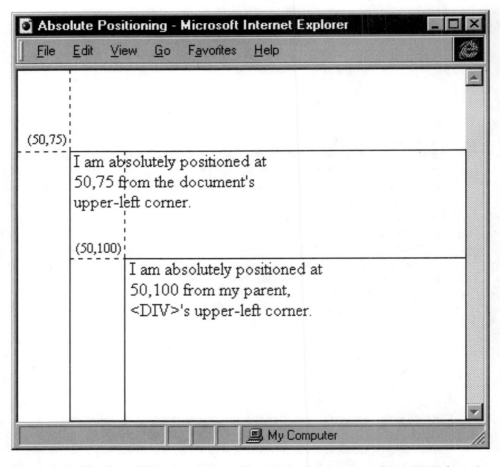

Figure 7–1   The first <DIV> element is positioned absolutely at coordinate 50,75 from the upper-left corner of the <BODY> element. The second <DIV> element is *inside the first*, so its coordinates are 50,100 from the *first <DIV> element*'s upper-left corner. I drew in the lines and coordinates by hand, for clarification.

The first <DIV> element in Figure 7–1 is positioned absolutely at coordinates 50,75 from the <BODY> element's upper-left corner. The second <DIV> element's coordinates are 50,100, but since its parent, the first <DIV> element, is positioned as well, its coordinates are from its parent's upper-left corner, not the <BODY> element. If it was not inside the first <DIV> element, its coordinates would have to be 100,175 from the <BODY> element's upper-left corner to end up in the same location.

This all sounds a bit confusing at first, but once you start playing around with it, you'll realize there is nothing to it. The essence of the situation is, if your positioned element is *not inside another positioned element*, its coordinates will be from the <BODY> element's upper-left corner. If, on the other hand, it *is inside another positioned element*, its coordinates will be from the first positioned element's upper-left corner instead. In a nutshell, the coordinate system "shifts."

Of course, there is nothing to stop you from always positioning based on the <BODY> element's coordinates. Just don't embed positioned elements inside other positioned elements. This brings me to the next feature of absolute positioning. When an element is absolutely positioned, it is *removed from the normal flow of the document*. In other words, an absolutely positioned element will happily overlap any other element or elements, without the elements affecting each other in any way, except, of course, making them slightly less readable. When an element is absolutely positioned, it is as if it were drawn on a transparency and gently laid on top of the document—actually a pretty good analogy, now that I think about it.

Absolutely positioned elements behave independently of the rest of your document, including the browser window's borders. If an absolutely positioned element goes off the edge of the browser window, text and images *will not wrap*. If the user wants to see the missing parts, he will have to manually scroll the window. I liked the transparency analogy so much, I think I'll use it again. When an element is positioned absolutely, the browser first "draws" it on a transparency the size of the original browser window. If the element reaches the edge of this transparency, it *will* actually wrap, but when the browser is finally done laying out the positioned element, its transparency is then *shifted* into the new position. If the edges of the element slide outside of the browser window, tough.

The position, top, and left Properties

To position your elements, you need the following three properties: position, top, and left. The "position" property tells the browser that this element will require positioning and should not be considered when laying out the rest of the document. The "top" and "left" properties give the actual coordinates of the positioned element. Take a look at the listing below and the resulting screen shot in Figure 7–2.

```
<HTML>
<HEAD>
<TITLE>Absolute Positioning</TITLE>
</HEAD>
<BODY>
```

```
<DIV STYLE="position: absolute; top: 75; left: 50; width:
2in">I am absolutely positioned at 50,75 from the document's
upper-left corner.

<DIV STYLE="position: absolute; top: 75; left: 50; width:
2in">I am absolutely positioned at 50,75 from my parent,
&lt;DIV&gt;'s upper-left
corner.
</DIV>

</DIV>

<P>This element is not positioned in any way, so the browser
draws it normally, as if the positioned elements never ex-
isted. This is a key point, and is why I think the trans-
parency analogy is so effective.</P>

</BODY>
</HTML>
```

This example is similar to the HTML used to generate Figure 7–1, with a few modifications. The document begins by positioning a <DIV> element at 50,75. Next, another
<DIV> element is positioned, this time inside the first <DIV> element. It is also at 50,75
but this time, its coordinates are from the first <DIV> element's upper-left corner, instead
of the document's <BODY> element. Both <DIV> elements have been given a width of
two inches, so they wrap nicely. This is one way to get around the "off the edge of the
browser" problem. Finally, there is a non-positioned <P> element, which is completely
oblivious to the existence of the two <DIV> elements! This is a key point in absolute positioning. In general, positioned and non-positioned elements are completely unaware of
each other's existence.

The first step to positioning an element is setting its position property. Since we're
currently working with absolute positioning, the position element should be set to "absolute." After that, it is simply a matter of giving the "top" property a Y-coordinate and
the "left" property a X-coordinate.

Coordinates can be given in any unit; however, pixels are the default and are generally
recommended. We're completely overriding the browser's instincts here, so we may as well
get as much precision as possible. Of course, you can use inches, centimeters, or even points
and ems without any ill effects. I just find it is a little tougher to predict exactly where my element will end up if I use anything other than pixels. Your mileage may vary.

You can also use a percentage value. For example, positioning an element at
50%,50% will put the element's upper-left corner exactly in the middle of the browser
window. If the user resizes the browser, the element will adjust its position on the fly to
keep it at the proper percentage. It's a weird, but very neat, effect. Be careful with this
one, though, because I can guarantee your element won't end up where you want it unless

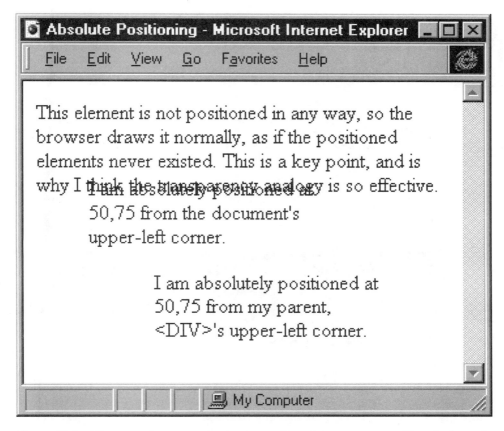

Figure 7–2 Element's that are completely positioned ignore non-positioned elements, and vice versa. The <P> element has no idea that anything is on the page except itself!

you're particularly careful. The "top" and "left" properties also accept the value "auto," which is interpreted by the browser as coordinate zero.

A few examples appear below, along with a screenshot in Figure 7–3. I increased the font size a little bit to make things easier to see.

```
<HTML>
<STYLE>
    DIV { font-size: 16pt }
</STYLE>
<HEAD>
<TITLE>Absolute Positioning</TITLE>
</HEAD>
<BODY>
```

```
<DIV STYLE="position: absolute; top: 50; left: 100">At
100,50</DIV>
<DIV STYLE="position: absolute; top: 5em; left: 2em">At
10em,5em</DIV>
<DIV STYLE="position: absolute; top: 1in; left: 1in">At
1in,1in</DIV>
<DIV STYLE="position: absolute; top: 50%; left: 50%">At
50%,50%</DIV>
<DIV STYLE="position: absolute; top: -10; left: -10; width:
2in"> I am at -10,-10 which means I am off the top edge of the
screen!</DIV>

</BODY>
</HTML>
```

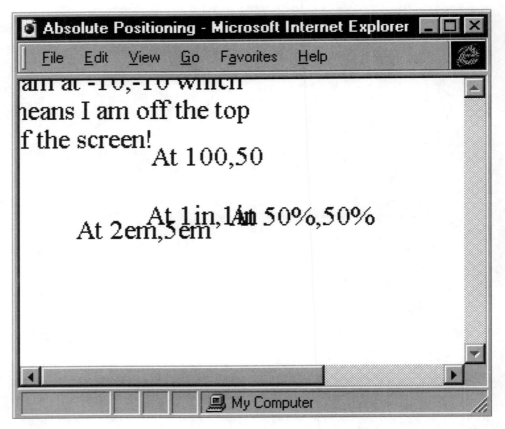

Figure 7–3 The "top" and "left" properties can be any unit, or even a percentage, but pixels are the default.

By the way, negative values are perfectly acceptable coordinates, as you can see in Figure 7–3. Just keep in mind that anything off the top or left edge of the browser window is gone forever! The user can't scroll to see them!

RELATIVE POSITIONING

Relative positioning works quite a bit differently from absolute positioning. Instead of specifying coordinates relative to upper-left corners, your coordinates are relative to where the element *would have been if it was not positioned.* And unlike absolute positioning, the positioned element and document are very aware of each other, and the element will reposition itself as the document changes. For example, if the browser is resized, the positioned element will reposition itself so it is still relative to the point where it should have been. Once again, this is easiest to understand with an illustration, so take a look at Figure 7–4.

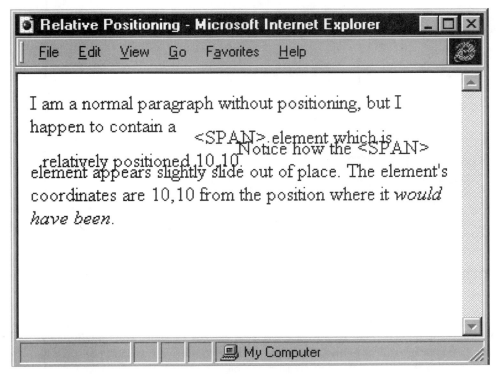

Figure 7–4   Relative positioning in action. The <SPAN> element is relatively positioned 10 pixels down and 10 pixels to the right from the position it would have been if it had not been positioned.

The best way to think about relative positioning is to picture the browser drawing the document *without* thinking about relative positioning. When the layout is complete, the browser takes a razor blade, cuts out the positioned elements, and then slides them to their new coordinates relative to where they were previously. The HTML used to create Figure 7–4 is below.

```
<HTML>
<HEAD>
<TITLE>Relative Positioning</TITLE>
</HEAD>
<BODY>

<P>I am a normal paragraph without positioning, but I happen
to contain a <SPAN STYLE="position: relative; top: 10px; left:
10px"> &lt;SPAN&gt; element which is relatively positioned
10,10.</SPAN> Notice how the &lt;SPAN&gt; element appears to
slide slightly out of place. The element's coordinates are
10,10 from the position where it <I>would have been</I>.</P>

</BODY>
</HTML>
```

To specify relative positioning, set the position property to "relative." Negative values for the top and left properties are valid, and in some cases the only way to get the desired effect.

STATIC POSITIONING

Static positioning is just a fancy way of telling the browser to position as normal. When the position property is set to "static," the top and left properties have no effect on the position of the element. Instead, the browser positions the element as it normally would.

CLIPPING AND OVERFLOWS

As you have seen, one of the problems with positioning is the possibility of your positioned element's contents overflowing into an area where you don't want it to go. In particular, there is always the danger of part of your element slipping off the edge of the browser window. To remedy this situation, you can use the "width" and "height" properties to define an area for the element to occupy. The problem is, what happens when the element is too big to fit into the area you just defined? Thankfully, with the "clip" and "overflow" properties, we can tell the browser exactly how to handle this situation.

clip: Property

Normally, when you set a positioned element's width and height, the browser does its best to fit the element's content into the defined area. Unfortunately, if the content is text and proves too large to fit into the given area, the browser's only choice is to let the content overflow past the boundaries you've set. The "clip" property gives you the ability to tell the browser to simply discard the extraneous information, instead of letting it overflow. In Figure 7–5, two <DIV> elements have been positioned next to each other and given a width and height of 2in. The first <DIV> element doesn't have clipping enabled, so its content overflows its height. The second <DIV> element *does* have clipping enabled, so its content is neatly truncated.

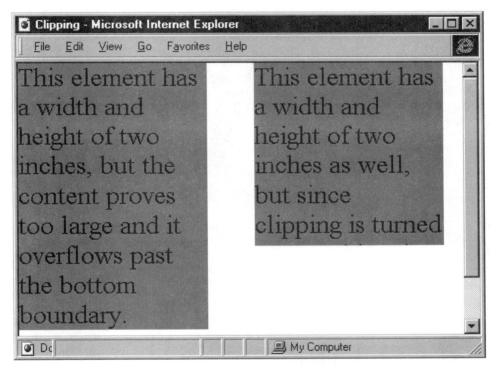

Figure 7–5   The left <DIV> element is not clipping, but the right one is.

The clip property accepts either a "shape" to clip, or the keyword "auto." The only valid shape, at this time, is a rectangle. To define a clipping area, you need to set each corner of the rectangle:

```
clip: rect(10 20 20 10)
```

In this example, a rectangle was defined with its top and left corners at 10px, its bottom and right corners at 20px. The order of the coordinates is: top, right, bottom, and left. A bit odd in my opinion, but that's the way it is. If your attempt at setting a clipping area results in the element missing completely, you may have accidentally switched the order of the rectangle's coordinates. Be careful!

The coordinates for each corner of your rectangle can be in any unit, with the default being pixels, starting relative to the upper-left corner of the element. Negative values are permitted. You can also specify the keyword "auto" for any of the corners, which tells the browser to enable the default clipping size for that corner: none.

The following listing was used to generate Figure 7–5.

```
<HTML>
<STYLE>
    DIV.a { position: absolute; top: 0; left: 0;
            width: 2in; height: 2in;
            background-color: gray;
            font-size: 20pt }
    DIV.b { position: absolute; top: 0; left: 2.5in;
            width: 2in; height: 2in;
            background-color: gray;
            font-size: 20pt;
            clip: rect(0 2in 2in 0) }
</STYLE>
<HEAD>
<TITLE>Clipping</TITLE>
</HEAD>
<BODY>

<DIV CLASS="a">
This element has a width and height of two inches, but the
content proves too large and it overflows past the bottom
boundary.</DIV>
<DIV CLASS="b">
This element has a width and height of two inches as well, but
since clipping is turned on, anything that doesn't fit is
eliminated, or "clipped"
from the element.</DIV>

</BODY>
</HTML>
```

overflow: Property

The "overflow" property is a little more convenient to use than "clip," because you don't have to define a separate rectangle for it. Instead, it takes its size from the element's width and height properties. Even better, overflow gives you three different options for dealing with overflowing text: visible, hidden, and scroll.

- **visible** allows overflowing content to be seen.
- **hidden** behaves like "clip," where overflowing content is hidden from view.
- **scroll** creates scrollbars to allow the user to scroll through overflowing content.

The three overflow values are illustrated in Figure 7–6. Check out the listing below to see how overflow can be applied to your elements.

```
<HTML>
<STYLE>
    DIV.a { position: absolute; top: 0; left: 0;
            width: 1.5in; height: 1.5in;
            background-color: gray;
            font-size: 18pt;
            overflow: visible }
    DIV.b { position: absolute; top: 0; left: 2in;
            width: 1.5in; height: 1.5in;
            background-color: gray;
            font-size: 18pt;
            overflow: scroll }
    DIV.c { position: absolute; top: 0; left: 4in;
            width: 1.5in; height: 1.5in;
            background-color: gray;
            font-size: 18pt;
            overflow: hidden }
</STYLE>
<HEAD>
<TITLE>Overflowing and Scrolling</TITLE>
</HEAD>
<BODY>

<DIV CLASS="a">
This element has overflow set to "visible," which means over-
flowing text will still be allowed to overflow like
normal.</DIV>
<DIV CLASS="b">
This element has overflow set to "scroll," which sets up
scroll bars so the user can view any overflowing text.</DIV>
<DIV CLASS="c">
This element has overflow set to "hidden," so overflowing text
is essentially clipped to the element size.</DIV>

</BODY>
</HTML>
```

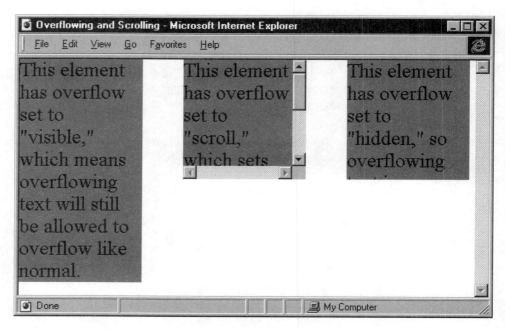

Figure 7–6   The three overflow values. The element on the left is set to "visible," the middle element is set to "scroll," and the right element is set to "hidden." The overflow property can act like a simple "clip" when set to "hidden," but the real power is the scrolling.

CONTROLLING OVERLAPPING: Z-INDEX AND VISIBILITY

Overlapping with positioned elements is almost a certainty, sometimes even a necessity. But when you're overlapping elements, which does the browser draw first? In general, the browser draws the elements in the order they appear in the document. The first element is drawn first, the second drawn second, and so on. The element that ends up on the top of the heap is the last one the browser encountered. Sometimes this is exactly the effect you're looking for, but many times it would be useful to shuffle the elements around. Take the bottom and shuffle it to the top, so to speak. This is called *z-ordering,* and is controlled by the "z-index" property.

z-index: Property

The z-index property accepts only one value, a positive or negative number representing the element's z-ordering. The higher the z-index, the higher its "layering" priority. The highest z-index is always on top, and the lowest z-index is always on the bottom. Everything else falls somewhere in between. Take a look at Figure 7–7.

To see a real example of z-index in action, take a look at the listing below and the screenshot shown in Figure 7–8. Three <DIV> elements have been given gray backgrounds and are set to overlap. Normally, the first element would be on the bottom, the

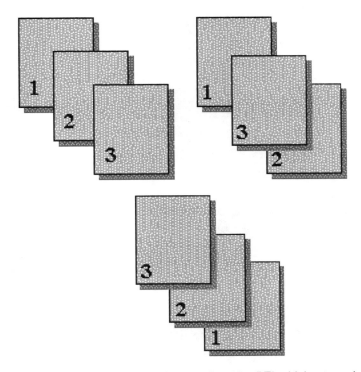

Figure 7–7   How an element's z-index affects its "layering." The highest number is on top, the lowest on the bottom.

second in the middle, and the third on top, but by changing the z-index the order has been changed as well. Now, the middle element is on top, with the others underneath.

```
<HTML>
<STYLE>
   DIV.a { background-color: gray;
           font-size: 18pt;
           width: 1.5in; height: 1.5in;
           position: absolute; top: .25in; left: .25in }
   DIV.b { background-color: silver;
           font-size: 18pt;
           width: 1.5in; height: 1.5in;
           position: absolute; top: .75in; left: .75in }
   DIV.c { background-color: gray;
           font-size: 18pt;
           width: 1.5in; height: 1.5in;
           position: absolute; top: 1.25in; left: 1.25in }
</STYLE>
<HEAD>
```

```
<TITLE>Controlling Overlapping</TITLE>
</HEAD>
<BODY>

<DIV CLASS="a" STYLE="z-index: 1">This is the first ele-
ment.</DIV>
<DIV CLASS="b" STYLE="z-index: 3">This is the second ele-
ment.</DIV>
<DIV CLASS="c" STYLE="z-index: 2">This is the third ele-
ment.</DIV>

</BODY>
</HTML>
```

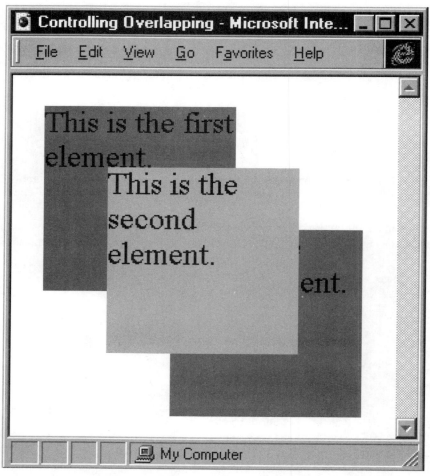

Figure 7–8   The middle <DIV> element would normally be under the third, but making its z-index higher than the others puts the middle one on top instead.

If two elements have the same z-index, the browser draws them in the order they are encountered in the HTML. The last element encountered will be on top, with the others underneath.

visibility: Property

The final positioning property actually affects the element's visibility, not its position. If you want an element to become completely invisible, set its "visibility" property to "hidden." The element will disappear, but unlike the "display" property, the space it previously occupied remains. Notice in Figure 7–9 the invisible image with the text happily flowing around it.

The visibility property accepts three values: visible, hidden, and inherit. A "visible" property can be seen, a "hidden" one can't. It's that simple. Normally, the child element's visibility is set to "inherit," so whatever state the parent element is in, so is the child. If the parent is invisible, the child vanishes as well. If the parent is visible, so is the child. If you want the child element to remain visible, even if its parent isn't, set its visibility property to "visible."

Figure 7–9 demonstrates the visibility property. At the top of the document is an image floating to the left, with text wrapping around it. The image is set "hidden," however, so the user can't see it. At the bottom of the document is an invisible paragraph, but

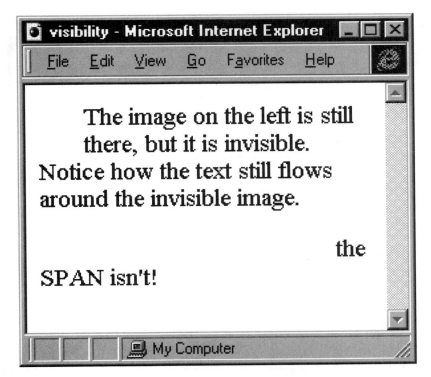

Figure 7–9 An invisible image and an invisible paragraph with its child set to "visible."

its child element is set "visible." You can see the child, but can't see the parent. The listing is below.

```
<HTML>
<STYLE>
   P { font-size: 14pt }
</STYLE>
<HEAD>
<TITLE>visibility</TITLE>
</HEAD>
<BODY>

<P><IMG SRC="picture.gif" STYLE="visibility: hidden; float:
left"> The image on the left is still there, but it is invisi-
ble. Notice how the text still flows around the invisible
image.</P>

<P STYLE="visibility: hidden">This paragraph is hidden, but
<SPAN STYLE="visibility: visible">the SPAN isn't!</SPAN> Weird
effect, huh?</P>

</BODY>
</HTML>
```

As you can see, the visibility property isn't just for positioned elements. Technically, any element can have its visibility set. Alone, this capability may not be very useful, but when compiled with dynamic styles, visibility can allow you to create a number of really neat effects. Positioned elements can be flipped through like a pack of cards when controlled by your script!

DYNAMIC STYLE CONSIDERATIONS

All of the style sheet properties, including the positioning properties, are available to your scripts through the document object model, so you can easily change your element positions on the fly. But there are a few quirks that are worth mentioning here. The most important quirk is that *you can only modify an element's position if it has been previously positioned.* In other words, you can't take a non-positioned element and turn it into a positioned element. It just doesn't work—the "position" property is read-only, and any attempts at changing it to "absolute" or "relative" will result in failure. With that in mind, here is how you can access your previously positioned elements.

Positions and Pixels

The "top," "left," "height," and "width" properties are all available, via the element's "style" property; however, they have been renamed slightly. The "top" property is now called "posTop," the "left" property is now called "posLeft," the "height" property is now called "posHeight," and the "width" property is now called "posWidth." Through these four properties, you can access the position and size of your elements in their original units. For example, if the "top" element was originally specified in "inches," the "posTop" property will contain the value in inches. Here comes another quirk: This is a floating point value and the unit names are not included. Any attempts to change the unit type once it has been set in your style sheet will fail utterly. In other words, if you originally defined the position in inches, you're stuck with inches.

```
document.all.MyElement.style.posTop = "1in"; // I will FAIL..
document.all.MyElement.style.posTop = 1.0;   // This is   correct..
```

The first line of code, above, is incorrect. Attempting to specify "in," or any other unit, will be interpreted as ZERO. The second line is correct. The "posTop" and related properties only accept floating point values, not strings.

This can be inconvenient, to say the least. If you want to position your element in inches, but use pixels to move it around, you're out of luck. But wait! Apparently, the designers realized this limitation and implemented a small concession: They gave us another set of properties specifically for pixels! The "pixelHeight," "pixelWidth," "pixelTop," and "pixelLeft" properties are analogous to the "pos*" properties, but always use pixels, regardless of the original units. Changing "posTop" will make the corresponding change, in pixels, to "pixelTop," and vice versa.

```
document.all.myElement.style.posTop += 1.0;  // Add 1.0 to units
document.all.myElement.style.pixelTop += 96; // Add 96 to pixels
```

Reading Offsets

Incidentally, the "offsets" of all your elements, positioned or non-positioned alike, can also be read directly from the element object using one of the following four properties: "offsetHeight," "offsetLeft," "offsetTop," and "offsetWidth." For all intents and purposes, these properties are the same as the "pixel*" properties, except they are read-only and available on the element object directly.

Speaking of offsets, the "offsetParent" property, also available on the element object, is a read-only property that can be used to determine what the parent element is when figuring out coordinates. For example, if an element is positioned inside the <BODY> element, its coordinates are based on the <BODY> element's upper-left corner. If, on the other hand, the element is positioned inside another positioned element, then its coordinates are based on that element's upper-left corner instead. The "offsetParent" returns the element object whose coordinate system is being used.

Putting It All Together

Just for fun, I decided to position an element and then read all of its position and offset properties. The results of my experiment, listed below, can be found in Figure 7–10.

```
<HTML>
<STYLE>
   DIV { position: absolute; top: 1in; left: 1in;
         width: 1.5in; height: 1.5in; }
</STYLE>
<HEAD>
<SCRIPT>
function report_settings()
{
    var myString = "";
    var myDiv = document.all.MyDIV;

    myString = "offsetHeight: " + myDiv.offsetHeight + "\n" +
               "offsetWidth : " + myDiv.offsetWidth + "\n" +
               "offsetParent: " + myDiv.offsetParent.tagName +
                 "\n" +
               "offsetTop   : " + myDiv.offsetTop + "\n" +
               "offsetLeft  : " + myDiv.offsetLeft + "\n\n";
    myString +="posHeight   : " + myDiv.style.posHeight + "\n" +
               "pixelHeight : " + myDiv.style.pixelHeight + "\n" +
               "posLeft     : " + myDiv.style.posLeft + "\n" +
               "pixelLeft   : " + myDiv.style.pixelLeft + "\n" +
               "posTop      : " + myDiv.style.posTop + "\n" +
               "pixelTop    : " + myDiv.style.pixelTop + "\n" +
               "posWidth    : " + myDiv.style.posWidth + "\n" +
               "pixelWidth  : " + myDiv.style.pixelWidth;

    alert(myString);
}
</SCRIPT>
<TITLE>Dynamic Style</TITLE>
</HEAD>
<BODY onLoad="report_settings()">

<DIV ID="MyDIV">
This is a sample of accessing positioning elements with dynamic
styles.
</DIV>

    </BODY>
    </HTML>
```

VISUAL FILTERS AND TRANSITIONS

Filters is a neat new style sheet feature that enables high-quality multimedia effects until now only seen in professional presentation software. A full suite of visual effects, transi-

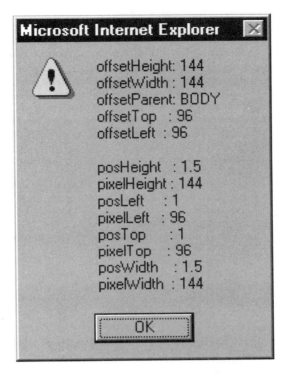

Figure 7–10 Positions and offsets.

tions, fades, blends, and wipes are available with one or two simple commands. Currently only available on Microsoft Internet Explorer 4.0, other modern browsers are sure to follow, or risk not being taken seriously.

Filters come in two varieties. The first group is known as the "visual" or "visual effect" filters, which handle special effects such as blurs, drop shadows, glow, and lighting effects. The other group is called "transition" filters, and handles blends, fades, wipes, splits, and other "slide show" type effects. With the combination of these powerful filters, style sheets, and dynamic content, your web browser finally becomes a true presentation platform!

Visual Filters

There are currently a total of fourteen preset visual filters, ready for instant application in your documents. Applying a filter is as easy as setting a style sheet property, but their effects can be rather dramatic. For example, the "light" filter simulates a fully customizable light source shining on one or more elements. The "glow" filter can be set to make an element glow. Drop shadows can be set with the "DropShadow" filter, and "wave" can be used to add ripples to an element. Better yet, filters can be combined on the same element, creating impressive compound effects. A list of all the visual filters and their descriptions can be found in Table 7–1.

Table 7–1   All Fourteen Preset Visual Filters

Filter Name	Description
Alpha	Sets an element's transparency level. A variety of subeffects are available, including uniform, linear graded, and radial graded transparencies.
Blur	Blurs an element to give it the impression of speed or movement.
Chroma	Sets an arbitrary color transparent.
DropShadow	Gives an element a "floating" effect by drawing a drop shadow.
FlipH	Flips an element horizontally.
FlipV	Flips an element vertically.
Glow	Surround an element with a glowing haze of the specified color and strength.
Gray	Convert the colors in an element to a grayscale.
Invert	"Invert" an element's colors. Picture a photographic negative.
Light	Shine an artifical light source on an element, from any position, intensity, or color.
Mask	Make an element's transparent color an arbitrary color, and make non-transparent colors transparent. Picture a silhouette.
Shadow	Put a shadow along one edge of an element, to give it the appearance of light shining on it from another direction.
Wave	Create wave patterns in your element.
Xray	Only shows the edges of an element, giving it the appearance of being viewed through an x-ray machine.

Not all elements can use filters, but the ones that do can be used as containers for the ones that don't, thus getting by this limitation to a large degree. Examples of elements for which filters are allowed are: BODY, BUTTON, DIV, IMG, INPUT, MARQUEE, SPAN, TABLE, TD, TEXTAREA, TFOOT, TH, THEAD, and TR. For DIV and SPAN to accept filters, they should have a specific width and height assigned, or be absolutely positioned. We'll go over these details a bit more in a moment. But first things first—let's set up a few filters!

filter: Property

Filters are set using the "filter" style sheet property. Let's use the "Blur" filter for our first example. In the code below, the text and image are both "blurred." Check out the screen shot in Figure 7–11, then look at the code. Most of these filters are rather difficult to reproduce in printed form, so if you're feeling ambitious, try out the code yourself. And by all means, experiment!

```
<HTML>
<STYLE>
    DIV { font-size: 32pt;
          width: 2in; height: 1in;
          filter: Blur(Direction=90, Strength=10) }
</STYLE>
<HEAD>
<TITLE>Visual Filters</TITLE>
</HEAD>
<BODY>
```

```
<DIV>I am blurred!</DIV>
<DIV><IMG SRC="image.gif"></DIV>

</BODY>
</HTML>
```

All the blurring work is happening because of the "filter" property in the <DIV> element. Notice how I gave <DIV> a width and height. For the <DIV> element to accept a filter, it must have a width and height defined! The "Blur" filter itself is called by the filter property and has two arguments. The first argument, "Direction," tells the browser which way to perform the blur, in degrees. The "Strength" argument is how many pixels long the blur should be. Most filters accept one or more arguments. If things don't quite work right, make sure your arguments are spelled correctly, are separated from their values with an equals sign, and are separated from each other with a comma. Quite a few times I've scratched my head wondering why a filter wasn't working until I realized I used semicolons instead of commas.

Figure 7–11 The "Blur" filter at work on some text and an image.

By the way, there is a reason I applied the filter directly to the <DIV> instead of the <IMG> element. As it turns out, filter effects end where the element ends, so if I applied the blur directly to the image, the blur "trail" would have terminated right at the edge of the image! But by putting the <IMG> into the <DIV> element, and applying the blur to the <DIV> instead of the image, we get around this little quirk completely. If your filter effect looks a little weird, this may be the reason. You can either insert the element into a slightly larger <DIV> element, or expand the element's margins so the effect has a little more "breathing room."

You can apply as many filters as you want to a single element. Just keep stacking them onto the filter property in the order you want them applied. Let's add some waves! Change the filter line in the previous example to read the following:

```
filter: Blur(Direction=90, Strength=10) Wave(Freq=6, Strength=5) }
```

Now our elements are blurred, and then a wave pattern is applied. Wave, by the way, is a very neat filter when combined with dynamic styles. You can easily change the frequency, strength, and phase in a loop to create some wild effects!

Scripting Your Filters

All of your filters are available via the "filters" collection located on the element object. You can access your filters from this collection in all the standard collection-accessing ways. For example, you can give the collection an index number for the filter—which is actually the easiest way since you rarely have more then one or two filters—or you can use the filter's name.

```
document.all.myElement.filters[0].strength = 25;
document.all.myElement.filters.Blur.strength += 10;
```

The first line is an example of accessing the first filter on the current element and setting its strength argument to 25. The second line uses the filter's name instead, and adds 10 to its strength argument. The next obvious question is how to access the filter's arguments, which, as you can see above, is as simple as specifying the argument's name as a property.

```
<DIV onClick="this.filters[0].strength += 5;">I am blurred!</DIV>
<DIV onClick="this.filters.Blur.strength += 10;"><IMG
SRC="image.gif"></DIV>
```

Adding a couple of onclick event handlers to the two <DIV> elements in the previous example gives us a quick way to test the dynamic nature of filters. Clicking on the first element adds 5 to its strength each time, and clicking on the second adds 10.

All filter objects also have an "enabled" property, which allows you to enable or disable that particular filter effect. Setting the "enabled" property to "false" turns the filter off, and setting it to "true" turns it back on again. In theory, you should be able to turn off individual filters without affecting other filters on the same element, but sometimes they all disable anyway. I imagine this minor bug will be fixed soon enough, but if it isn't, you should keep this problem in mind.

Another way to access filters is via the style sheet "filter" attribute. That's the singular "filter." It's easy to confuse it with the plural "filters" collection, so be careful. This is no-frills access—you get the entire filter string, and changes are made by rewriting the entire line. There are no properties to access, so getting at an individual filter can be a royal pain. But the capability is there if you need it.

```
document.all.myElement.style.filter = "Wave(strength=100)";
```

Accessing the filter property this way can be used to add or remove filters from an element, but there is an easier way. All filters accept the "enabled" *argument*, which can be set directly in the style sheet. For example, the following style has an enabled wave filter and a disabled blur filter. Now it's just a matter of turning filters on and off with the "enabled" *property*.

```
filter: Wave(strength=100, enabled=true) Blur(direction=90,
strength=15, enabled=false)
```

Important Performance Issues

Filters really don't take much processing power, but it *does* add up. If you have dozens of filters on one document, particularly on large or complex elements, the user's computer may start feeling the pressure. Remember, these filters are calculated *on the fly*, and not everyone has a high-end workstation. Don't worry about a half-dozen or so filters—it shouldn't be a problem—but try not to go overboard!

Table 7–2 Visual Filters Reference

Alpha   Sets an element's transparency level. A variety of subeffects are available, including uniform, linear graded, and radial graded transparencies.

Argument	Description
opacity	How transparent? 0 is fully transparent, 100 is fully opaque. The default is 0. When used with "finishopacity" to create a graded effect, this argument doubles as the "start" opacity.
finishopacity	Same "opacity," above, but is used as the ending opacity when creating a graded effect.
style	Shape of gradient: 0 = uniform 1 = linear 2 = radial 3 = rectangular
startX	X coordinate to start gradient.
startY	Y coordinate to start gradient.
finishX	X coordinate to end gradient.
finishY	Y coordinate to start gradient.

Table 7–2   (*Continued*)

Blur   Blurs an element to give it the impression of speed or movement.

Argument	Description
add	Set to "true" if original image should be added back to the blurred image, and "false" if only the blur should be shown.
direction	Which way the blur should travel, in 45-degree increments. If you go above 360 degrees or less then 0 degrees, the direction will "wrap" automatically.
strength	The length of the blur, in pixels.

Chroma   Sets an arbitrary color transparent.

Argument	Description
color	The color to turn transparent. Colors should be specified as an RGB hexadecimal triple. For example, red is #FF0000.

DropShadow   Gives an element a "floating" effect by drawing a drop shadow.

Argument	Description
color	The color of the drop shadow. Colors should be specified as an RGB hexadecimal triple, or a color name. For example, red is #FF0000.
offX	Horizontal offset of the drop shadow, in pixels. Negative values OK.
offY	Vertical offset of the drop shadow, in pixels. Negative values OK.
positive	If "true," a drop shadow is created for any nontransparent pixel. If "false," a drop shadow is created for any transparent pixel. Default is "true."

FlipH   Flips an element horizontally. Yes, text in your element will flip as well.

Argument	Description
No arguments.	

FlipV   Flips an element vertically. Yes, text in your element will flip as well.

Argument	Description
No arguments.	

Glow   Surrounds an element with a glowing haze of the specified color and strength.

Argument	Description
color	The color of the drop shadow. Colors should be specified as an RGB hexadecimal triple or a color name. For example, red is #FF0000.
strength	How bright? Valid values are 1 (weakest) to 255 (strongest). This appears to be in pixels, so a value of 5 or 6 is usually a nice glow. 255 is simply insane.

Gray   Converts the colors in an element to a grayscale.

Argument	Description
No arguments.	

Invert   "Inverts" an element's colors. Picture a photographic negative. Careful, because black text turns white, which is completely unreadable on a white background.

Argument	Description
No arguments.	

Light   Shines an artificial light source on an element, from any position, intensity, or color. See the following section after this table for more information. This is a strange filter and requires a completely separate section to properly describe.

Argument	Description
No arguments.	

Mask   Makes an element's transparent color an arbitrary color and makes non-transparent colors transparent. Picture a silhouette.

Argument	Description
color	The color of the drop shadow. Colors should be specified as an RGB hexadecimal triple or a color name. For example, red is #FF0000.

Shadow   Puts a shadow along one edge of an element to give it the appearance of light shining on it from another direction. This is a great filter for text, and the defaults are just perfect!

Argument	Description
color	The color of the drop shadow. Colors should be specified as an RGB hexadecimal triple or a color name. For example, red is #FF0000.
direction	Which way the shadow should face, in 45-degree increments. If you go above 360 degrees or less then 0 degrees, the direction will "wrap" automatically

Wave   Creates wave patterns in your element. Waves always travel vertically.

Argument	Description
add	If "true," insert the original image on top of the waves. If "false," only display the waves.
freq	Number of waves to use.
light	How light should the waves be? Valid values are 0 (least) to 100 (most)
phase	At what point in the sine wave's phase should the distortion begin, specified as a percentage of the wavelength? If that doesn't make sense, just keep the default value. For a wild effect, have a script cycle through the phase from 0 to 100 and back again . . .
strength	How intense are the waves? This appears to be in pixels.

Xray   Only shows the edges of an element, giving it the appearance of being viewed through an x-ray machine. This makes a mess out of black and white images.

Argument	Description
No arguments.	

The "Light" Filter

With the "light" filter, you can create some really interesting lighting effects on your elements, including ambient lighting, cones of light, and "spots" of light. But this is also the strangest filter, as far as syntax and implementation go, so it gets its own section. This filter is not "the norm," so don't panic thinking that all filters are this tough to get a handle on. As a matter of fact, I would recommend going back to the previous section first, if you haven't done so already, and revisiting the "light" filter later. Get a little experience dealing with the other filters first, then try your hand at "light."

The filter starts out innocently enough. It accepts no arguments, and can be applied via the "filter" property, just like any other filter.

```
filter: Light()
```

Unfortunately, what this gives you is a completely blacked out element. No light. Here's where the fun starts: You have to manually set up each "light source" for your element, inside a script. Yikes! The "light" filter actually creates a "light collection" of sorts, where it keeps track of up to ten separate light sources for your element. Adding and removing light sources requires the use of no less then *seven* methods.

```
<HTML>
<STYLE>
    DIV { font-size: 32pt; background-color: white;
        width: 2in; height: 1in;
        position: absolute; top=0; left=0;
        filter: Light() }
</STYLE>
<HEAD>
<SCRIPT LANGUAGE="JavaScript">
function light_effect()
{
    var myFilter = document.all.myDiv.filters.Light;

    myFilter.addAmbient(255,255,255,25);
}
</SCRIPT>
<TITLE>Visual Filters</TITLE>
</HEAD>
<BODY onLoad="light_effect()">

<DIV ID="myDiv"><IMG SRC="image.gif"> Light this element!</DIV>

</BODY>
</HTML>
```

The listing above will be our "base" document, from which we will do all of our experimentation. It has a single <DIV> element, with the filter set for "Light." I specifically told the background color to be white, because otherwise the lighting effects won't work quite right for the text. Anyway, setting up the light sources will be done in the light_effect() function, which is called after an onload event.

The first experiment is "ambient lighting," using the "addAmbient()" method. All of these methods are called directly on the "Light" filter object. Ambient lighting is a "generic" light source that appears to come from everywhere at once, or from nowhere in particular, depending on your point of view. The addAmbient() method accepts four arguments and will add an ambient light to your element. The four arguments are: red-value, green-value, blue-value, and strength. As you can see, things have already gotten weirder. Instead of giving a color name, we're forced to specify each level of red, green, and blue separately. Valid values for the colors are 0, meaning none of that color, to 255, meaning the most of that color. If you want white light, set all three to 255. The strength value is from 0, meaning no light, to somewhere around 100.

The "addCone()" method adds a "cone" light source. Picture a flashlight held at an angle to your wall, and you're looking at the cone-of-light effect. We only need *ten* arguments to generate this effect: source-x, source-y, source-z, target-x, target-y, red-value, green-value, blue-value, strength, and focus. The source coordinates tell the browser where the light is originating from, and the target coordinates are where the light is being aimed at. The focus is a value from 0 to 90, indicating the angle of divergence of the "beam" of light. The greater the angle, the wider the cone. Figure 7–12 shows two crossing cones of light, added with the two lines of code below.

```
myFilter.addCone(0,0,10,  100,100,  255,255,255,  50,  20);
myFilter.addCone(200,0,10,  0,100,  255,255,255,  50,  10);
```

For the effect of a bare light bulb over your element, you can use the "addPoint()" method. It accepts only five arguments: x, y, z, red-value, green-value, blue-value, strength. Note that the larger the "z" coordinate, the more area the light will cover, but at less of an intensity.

```
myFilter.addPoint(0,0,50,  255,255,255,  100);
myFilter.addPoint(125,50,40,255,255,255,  100);
```

The remaining four methods are for changing some aspect of your existing lighting. For example, the "ChangeColor()" method is used to alter a light's color. This method accepts five arguments: the lightnumber, red-value, green-value, blue-value, and absolute. The lightnumber is which of the light filter's light sources you are modifying. For example, to modify the first light, the lightnumber would be 0. If you have two light sources, the first would be 0 and the second would be 1. The last argument, "absolute," is a flag that determines if the color values should be *added* to the current values (false) or if the new values should *replace* the current values (true). The example below adds a white "point" light source, and then changes its color to red.

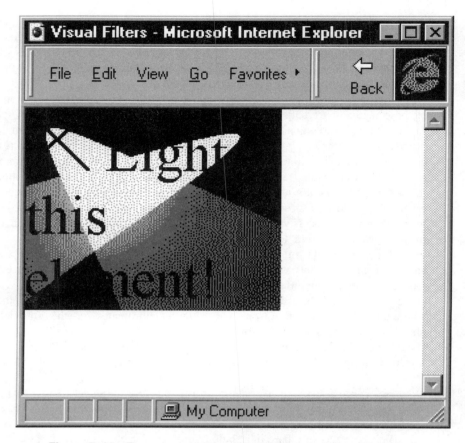

Figure 7–12 Two cones of light added with the "addCone()" method.

```
myFilter.addPoint(125,50,40,255,255,255,100);
myFilter.ChangeColor(0, 255,0,0, true);
```

The "ChangeStrength()" method is similar to ChangeColor(), except it modifies the strength of the light instead of its color. Its three arguments are lightnumber, strength, and absolute. If "absolute" is set to "true," the new strength value replaces the old one. If "false," the new value is added to the old one. The example below sets a bright white "point" light, and then dims it down a bit.

```
myFilter.addPoint(125,50,40,255,255,255,100);
myFilter.ChangeStrength(0, 50, true);
```

The "Clear()" method removes all of the Light filter's light sources. It accepts no arguments. Once a Light filter's lights have been cleared, the browser instantly plunges the element into darkness.

```
myFilter.Clear();
```

The final method is "MoveLight()," which moves the light source. It accepts three arguments: lightnumber, x, y, z, and absolute. You know the drill by now, I'm sure. If the light source is a cone, the position of its *target* is modified. Since the target for a cone light only has an X and Y coordinate, the Z coordinate is thrown away. Below is the same white "point" light, this time being moved a bit to the left and "up."

```
myFilter.addPoint(125,50,40,255,255,255,100);
myFilter.MoveLight(0, 50,50,20, true);
```

I wouldn't get *too* comfortable with these methods. They are a bit complex and unnecessarily cumbersome, so I would bet they will be cleaned up a little bit before too long.

TRANSITIONS

Transitions are special filters that create animated effects, such as blends, fades, and wipes. For example, when changing an image, the new image loads and instantly replaces the old one. But if you applied the "blend" transition filter, the old image would slowly fade out while the new image faded in. This is just one of twenty-five built-in transitions.

There are two types of transitions: blend and reveal. The blend transition performs only simple fades, but the reveal transition is capable of applying twenty-four different transition styles.. We'll look at the blend transition first, and then move on to the fancy reveal transitions once we have the basics down.

The Blend Transition: Applying a Basic Transition

The first thing to keep in mind when dealing with transitions is that they aren't like the visual effect filters we studied earlier. You can't just "apply" a transition to an element and expect to see something happen, because transitions can only occur when an element has changed in some way; for example, using a script to replace an image, or changing the text inside an element. This means that to apply a transition you will need to do a little scripting.

Setting up a transition is a four-step process:

1. Defining the transition on the filter: property.
2. "Freezing" the element with the Apply() method.
3. Changing the element in some way.
4. "Playing" the transition with the Play() method.

Let's create a simple document and step through the process. First, I defined a short document, below. The document's body contains a single <DIV> element with some text that changes when the user clicks on it. Remember, when working with <DIV> and filters, you must give the <DIV> element a width and height!

```
<HTML>
<STYLE>
    DIV { width: 1.5in; height: 1.5in;
        font-size: 24pt;
        }
</STYLE>
<HEAD>
<SCRIPT LANGUAGE="JavaScript">
function do_change(myElement)
{
    myElement.innerText = "I am some new text! Yippee!";
}
</SCRIPT>
<TITLE>Transition Filters</TITLE>
</HEAD>
<BODY>

<DIV onClick="do_change(this)">
Click me to change this text!</DIV>

</BODY>
</HTML>
```

When the user clicks on the text, it instantly changes. The goal is to create a slower, smooth transition from the old text to the new. The first step is to define the blend filter in the <DIV> element's style sheet.

```
filter: blendTrans(Duration=2.000)
```

The blend transition is defined using "blendTrans," which accepts a "duration" as its only argument. The duration is in seconds and milliseconds, so in the example above we are requesting a two-second duration. The duration specifies how long the blend will take to complete, from start to finish. The longer the duration, the slower the transition.

You would think that this would be it, but we still have a few more steps to go. Clicking the element now will still result in an instant change. To get the transition to work properly, the next step is to "freeze" the element with the Apply() method. Freezing the element actually has two effects. First, it tells the browser that the change should be made through the transition. This keeps our changes from happening immediately, giving us the opportunity to load images, manipulate text, and otherwise modify the element in some creative way.

The Apply() method is performed in our do_change() function, before we modify the element. Now, any changes we make to the element will be "cached," instead of being displayed immediately. If you make the following changes to the do_change() function, it will appear as if nothing happens when the user clicks the element.

```
function do_change(myElement)
{
    myElement.filters[0].Apply();
    myElement.innerText = "I am some new text! Yippee!";
}
```

To get the changes to take effect and finally run the transition, we need to apply one last method: Play(). The Play() method takes all the changes made to the element since the Apply() method and runs them through the transition. With no arguments, the Play() method will use the duration you set for the filter in the style sheet, but you can also give Play() a new duration, which overrides any other setting.

```
function do_change(myElement)
{
    myElement.filters[0].Apply();
    myElement.innerText = "I am some new text! Yippee!";
    myElement.filters[0].Play();
}
```

Now we're ready! When the user clicks on the text, the do_change() function is called, which runs the Apply() method. Any changes made to the element are now cached until the Play() method, at which point the transition beings. The old text will slowly fade out of view, turning more and more transparent. At the same time, the new text will start out completely transparent and slowly become opaque. After about two seconds, the length of our duration, the old text will have completely faded out of view and the new text has taken over. The blend is complete.

Don't forget to use the Apply() method in your transitions! The Play() method counts on the Apply() method being called before it. If you forget it, you will get an error message, because the Play() method won't have any idea what changes need to be handed to the transition.

Transitions work just as well on images as they do on text. The code below takes the first image, "image.gif," and slowly blends it into the new image, "new-image.gif," when the user clicks on it. This is exactly the same as the previous example, except this time the filter is applied inline directly to the <IMG> element.

```
<HTML>
<HEAD>
<SCRIPT LANGUAGE="JavaScript">
function do_change(myElement)
{
```

```
        myElement.filters[0].Apply();
        myElement.src = "new-image.gif";
        myElement.filters[0].Play();
}
</SCRIPT>
<TITLE>Transition Filters</TITLE>
</HEAD>
<BODY>

<IMG onClick="do_change(this)" SRC="image.gif"
     STYLE="filter: blendTrans(Duration=2.500)">

</BODY>
</HTML>
```

Reveal Transitions

The reveal transitions are the same as the blend transition, with the exception of being able to perform more complex fades and wipes. Other then that, calling them requires the same steps and has the same end result: a graceful transition to the new element.

Reveal transitions require two arguments to function properly. The first is the duration, just like the blend transition. The second argument, however, controls the "style" of the transition. For example, should the transition "circle in" or should it wipe to the left? There are twenty-four possible transition styles, numbered 0 through 23. The following example sets a reveal transition to the tenth style, "checkboard across." The transition will complete in three seconds.

```
filter: revealTrans(duration=3.000, 10)
```

For a complete list of the built in transitions, check out Table 7–3. As you can imagine, screen shots of transitions are a bit difficult to produce, so if you're curious what one of these transitions really does, try it out!

Table 7–3   The Reveal Transition Filter Types

Transition Number	Description
0	Box in
1	Box out
2	Circle in
3	Circle out
4	Wipe up
5	Wipe down
6	Wipe right

Table 7–3 (*Continued*)

Transition Number	Description
7	Wipe left
8	Vertical blinds
9	Horizontal blinds
10	Checkerboard across
11	Checkerboard down
12	Random dissolve
13	Split vertical in
14	Split vertical out
15	Split horizontal in
16	Split horizontal out
17	Strips left down
18	Strips left up
19	Strips right down
20	Strips right up
21	Random bars horizontal
22	Random bars vertical
23	Random

Let's look at a slightly more complex example, this time with a reveal transition. When the <DIV> element is clicked in the example below, the "wipe right" reveal transition is applied, slowly changing the text and colors as it goes.

```
<HTML>
<STYLE>
    DIV { font-size: 32pt;
        width: 1in; height: 1em;
        background-color: white; color: black;
        filter: revealTrans(Duration=5.000,Transition=6)
    }
</STYLE>
<HEAD>
<SCRIPT LANGUAGE="JavaScript">
function do_change(myElement)
{
    myElement.filters[0].Apply();
    myElement.innerText = "World!";
    myElement.style.backgroundColor = "black";
    myElement.style.color = "white";
    myElement.filters[0].Play();
}
function do_stop(myElement)
{
```

```
        if (myElement.filters[0].status == 2)
        {
            myElement.filters[0].Stop();
        }
    }
</SCRIPT>
<TITLE>Transition Filters</TITLE>
</HEAD>
<BODY>

<DIV onClick="do_change(this)"
     onMouseOut="do_stop(this)">Hello!</DIV>

</BODY>
</HTML>
```

With a five-second duration, the transition may be a little too slow, so I included an alternative for the user. When the user moves the mouse off of the element, the do_stop() function is called. If the transition is still running, the Stop() method is applied, immediately finishing the transition. This involves two new concepts: the status property and the Stop() method.

The status property contains information on what the transition is currently doing. A value of 0 means the transition isn't currently running, and a value of 2 means the transition is still doing its thing. There is also supposed to be a value of 1, which means that the transition has been applied, but honestly, I couldn't convince the filter to ever return this value. No matter, because the only important values are "it's stopped" and "it's going." In our example, if the status is 2, meaning the filter is still running, we apply the Stop() method.

The Stop() method tells the transition to finish up immediately, regardless of how much time is left. Don't worry, because it won't leave you mid-transition! It actually fast-forwards the transition to the end.

When a transition starts or finally completes, it triggers an onfilterchange event on the object to which the filter was applied. This is a great way to create "bouncing" filter effects, for example. Let's make a few modifications to the previous example, and create some "bouncing" filters.

```
<HTML>
<STYLE>
    DIV { font-size: 32pt;
          width: 1in; height: 1em;
          background-color: white; color: black;
          filter: revealTrans(Transition=7, Duration=1.000)
        }
</STYLE>
<HEAD>
```

```
<SCRIPT LANGUAGE="JavaScript">
function do_change(myElement)
{
    if (myElement.filters[0].status == 2)
    {
        return; // I am already running!
    }

    myElement.filters[0].Apply();
    if (myElement.filters[0].transition == 7)
    {
        myElement.filters[0].transition = 6;
        myElement.innerText = "World!";
        myElement.style.backgroundColor = "black";
        myElement.style.color = "white";
    }
    else
    {
        myElement.filters[0].transition = 7;
        myElement.innerText = "Hello!";
        myElement.style.backgroundColor = "white";
        myElement.style.color = "black";
    }
    myElement.filters[0].Play();
}
function do_stop(myElement)
{
    if (myElement.filters[0].status == 2)
    {
        myElement.filters[0].Stop();
    }
}
</SCRIPT>
<TITLE>Transition Filters</TITLE>
</HEAD>
<BODY>

<DIV onMouseOver="do_change(this)"
    onMouseOut="do_stop(this)"
    onFilterChange="do_change(this)">Hello!</DIV>

</BODY>
</HTML>
```

Creating a "bouncing" filter effect isn't too difficult. First, I set the <DIV> element to listen for onfilterchange events. When it catches one, it calls the do_change() function again, to start the new transition.

There have also been a few changes in the do_change() function. The first thing I do is check the filter's status. Starting a new filter on an element where a filter is already running is not good, so it is always a good idea to double-check before applying a new filter. After the Apply() method, the function now has a choice. Should it apply transition 6 or transition 7? By checking the current transition number, the function knows what transition was just completed and picks the opposite filter instead. All that remains now is the Play() method, and we have a bouncing transition!

Incidentally, the Stop() method will *not* trigger an onfilterchange event, so when the user moves the mouse pointer away from the <DIV> element, the bouncing effect will immediately halt. Visual filter effects, when applied or enabled, also trigger onfilterchange events.

Interpage Transitions

Transitions on an entire page? You bet! And without scripting, too! Interpage transitions take advantage of the <META> element to apply a transition when a page is loaded or unloaded, a page from another site is loaded, or when someone is loading your page from another site. Here's how it works.

For each interpage transition, place a <META> element in the document's <HEAD>. The "HTTP-EQUIV=" attribute should be set to one of the following interpage transition types: Page-Enter, Page-Exit, Site-Enter, or Site-Exit.

- **Page-Enter** applies the transition any time the page is loaded.
- **Page-Exit** applies the transition when the user unloads the page.
- **Site-Enter** applies the transition when the user has loaded your page after coming from someone else's server. The transition isn't applied if the user visits this page from another page on your server.
- **Site-Exit** applies the transition when the user goes to someone else's server. The transition isn't applied if the user visits another page on your server.

Next, set the "CONTENT=" attribute to the transition filter you want to apply. For example, if you want your home page to "circle in" when the user visits it from another web site, you would put the following line in your document's <HEAD> element:

```
<META HTTP-EQUIV="Site-Enter"
CONTENT="revealTrans(Duration=2.000,Transition=2);
```

That's all there is to it! No scripting, no hassle. Whenever the user visits the document with this <META> element from another server, the page will "circle in."

The only caveat is that the maximum duration for any transition applied in this fashion is 30 seconds.

CONCLUSION

Hopefully, this was a fun chapter! Positioning is a very powerful tool that when used properly allows for precise layout and design. Combined with filters and transitions, you have unprecedented flexibility to create some pretty stunning pages.

CHAPTER 8

Netscape's View
of Dynamic HTML

Until this point, I've mostly concentrated on how Dynamic HTML works on the Internet Explorer 4.0 side of things. The reason for this is twofold: IE 4.0 has, in my opinion and that of the W3C, a better model and Netscape Communicator 4.0 would at some point in the near future support most of these features anyway. The truth is, I am both right and wrong with these assumptions. Netscape already supports cascading style sheets and positioning and, of course, JavaScript, but there are still some differences that make the two browsers incompatible in many of these areas. This chapter will discuss some of these differences, as things currently stand, and offer some insights on how to get around a few of the incompatibilities.

JAVASCRIPT OBJECT AND EVENT MODEL

Netscape was the first browser to offer a scripting language. At the time, it was called LiveScript, but the name was changed to JavaScript, capitalizing on the popularity of the up-and-coming Java language. As far as I can tell, the two languages are about as far removed from each other as two languages could possibly be. No matter, because the name change worked and JavaScript caught on in a big way. Even Microsoft stood up and took notice, pushing aside its VBScript language for a while to create its own JavaScript implementation, which they called JScript. Right now, JavaScript is well on its way to becoming an official specification, which is probably a good thing.

JScript is mostly compatible with JavaScript, but recently the two languages have begun to diverge. Most notable is the object model. Netscape still doesn't support the new document object model, and that can create a bit of a problem. Not to worry, though, because there are some tricks and techniques we can use to write code that will work, to at least some degree, in both browsers. The biggest problem, however, is that Netscape simply isn't capable of the dynamic content features that make Dynamic HTML so powerful. We'll look at ways around that shortly. First, let's see how the object model differs.

JavaScript Object Model

Netscape still uses the older JavaScript Object Model, which isn't nearly as powerful or all-encompassing as the new document object model (see Figure 8–1).

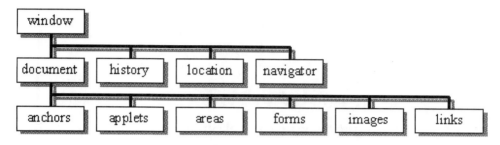

Figure 8–1 The JavaScript Object Model.

One thing missing is the "all" collection. Strictly speaking, you can't access all the elements anyway, so this isn't surprising. As a matter of a fact, the only time you can access elements other than form elements, links, and so forth, is when the element has been positioned using style sheets. For example, you normally can't access the <DIV> element directly, but if it has been positioned you can.

```
document.myElement.visibility = "hidden";
```

Here, we are changing the visibility property of the element "myElement" to "hidden." The only properties available for your manipulations are the style sheet positioning properties. There is no style object, so the positioning properties are called directly from the element object. The example below shows how you can toggle a positioned element's visibility. Check out Figure 8–2 for a screen shot.

```
<HTML>
<STYLE TYPE="text/css">
    DIV { position: absolute; top: .5in; left: 1in;
        width: 1in;
        background-color: silver;
        font-size: 18pt;
        border-width: thin; border-color: black; }
</STYLE>
<HEAD>
<SCRIPT LANGUAGE="JavaScript">
```

```
function do_click()
{
    if (document.MyDiv.visibility == "hide")
    {
        document.MyDiv.visibility = "visible";
    }
    else
    {
        document.MyDiv.visibility = "hidden";
    }
}
</SCRIPT>
<TITLE>Netscape's Object Model</TITLE>
</HEAD>
<BODY>

<DIV ID="MyDiv">Netscape does things differently.</DIV>

<FORM><INPUT TYPE="button" VALUE="Click"
onClick="do_click()"></FORM>

</BODY>
</HTML>
```

So Netscape can do some of the things that Internet Explorer can, but even when it does, the syntax for doing so is different. Writing pages that work in both browsers, even when the browsers have similar capability, can be a real challenge. It's almost easier to write separate pages for each! But at least there is one trick you can use.

Our previous example works in Netscape, but not in Explorer, even though both browsers have the ability to position and modify the positioning properties via scripting. Instead of writing separate pages for each browser, one solution is to check the browser version at the top of your script and use that information to offer each browser an alternate object. For example, if the browser is Netscape, you would use "document.myElement" to access the properties. If it is Explorer, you would use "document.all.myElement.style" instead. Actually, this doesn't have to be as intrusive as it sounds.

```
var is_Nav = (navigator.appName == "Netscape");
```

If you put this simple line at the top of your script, before anything else, the "is_Nav" variable will check the browser version and assign "true" if it is Netscape, or "false" if it is any other browser. You now have a quick way to check the browser version in your script. Later, when you need to change a positioning property, you could use the following "tertiary operator" to ensure the right syntax is used every time.

```
var myStyle = (is_Nav) ? document.MyDiv : document.all.MyDiv.style;

myStyle.visibility = "hidden";
```

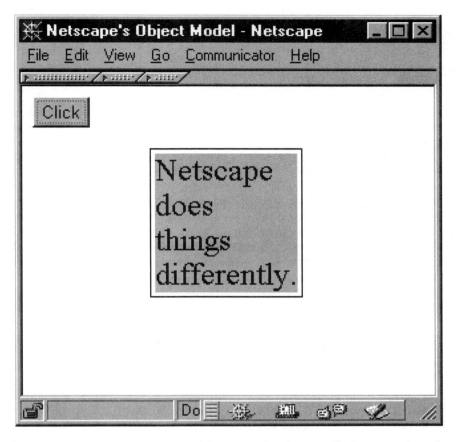

Figure 8–2 Netscape can do some of the things that Internet Explorer can, but when it does, the syntax is different anyway. Notice how Netscape *does* do borders, though!

The first line of code checks the "is_Nav" variable. If it is true, it will assign the "document.MyDiv" object to "myStyle," otherwise it will use the "document.all. MyDiv.style" object. Now all you can access the "visibility" property directly from the "myStyle" variable. This is a lot easier than writing two separate functions, one for Netscape and the other for Explorer.

```
<SCRIPT LANGUAGE="JavaScript">
var is_Nav = (navigator.appName == "Netscape");

function do_click()
{
    var myStyle = (is_Nav) ? document.MyDiv :
document.all.MyDiv.style;
```

```
        if (myStyle.visibility == "hide" ||
            myStyle.visibility == "hidden")
        {
            myStyle.visibility = "visible";
        }
        else
        {
            myStyle.visibility = "hidden";
        }
    }
    </SCRIPT>
```

If you replace the previous <SCRIPT> element with the new one above and try the document again, it will work in both browsers. Notice in the conditional, where I check to see if the element is already hidden or not, I have to check for "hide" and "hidden." This is because Netscape incorrectly returns "hide" when the visibility is set to "hidden." Little inconsistencies like this are going to drive you nuts when writing your documents for both browsers. The obvious differences aren't so bad when compared to this kind of insidious little bug.

I wouldn't be too concerned about any of these problems right now. Granted, making your pages work in both browsers could be a hassle at first, but things should change for the better before you know it. Microsoft and Netscape have both sworn to make their browsers more compatible in the future, and I imagine Netscape will slowly begin to adopt the new object model, particularly when the W3C finally pronounces the new model "standard." It would be death for Netscape to have a "non-standard" browser, and the new object model is well on its way to becoming the standard.

Netscape's Event Model

Netscape also has a vastly different event model from Internet Explorer—different enough to make complex scripts almost impossible to reconcile between the two. For one thing, Netscape won't listen for events directly on elements like <P> or <DIV>, which makes the kind of "advanced" user interface design we're used to by now nearly impossible.

Netscape supports the following events, listed in Table 8–1. Thankfully, most of these do have corresponding events in Internet Explorer.

Table 8–1   Netscape's Events

onAbort	onKeyDown	onMouseUp
onBlur	onKeyPress	onMove
onClick	onKeyUp	onReset
onChange	onLoad	onResize
onDblClick	onMouseDown	onSelect
onDragDrop	onMouseMove	onSubmit
onError	onMouseOut	onUnload
onFocus	onMouseOver	

Binding event handlers is done a bit differently with Netscape. First, you are very limited in what elements and objects will accept event handlers. For example, "onclick" can only be bound to links and form elements. Attempting to bind "onclick" to a <DIV> element simply won't work. The actual binding is usually done inline using element attributes, like we're used to.

```
<INPUT TYPE="button" VALUE="Click Me!" onClick="do_click()">
```

Unfortunately, the for-event method of event handler binding doesn't work in Netscape. To make up for this, an entirely different way of binding was developed, which is not at all recognized by Internet Explorer. The event handler is exposed to your script as an element property. Interesting. Take a look at the example below.

```
<HTML>
<HEAD>
<TITLE>Netscape Events</TITLE>
<SCRIPT LANGUAGE="JavaScript">
function do_click()
{
    alert("Clicked!");
}
</SCRIPT>
</HEAD>
<BODY>
<FORM>
<INPUT NAME="myButton" TYPE="button" VALUE="Click Me">
</FORM>

<SCRIPT LANGUAGE="JavaScript">
    document.forms[0].myButton.onclick = do_click;
</SCRIPT>

</BODY>
</HTML>
```

The form button, "myButton," is actually listening for the "onclick" event, even though there is no "onClick=" attribute set on the element. The event handler is actually bound to the element in the short script underneath the form. The "onclick" property can be used to bind a function to the button. This means you can actually change the event handler *on the fly*. I like it, but it's not as powerful as it looks, because you can't pass arguments to the event handler when using this method. If you try, the assignment will actually *call* the function and attempt to bind the function's return value instead of the function itself. Be careful not to put parenthesis after the function name, or any arguments for that matter, or the function will be called on the spot, not bothering to wait for an event. Another pitfall is attempting to bind the event handler *before* the element is defined.

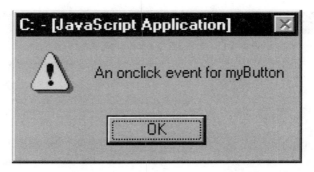

Figure 8–3   The event object can return a bunch of useful information about your event.

Make sure the document has completely loaded, or the <SCRIPT> element where you do the binding is after the element you're binding to, or you will get an error.

This is not to say that nothing is passed to your event handler when using this method. On the contrary, Netscape automatically passes a copy of the event object, which is much like Internet Explorer's event object, at least in theory.

```
function do_click(e)
{
    alert("An on"+e.type+" event for "+e.target.name);
}
```

Rewriting the event handler function from the previous example, we can now access the properties on the event object (see Figure 8–3). Before moving on, take a look in Table 8–2 for a list of all the event object properties.

Table 8–2   The Netscape Event Object Properties

Property	Description
data	An array of strings containing the URLs of objects passed by the onDragDrop event.
layerX	If the layer was resized, this will be its width. Otherwise, this will be the mouse position relative to the event's layer.
layerY	If the layer was resized, this will be its height. Otherwise, this will be the mouse position relative to the event's layer.
modifiers	Modifiers are keys like SHIFT, ALT, etc. If a modifier key was pressed during the mouse or key event, this will contain a string with the following values, as appropriate: ALT_MASK, CONTROL_MASK, SHIFT_MASK, or META_MASK.
pageX	Mouse's position relative to the page.
pageY	Mouse's position relative to the page.
screenX	Mouse's position relative to the entire screen.
screenY	Mouse's position relative to the entire screen.
target	The object which caused the event.
type	The event name, without the "on" prefix. For example, "click" for the "onclick" event.
which	The mouse button pressed, or the ASCII code for the keyboard key pressed.

The event object can also be explicitly passed to an event handler, using the "event" keyword, if you decide to bind inline.

```
<INPUT NAME="myButton" TYPE="button" VALUE="Click Me"
onClick="do_click(event) ">
```

Unfortunately, "event" isn't a real object unless it is passed as a parameter to an event handler, as in the example above. Attempts at calling it directly from inside a function won't work!

```
var e = event;  // This won't work!
```

This example will fail, because "event" doesn't truly exist.

These aren't the only event model differences. Netscape also has its own version of event bubbling, which it calls "event capturing." Unfortunately, it works in reverse compared to Internet Explorer's bubbling. Instead of the event being processed on the original element and bubbling up to the window object, it can be "captured" and processed on the window object or allowed to "trickle down" to the original element.

Four methods are used with event capturing: captureEvents(), releaseEvents(), routeEvent(), and handleEvent().

```
HTML>
<HEAD>
<TITLE>Netscape Events</TITLE>
<SCRIPT LANGUAGE="JavaScript">
function captured_click(e)
{
    alert("Pass it on...");
    window.routeEvent(e);
}
function do_click(e)
{
    alert("I finally got the click!");
}

window.captureEvents(Event.CLICK);
window.onclick = captured_click;
</SCRIPT>
</HEAD>
<BODY>
<FORM>
<INPUT NAME="myButton" TYPE="button" VALUE="Click Me"
onClick="do_click()">
</FORM>

</BODY>
</HTML>
```

This is an example of how to force the window object to capture all onclick events. When the user clicks on the button, the onclick event first goes to the window's captured_click() function. It sends a message and then "routes" the event on to the next event handler. Now the do_click() function has a shot at it, and it sends another message.

The captureEvents() method is used to force the window object to intercept events bound for other objects. It accepts one argument, the event to capture. In this case, we are capturing onclick events.

```
window.captureEvents(Event.CLICK);
```

If you want to capture more then one kind of event, you can specify these as well, separating each with a vertical bar. For example, the following line will capture all onclick, onfocus, and onblur events:

```
window.captureEvents(Event.CLICK | Event.FOCUS | Event.BLUR);
```

Once the window object has been set up to capture events, you need to bind event handlers to the window object for these events.

```
window.onclick = captured_click;
```

Now the window object will capture all onclick events and handle them with the captured_click() event handler. When it's done with the event, it can then decide to pass it on down the line, to the next event handler, with the routeEvent() method.

If you want to "undo" capturing, you can use the releaseEvents() method. By giving it the event to release, the window object will stop capturing that event, and it will default back to its normal routing.

```
window.releaseEvents(Event.CLICK);
```

Speaking of routing, the routeEvent() method accepts one argument—the event object—and passes the event down to the next event in line, if there is one. In our example, the do_click() function is next in line to receive the event. When do_click() has completed, control is passed *back* to the captured_click() function, and routeEvent() returns the return value sent by the do_click() function. You thought event bubbling was complex!

The handleEvent() method is interesting in that it can be used to pass an event to *any* event handler, regardless of whether it was in line for the event or not. For example, you can essentially send an onclick event from one link to another link that wasn't event clicked!

```
<HTML>
<HEAD>
<TITLE>Netscape Events</TITLE>
```

```
<SCRIPT LANGUAGE="JavaScript">
function do_click_one(e)
{
    alert("Pass it on...");
    document.links[1].handleEvent(e);
    return false;
}
function do_click_two(e)
{
    alert("Now I handle the event!");
    return false;
}
</SCRIPT>
</HEAD>
<BODY>
<A HREF="document_1.html" onClick="do_click_one(event)">I'll
  pass it on!</A>
<P><A HREF="document_2.html" onClick="do_click_two(event)">I
  got it!</A>
</BODY>
</HTML>
```

In this strange example, if the first link is clicked, the do_click_one() event handler is called. But do_click_one() decides to pass the event over to the second link's event handler, so do_click_two() is called as well. Weird.

LAYERS AND STYLE SHEET POSITIONING

Netscape developed layers in response to the need for the dynamic positioning of elements. Now that Netscape supports style sheet positioning, however, layers have been pushed off to the side and will likely fade away at some point in the future. Everything you can do with Netscape layers can also be done with style sheet positioning. As a matter of fact, layers are so closely related to positioning that many of the features will already be familiar to you.

The <LAYER> Element

With style sheet positioning, any block element and its contents, such as <DIV>, can be positioned on the browser window. Layers, on the other hand, require the special <LAYER> element. Anything inside the <LAYER> element is part of that layer, including other layers. Essentially, a layer is an element that defaults to absolute positioning.

```
<HTML>
<STYLE>
    P { font-size: 24pt; }
```

```
</STYLE>
<HEAD>
<TITLE>Layers</TITLE>
</HEAD>
<BODY>

<P>I am not in a layer.</P>

<LAYER LEFT=20 TOP=20><P>And I am in a layer.</P></LAYER>

</BODY>
</HTML>
```

Figure 8–4

In this example, the second paragraph is inside a layer, positioned 20 pixels from the top of the browser window and 20 pixels from the left. The second paragraph slightly overlaps the first, as seen in Figure 8–4. Right away, the similarity between layers and style sheet positioning should be apparent. The "TOP=" and "LEFT=" attributes directly correspond to the style sheet properties of the same name.

The <LAYER> element has thirteen attributes, most of which directly mirror the style sheet positioning properties. A list of each attribute and its function can be found in Table 8–3.

Table 8–3   <LAYER> Element Attributes

Attribute	Value	Description
ABOVE	string	Name of the layer immediately above this one.
BACKGROUND	A URL	Background image.
BELOW	string	Name of the layer immediately below this one.
BGCOLOR	color value	Background color. Default is transparent.
CLIP	four integers separated by commas	Left, top, right, and bottom coordinates for the clipping region.
HEIGHT	number of pixels or percent	Height of layer.
LEFT	number of pixels or percent	Left position of layer relative to parent layer or window.
NAME	string	The name of the layer. Must be unique.
PAGEX	number of pixels	Left position of layer *relative to window*, not the parent layer.
PAGEY	number of pixels	Top position of layer *relative to window*, not the parent layer.
SRC	A URL	URL to load into layer for content.
TOP	number of pixels or percent	Top position of layer relative to parent layer or window.
VISIBILITY	SHOW, HIDE, or INHERIT	Visibility of layer.
WIDTH	number of pixels or percent	Width of layer.
Z-INDEX	positive integer	Z-index relative to other layers.

Most of the attributes in Table 8–3 are self-explanatory or behave like their style sheet counterparts. The "ABOVE=" and "BELOW=" attributes are simply additional ways to specify the z-index. When the layer is first created, it will be placed either *beneath* the layer specified by the "ABOVE=" attribute, *above* the layer specified by the "BELOW=" attribute, or at the exact z-index specified by the "Z-INDEX=" attribute. These three attributes are mutually exclusive.

The "SRC=" attribute is another new one, with an interesting application. Give it a URL and the <LAYER> element will load that document and use it for its content. As I found out the hard way, the style sheet properties on the document with the <LAYER> element *will* apply to the new document loaded with the "SRC=" attribute. I don't know why, but it caught me by surprise, so I thought I would mention it.

With the exception of the "SRC=" attribute, if you can do it with layers, you can do it with style sheets, as the code below demonstrates. The <DIV> element is positioned with style sheets, and the equivalent <LAYER> element is to the right. The screen shot is in Figure 8–5.

```
<HTML>
<STYLE>
    DIV { position: absolute; top: 25; left: 25;
        width: 150;
        }
</STYLE>
<HEAD>
<TITLE>Layers</TITLE>
</HEAD>
<BODY>
```

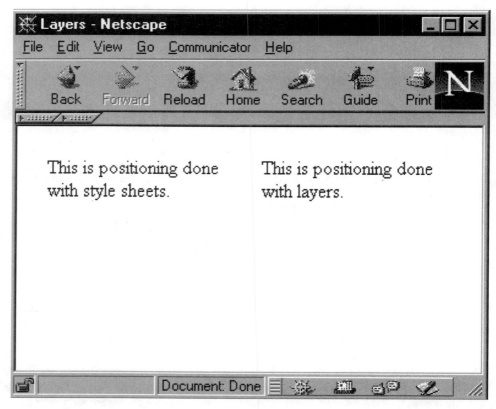

This is positioning done with style sheets.

This is positioning done with layers.

Figure 8–5   The <DIV> on the left was positioned with style sheets. The equivalent <LAYER> is on the right.

```
<DIV>This is positioning done with style sheets.</DIV>

<LAYER TOP=25 LEFT=200 WIDTH=150>
This is positioning done with layers.
</LAYER>

</BODY>
</HTML>
```

Accessing Layers with JavaScript

Your layers can be accessed using the "layers" collection on the document object. You can use either the index number of the layer or the layer's name. The layer's collection has one property, "length," which contains the number of layers in the current document. For example, to access the third layer in a document named "layerThree," you could use any of the following lines:

```
var myLayer = document.layers[2];
var myLayer = document.layers["layerThree"];
var myLayer = document.layers.layerThree;
```

Each layer object has its own set of properties for accessing its various attributes. Some of these properties can be written to as well as read, and some are read-only. Table 8–4 lists each layer property, its description, and if it can be modified.

Table 8–4   Layer Object Properties

Property	Write?	Description
clip.bottom	yes	Bottom corner of clipping region; CLIP=
clip.height	yes	HEIGHT=
clip.left	yes	Left corner of clipping region; CLIP=
clip.right	yes	Right corner of clipping region; CLIP=
clip.top	yes	Top corner of clipping region; CLIP=
clip.width	yes	WIDTH= attribute
document	no	Each layer is treated as its own document. This is how you get at the document properties, collections of images and links, etc.
layers	no	A collection of any layers inside this one
left	yes	LEFT= attribute
name	no	NAME= attribute
parentLayer	no	If this layer is inside another, the parent layer
siblingAbove	no	The layer above this one in z-order. Is "null" if none.
siblingBelow	no	The layer below this one in z-order. Is "null" if none.
top	yes	TOP= attribute
visibility	yes	VISIBILITY= attribute

The "WIDTH=" and "HEIGHT=" attributes are interesting, because they are included with the "clip" properties. With Netscape, once a document is laid out, the layout can't be modified. Sure, you can move layers around and use style sheet positioning to move around other elements as well, but the *layout*, or "document flow," can't be changed. Ever notice what happens when you replace a smaller image with a larger one in Netscape? The new image overlaps any surrounding text or images, because the document is not adjusted for the change in size. The same thing is true with layers. Once the content of a layer has been written, the browser will not lay it out again, even if the width or height is changed. If you make the layer wider, the text is not reflowed to fit the new space. The same holds true if you make the layer smaller—the text will not reflow. Compare this to Internet Explorer, which *does* reflow text when a positioned element is resized. This is why width and height are included with the "clip" properties. If you decrease the layer's width or height, the contents of the layer are actually *clipped* to fit the new dimensions, not reflowed. So width and height become clipping properties. Take a look at Figure 8–6 and compare it to the code below. When the width and height are reduced, the layer's contents are clipped, not reflowed.

```
<HTML>
<HEAD>
<TITLE>Layers</TITLE>
<SCRIPT>
function do_clipLayer()
{
    var myLayer = document.layers.MyLayer;

    myLayer.clip.width -= 50;
    myLayer.clip.height -= 50;
}
</SCRIPT>
</HEAD>
<BODY onLoad="do_clipLayer()">

<LAYER NAME="MyLayer" TOP=25 LEFT=50 WIDTH=150>
This is positioning done with layers. This is positioning done
with layers. This is positioning done with layers. This is
positioning done with layers. This is positioning done with
layers.
</LAYER>

</BODY>
</HTML>
```

The layer object also has six methods to help take some of the drudge work out of moving and resizing your layers. These are listed in Table 8–5.

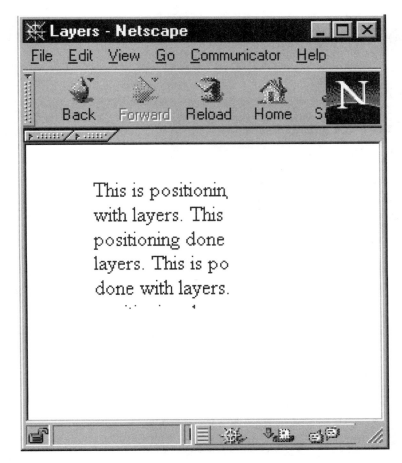

Figure 8–6 When a layer's width and height are decreased, the layer's contents are clipped, not reflowed to fit the new size.

Table 8–5 Layer Object Methods

Method	Description
moveBy(x-pixels, y-pixels)	Move the layer *by this number of pixels,* not to this location.
moveTo(x-pixels, y-pixels)	Move the layer to these coordinates.
resizeBy(width,height)	Resize the layer *by this number of pixels,* not to this exact size.
resizeTo(width,height)	Resize the layer to this exact size.
moveAbove(layername)	Move the layer's z-index *above* the specified layer.
moveBelow(layername)	Move the layer's z-index *below* the specified layer.

The methods are easy to use and take a bit of the work out of resizing and moving your layers around. For example, to shrink the layer named "myLayer" by 20 pixels vertically, the following line would do the trick:

```
document.layers.myLayer.resizeBy(0,-20);
```

The <NOLAYER> Element

Only Netscape Communicator supports layers. If you would like to display a message for users of other browsers, you can use the <NOLAYER> element. Anything inside the <NOLAYER> element will be ignored by Netscape, but other browsers will display it without a complaint. This gives you the opportunity to explain how to get to a non-layer version of your pages, but not bother Netscape users with this extra information.

```
<NOLAYER>
    <P>These pages make extensive use of layers. Since your
browser can not view layers, you may want to <A HREF="no-
layers.html"> visit this no layers version</A> instead.</P>
</NOLAYER>
```

Layer Events

The most exciting news about layers is that they can listen for events! The following five events are available on all your layers:

- **onMouseOver** is triggered when the mouse moves over a layer.
- **onMouseOut** is triggered when the mouse is moved off a layer.
- **onFocus** is triggered when the layer receives focus. This can double as onclick, if you're creative.
- **onBlur** is triggered when the layer receives focus, for example, if you click outside a layer.
- **onLoad** is triggered when the layer has finished layout, or when the document loaded by the "SRC=" attribute is finished loading.

Events are bound to layers in all the usual ways. For example, the following code binds a function to the onMouseOver event:

```
<LAYER onMouseOver="alert('Event triggered!')">
```

Absolute or Relative Positioning? The <ILAYER> Element

The <LAYER> element defaults to absolute positioning. If you want the same functionality of relative positioning, you can use the <ILAYER> element instead (see Figure 8–7).

The <ILAYER> element accepts all the same attributes and methods of the <LAYER> element, with the following two exceptions:

- No "PAGEX=" or "PAGEY=" attributes.
- No events can be bound to <ILAYER>

Moving on . . .

This is about all I am going to say about layers. Since Netscape supports style sheet positioning, you should avoid creating new documents using the <LAYER> element. Instead, use this information to help convert older documents from a layers format to the style sheet methods. Layers are on the way out, and creating new layers will just make it harder to convert in the future.

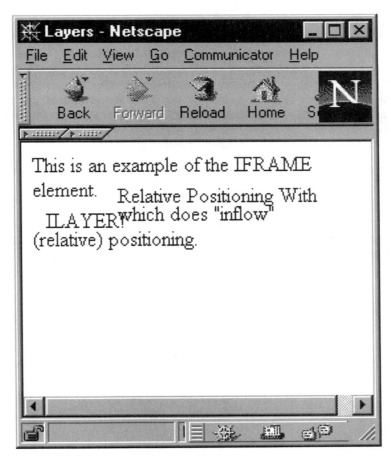

Figure 8–7 Relative positioning with the <ILAYER> element.

JASS: JAVASCRIPT STYLE SHEETS

JavaScript Style Sheets (JASS) is an alternate style sheet syntax developed, and only supported by, Netscape. I scoured Netscape's site for information on the genesis of, or at least the reasoning behind, JASS, and I couldn't turn up a thing. As a matter of fact, I barely found *any* information on JASS at all. I include information on it here only for your information. I don't claim, and I doubt Netscape does either, that JASS is well suited for any particular task. You be the judge; however, I must warn that if you use JASS, other browser won't be able to view your styles. Actually, seeing how little information is on Netscape's site about it, I'm beginning to doubt that even Netscape will understand JASS in another release or two.

The concept behind JASS is that JavaScript can be used to specify styles. You define a JavaScript Style Sheet the same way you define regular style sheets, in the <STYLE> element. This time, however, instead of using "text/css" for the type, you will use "text/javascript."

```
<STYLE TYPE="text/javascript">
```

The document object has a "tags" property, which can be used to access a list of tagnames that the document supports. You will use this tags property to access a particular type of tag, and "assign" a style to it. For example, to set the font size of your <P> elements to 24pt, you would do the following:

```
<STYLE TYPE="text/javascript">
   document.tags.P.fontSize = "24pt";
</STYLE>
```

Since Netscape always assumes the current document, you can omit the "document" part, before the "tags" property. By the way, the browser is executing *actual* JavaScript code. Just for laughs, I tried inserting an alert() method into a JavaScript Style Sheet. When the document loaded, the alert() method was called! Try doing *that* with regular style sheets!

```
<STYLE TYPE="text/javascript">
   tags.P.fontFamily = "arial";
   tags.P.fontSize = "16pt";
</STYLE>
```

You can group declarations by using the "with()" function, but there is no way I can tell to group selectors. Contextual selectors seem to be out of the question as well.

```
<STYLE TYPE="text/javascript">
   with (tags.P)
   {
```

```
        fontFamily = "arial";
        fontSize = "32pt";
        fontWeight = "bold";
    }
</STYLE>
```

The with() function accepts only one argument—the tag you are attempting to style. After the with() function, you can then include your declarations inside curly braces, but without all the hassle of putting the tag name before each one.

Can you change these values in a script later? No, unfortunately not. Once the document is laid out, that's it. But for what it's worth, you *can* at least read them later. The following code will report the font family of the <P> element:

```
alert(document.tags.P.fontFamily);
```

You can also link to an external JavaScript Style Sheet with the <LINK> element. External JavaScript Style Sheets use the extension ".js" instead of ".css" for cascading style sheets.

```
<LINK REL="stylesheet" TYPE="text/javascript"
SRC="mystyle.js">
```

Internet Explorer simply ignores JavaScript Style Sheets, but other browsers, particularly older browsers that don't support style sheets at all, will probably end up a mess. The worst part is, you can't enclose the contents of the style sheet inside HTML comments, because *Netscape will give you an error*! My advice—don't use JavaScript Style Sheets!

CONCLUSION

Netscape and Microsoft have their differences, it's true. But soon enough I expect to see these differences resolved, for the most part, and Dynamic HTML work properly in both browsers. Of course, expecting complete compatibility is fantasy, but already there have been great strides made to bring Netscape and Microsoft closer together. For example, Netscape has already begun phasing out JASS and <LAYERS> in favor of the more robust style sheet positioning standard. It is just a matter of time before Netscape adopts the document object model. The recent cooperation between Microsoft and Netscape to develop the style sheet positioning standards bodes very well for all of us.

Before we move on, I would like to state that I know I sounded a bit hard on Netscape throughout this chapter and even throughout the rest of this book. The truth is, I like Netscape—it is what I use at home and work, and there is nothing more I would like to see than Netscape continue to be the leading Web browser. I have supported them since NCSA Mosaic was the hot browser, and only a handful of hackers knew about Netscape.

However, this time Microsoft has standards on its side, and Internet Explorer has finally become a very powerful and robust browser. I admit it's buggy, slow at times, and a little bloated—but in reality, they *both* are.

Both Microsoft and Netscape took a gamble on what they thought was the best route to take for dynamic HTML. In the view of the W3C and a rapidly growing number of webmasters, Microsoft's ideas were better. With patience, our support, and constant feedback to both companies, we can all participate in shaping the future of the Web!

CHAPTER 9

Fonts

Ahh, fonts! They give your pages style and personality! Good fonts can give your pages a high-quality polished appearance. Bad fonts can make your pages look unreadable and foolish. This is where the amateurs separate themselves from the professionals, and if you make your living doing this stuff, it separates the employed from the unemployed. It's no wonder I decided to give the topic of fonts a chapter all to itself.

THE FONT PROBLEM

So you've been up all night, picking the perfect fonts for your pages. They look great in your browser, and you're really pleased with yourself. Arriving at your day job, bursting with pride, you drag the nearest coworker, willing or not, to your cubicle and load up your pages for him to critique. But what the . . . ?! The fonts are suddenly all wrong! Your fabulous "Farfel ICG Felt Tip" font . . . forsaken! The glorious "Garamond" font . . . gone! And worse of all, your perfect "Perpetua" font . . . purged! All of them, unceremoniously replaced with the system's default "Times" font. Your coworker smirks, says "Yeah, real nice," and wanders off, chuckling. "But . . . but," you stammer, "they were working last night!" Welcome to the world of Web fonts.

Much to your boss's chagrin, you spend the remainder of the morning attempting to piece together the solution. Your home computer is a Windows 95 machine, but the one at work is a Mac. Maybe that is the problem. You find a Windows 95 machine and try again. A glimmer of hope! Farfel and Perpetua are still missing, but Garamond is there. "Maybe it's the browser," you think. You use Internet Explorer at home, but this machine has Netscape Communicator installed. You finally manage to hunt down a machine with Internet Explorer and try one last time . . . success!

If you change the fonts in your document using style sheets, this scenario will not be uncommon. The world of fonts is a strange one, and straying from the defaults is almost guaranteed to get you in trouble, unless you understand some of the issues involved. Even then, it's almost a no-win situation. The problem is, the fonts on one user's machine are likely to be different from another's, almost without rhyme or reason.

DIFFERENT USERS == DIFFERENT FONTS

The sad fact is, different users are almost guaranteed to have different fonts installed. And this isn't as simple as "Mac vs. Windows," or even "Netscape vs. Microsoft," but much more insidious. For example, does the user have Microsoft Office installed, or another word processor? Microsoft Office adds new fonts, and other word processors might add different ones instead. Did she remove fonts to save space on a bloated hard drive, or add fonts to assist in desktop publishing? Did *you* add fonts to your own system? Many webmasters are also heavily into desktop publishing and have hundreds of additional fonts. Are you using one of these extra fonts that other users probably don't have? Do you even remember which fonts came with your system and which were added later? These are some of the issues we have to deal with when adding fonts to web documents.

When new browser features started popping up, we either had to resign ourselves to stick with the lowest common denominator or risk alienating an entire segment of our audience—for example, create HTML just for Netscape or just for Internet Explorer. If you've been browsing the Web for any length of time, surely you've seen the infamous "Best viewed with . . ." messages. But with fonts, the situation is much worse! You can't just design for Netscape or Microsoft, because your font selection is only based *in part* on the user's browser. You have to design for operating system, browser type, word processor, obscure applications, and so on. You could very well end up with a page that is only viewable "properly" for users with Internet Explorer 4.0 on Windows 95 with Microsoft Office 97 installed and XYZ Corporation's Mega-Font Expansion pack.

Sound hopeless? It gets worse, because even if the user has the font you want, there are no real font-naming conventions. The prime example is the default font for Netscape and Microsoft—one uses "Times" and the other uses "Times New Roman." They are, essentially, the same fonts, but their names are different. Macs call it "Times," and Windows call it "Times New Roman." It really is a nightmare.

Some Solutions

When picking fonts for your documents, there are a few guidelines you can use to *minimize* the font problem. I call these the Four Rules of Font Selection:

1. **Pick "best guess" fonts.**
2. **Supply alternate fonts.**
3. **Supply a generic family.**
4. **Assume the worst.**

Macs and Windows 95 both install a default set of fonts. They're not the same, but at least you will know that if the user has Windows 95 or a Mac, she will *almost certainly* have installed one of the two groups of fonts in Table 9–1. That is, if she didn't remove one, for some reason.

Table 9–1   Default Fonts Installed on Macs and Windows Machines

Windows 95, Windows 3.x and Windows NT	Macintosh
Arial	Chicago
Comic Sans	Courier
Courier New	Geneva
Modern	Helvetica
MS Sans Serif	Monaco
Symbol	New York
Times New Roman	Palatino
Wingdings	Symbol
	Times
	Zapf Dingbats

Of all these fonts, there are exactly four that can be considered close enough to be interchangeable between systems:

- **Arial** on Windows and **Helvetica** on the Mac are very close in appearance.
- **Courier New** on Windows and **Courier** on the Mac are the same.
- **Symbol**
- **Times New Roman** on Windows and **Times** on the Mac are the same.

You don't have to choose between "Mac" or "Windows" to use these fonts. Style sheets allow you to specify more than one font: the primary font and one or more alternatives. You can use this feature to ensure that Windows users get Arial and Mac users get Helvetica. Just specify *both* in the style sheet with the font-family property.

```
font-family: arial, helvetica
```

If the first font, in this case Arial, isn't available, the browser will then try Helvetica. If the user doesn't have Helvetica either, only then will the browser use the default font. This feature can be an absolute lifesaver! This brings me to my second Rule of Font Selection: Supply alternate fonts.

If you really *must* use a weird or out of the ordinary font, you should always supply an alternate font as well. If you don't, your users may very well end up being stuck staring at the system's default font, instead of your lovely Super-Deluxe-Fancy font. For example, if you want to use Centaur in your document, set an alternate font of Garamond, because

Garamond looks very similar to Centaur, and your users are a little more likely to have it since it comes with Microsoft Office for every platform except Mac. If they don't have either of those, Times/Times New Roman is the closest "default" shared by both Mac and Windows. Be careful when using fonts with more then one word in its name. Always enclose multi-word fonts in quotes and convert any uppercase characters to lowercase.

```
font-family: centaur, garamond, "times new roman", times
```

Wow, that certainly is a mouthful. The browser first tries Centaur, and if that is unavailable it will check for Garamond. If even that is unavailable, Times New Roman is also checked. Macs and Windows should both have that one, but it is called Times on the Mac, so it will check for that one as well. Technically, Times New Roman is the "default" font for Netscape and Microsoft, but no sense taking chances. Figure 9–1 illustrates this process.

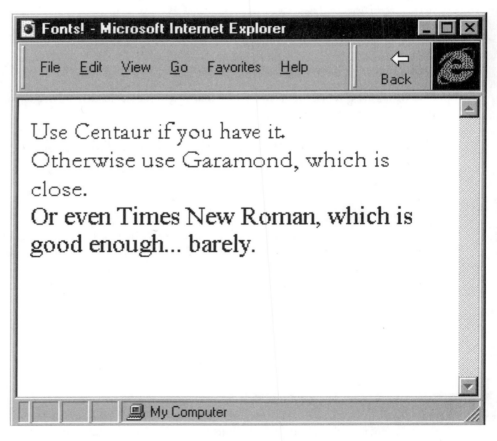

Figure 9–1   Give the browser a "failure path." If Centaur isn't available, Garamond is good enough . . .

Of course, as your fonts get weirder, it's going to be harder to find viable alternatives. I have this really neat font called "Critter," which is made of various animal faces and poses. Try finding a replacement for *that*. And you can just forget about those "symbol" and "dingbat" fonts, where the letters are little pictures of airplanes and dogs and houses and smiling faces.

My third Rule of Font Selection says you should also supply a generic font family. All fonts are classified in families, starting with a "generic font family" and becoming more and more specific. Families group fonts together based on their overall properties. For example, the generic "sans-serif" family covers font families without "serifs," such as Arial, Helvetica, and Gill Sans. Each of these three font families have one thing in common: no serifs. Serifs, if you're curious, are the little extra "bits" on the top and bottom of the vertical lines (stems) that make up each character (see Figure 9–2). For example, the letter "H" has two stems and the letter "I" has one.

If you always supply a generic font family along with the specific fonts, you'll be certain to at least get *something* that looks *remotely* like what you want.

```
font-family: centaur, garamond, "times new roman", times, serif
```

Centaur, Garamond, and Times New Roman are all "serif" fonts, because they have those little extra "bits" on their stems. Now, if absolutely none of our requested fonts are on the user's system, the browser will at least use a serif font of some sort. It's better than nothing, I guess, but it is still a very last ditch effort. It's somewhat akin to ordering something to drink at a restaurant. You prefer orange juice, but if they don't have that, any type

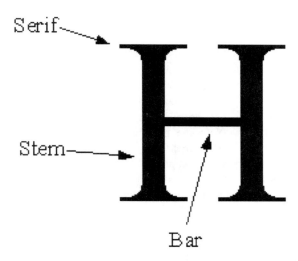

Figure 9–2   The "extra bits" at the top and bottom of the stems are called "serifs." This is a Times New Roman letter "H." This type of serif is called a "slab bracketed serif," because of its thickness and the curved arch that "brackets" it. The world of fonts and typography is rife with this kind of jargon.

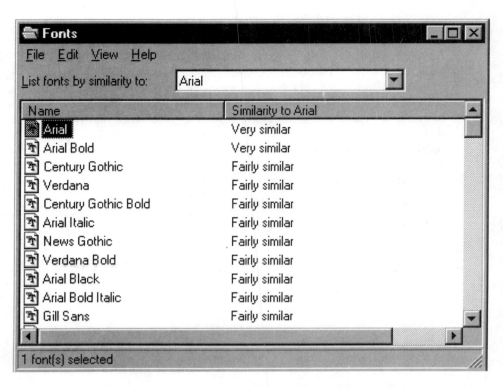

Figure 9–3 In Windows 95, you can have your fonts automatically sorted by "similarity." Go to C:\WINDOWS\Fonts and under "View" select "Listing Fonts By Similarity." Neat feature!

of juice will do. If they don't have *any* juice, you'll just have to settle for a glass of water—it is a horrible substitute for a glass of orange juice, but at least it will quench your thirst. Better to get a glass of water than a bucket of sand.

There are five main generic font families: serif, sans-serif, cursive, fantasy, and monospace. Currently, Netscape and Microsoft will only understand serif, sans-serif, and monospace. Table 9–2 describes each of these families, some common fonts in them, and what you can expect Netscape and Microsoft to give you right now.

The final Rule of Font Selection is to always assume the worst. The user will definitely not have the font you want, any fonts that even closely resemble your font, or even fonts in the same generic family. There's absolutely nothing you can do about it—or is there? Read on!

Bring the Fonts to the Users!

As you can imagine, a lot of people are working very hard on solving this problem once and for all. One of the solutions is to standardize what fonts everyone should have, or at

Table 9–2 Generic Font Families

Generic Family	Description	Netscape	Microsoft
serif	Fonts in this family have "serifs." They include Times New Roman and Garamond.	Times Times New Roman	Times Times New Roman
sans-serif	Fonts in this family don't have "serifs." They include Arial and Gill Sans.	Arial (Windows) Times (Mac)	Arial
cursive	These fonts have a flowing, curving, hand-writing feel to them. They include Brush Script and Zapf Chancery.	Times New Roman	Brush Script
fantasy	These are classified as "weird" fonts, usually following some sort of theme. Critter and Ransom fall into this one.	Arial (Windows) Times (Mac)	Arial
monospace	These are fonts where each letter takes up the same width. Courier and Monaco are two.	Courier New (Windows) Times (Mac)	Courier New

least standardize naming conventions. But we all know this isn't going to happen, at least not any time soon. The real solution is to ship the document's fonts *with the document.*

When you think about it, we've been doing this for years with our other applications. For example, when you send a user a Microsoft Word document, the fonts go with it. The user you're sending it to doesn't need to have the fonts installed, because any weird fonts you happen to use will be "embedded" in the document. There's absolutely no reason we can't apply the same technique to our web documents and have the user download our fonts at the same time as the document, just the way images are downloaded now. No problem, right?

Almost no problem. First, have you checked out the size of a relatively complex Microsoft Word document, lately? They can be a tad large, and all that isn't just text. A single "glyph," more typography lingo for a character, doesn't require much space, but all the characters in an entire font family, like Arial, can take up several kilobytes—easily in the 100k range, depending on the type of font. Arial is 64k alone. Now imagine a document with three or four different fonts! No one wants to download 250k of fonts just to read a short document. Add a few images, and you can end up pushing 350k to 400k for a single document. Not good for user relations. Particularly if the user happened to have that font already installed on her system.

And there are other issues, as well. Fonts aren't free. They can be copyrighted and usually are. Letting your users download copyrighted fonts could land you on the wrong end of a lawsuit, and frankly, I don't want to end up thousands in debt so people can read my latest caving exploits in a fancy font.

In spite of these issues, there are a few solutions already available. Each addresses these issues in different ways, and, of course, the solutions are all incompatible. But it is a start, and in time a standard is bound to emerge. For now, let's look at two of the current solutions: Netscape downloadable fonts and Microsoft font embedding technology.

NETSCAPE DOWNLOADABLE FONTS

Netscape's solution was to adopt a system called TrueDoc from a company called Bitstream. Essentially, TrueDoc takes your TrueType or Postscript Type 1 fonts and jams them into a Portable Font Resource (PFR) file, which can then be downloaded by your users. Because of the type of encoding, PFR files tend to be a bit smaller than the original font file, sometimes only half the size, so download times should be relatively snappy.

The general sequence of events is that you first design your documents with all the weird fonts you want. When you're done, you then run a special "font definition file authoring tool" that "burns" the selected fonts into a PFR file. Finally, you link to the PFR in your document, using either the <LINK> element or the proprietary "@fontdef" style sheet command. Let's look at each step.

Creating Font Definition Files

After creating your document, inserting fonts with reckless abandon, you need to make a PFR file that will contain the font definitions for all your weird fonts. For this, you'll need a special tool, called a *font definition file authoring tool*. The one Netscape seems to be pushing is a program called Typograph from HexMac. Thankfully, this program is available for both Macs and Windows.

The procedure is to start up Typograph and tell it which fonts you want to "burn" into a PFR file. As a security precaution, to ensure that other users can't steal or use the PFR file in their own documents, you must tell Typograph the domain name of the server where the PFR file will be located. For example, if your server's domain name is "www.prenhall.com," you would give this name to Typograph. The PFR file will work fine when served from that domain, but if someone tries to copy it and serve it from another domain, it will fail.

Finally, you tell Typograph to burn the fonts, and after a few moments, you have a PFR file. There are a few caveats, however. First, if you look at Figure 9-4, you will see the Typograph "burn menu," which contains the fonts available for burning. Notice how it says "Perpetua," "Perpetua Bold," and "Perpetua Bold Italic" in the menu on the left? One way that Typograph cuts down on PFR file size is to leave out the bold and italic version of a font, so if you have italics or bold *or bold italics*, you need to include that specific subset. Obviously, if you are using all those variations of the font, your PFR files can start

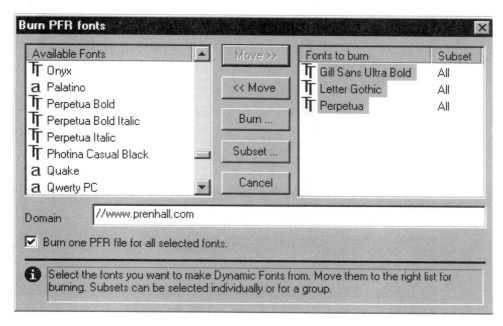

Figure 9–4 Selecting fonts for burning with HexMac's Typograph.

getting a little hefty. It's not that big a deal, but if you are wondering where all your bold and italics went, that may be the answer!

Linking to a PFR File

After burning your PFR file and uploading it to your server, you then need to link your documents to it. There are two ways to do this. You can use the <LINK> element, or do it in style sheets.

If you use the <LINK> element, you will set the "REL=" attribute to "FONTDEF," meaning this is a font definition file, and "SRC=" to the URL of the PFR file. For example, if you created a PFR file called "myfonts.pfr," which contains Gill Sans Ultra Bold, your document might look something like this:

```
<HTML>
<STYLE>
    P { font-family: "gill sans ultra bold" }
</STYLE>
<HEAD>
<TITLE>Fonts!</TITLE>
<LINK REL=FONTDEF
SRC="http://www.prenhall.com/fonts/myfonts.pfr">
```

```
</HEAD>
<BODY>
<P>This is Gill Sans Ultra Bold!</P>
</BODY>
</HTML>
```

After the PFR file is linked to the document, you can specify the font names as you normally would. If all goes well, all your text will be in exactly the fonts you specified—of course, only if the user happens to be using the latest version of Netscape Communicator 4.0 or another browser that supports PFR files. Hint: There are no other browsers that support PFR files. Because not everyone uses Netscape, or in case the PFR file can't be downloaded or is broken in some other way, it is always a good idea to give the user a list of alternative fonts.

If you don't want to use the <LINK> element or want to import the font directly from the style sheet, you can use the proprietary "@fontdef" style sheet command. This is *not* an "official" command, but was implemented for the use of PFR files only. To use it, your document may look something like this:

```
<HTML>
<STYLE>
    @fontdef url(http://www.prenhall.com/fonts/myfonts.pfr);
    P { font-family: "gill sans ultra bold" }
</STYLE>
<HEAD>
<TITLE>Fonts!</TITLE>
</HEAD>
<BODY>
<P>This is Gill Sans Ultra Bold!</P>
</BODY>
</HTML>
```

That's all there is to it! Well, almost. If your Web server isn't set up to recognize PFR files, you're not going anywhere. If you have access to your Web server's configuration, this is easy to fix. If you don't, I hope you're on good terms with your system administrator! All that is required is to set the server to recognize the "application/font-tdpfr" MIME-type, and associate it with the ".pfr" extension. Every Web server does this differently, so check your user's manual if you're not sure.

Further Information on Netscape Downloadable Fonts

Netscape has some good information on its site, of course, but ironically those examples didn't work the last time I checked. It's a good starting point, however, so check out the following URL:

```
http://home.netscape.com/comprod/products/communicator/fonts/
```

Bitstream, the developer of TrueDoc and PFR files, can be found at the address below. There is some pretty good information there, and their demos actually work.

```
http://www.bitstream.com/
```

If you want to get your hands on a copy of HexMac's Typograph, you can visit their site at:

```
http://www.hexmac.com/
```

MICROSOFT FONT EMBEDDING

Of course, Microsoft has its own view of how to do things. Their solution is called "font embedding," and it works a little differently than Netscape's downloadable fonts. To reduce size of the embedded font files, only the glyphs that your documents use are encoded. In other words, if the only word in Gill Sans Ultra Bold is "Welcome!," then only those eight characters are embedded. This means you have more freedom to include additional fonts in your documents without running the risk of having 500k of embedded fonts. It also means that if you later change your document to use some characters that weren't previously embedded, you'll have to redo your font files. Perhaps a small price to pay for quicker downloads.

For copyright and security concerns, font embedding doesn't have the restriction of encoding the domain name into the font file, so you can use it on other sites. The drawback to this is that you can end up limited in the number of fonts available for embedding, since the font has to be free, in the public domain, or give embedding permission. It is pretty frustrating when you've found the perfect font, only to discover you don't have permission to use it in your documents! Right now, Microsoft only supports embedded TrueType fonts.

The procedure for creating embedded fonts is actually similar to Netscape's downloadable fonts: You create your document with your weird fonts, use a special program to extract and encode those fonts into a "font object," and then link the fonts to your document.

Creating Embedded Fonts with WEFT

Microsoft provides its own tool for creating the "font objects" that contain your document's embedded fonts, called the Web Embedding Fonts Tool, or WEFT for short. WEFT has the charm of actually being free, which MacHex's Typograph *isn't*. Of course, free doesn't necessarily mean better, but it certainly helps. Anyway, after your documents are created, you need to load up a copy of WEFT and create your font objects.

Since WEFT only embeds the fonts your documents are actually using, instead of the entire character set, you will need to provide WEFT with the URL of the document or documents that are to be processed. WEFT then uses Internet Explorer 4.0 to open each document, figure out what fonts are needed, and create your embedded font objects. When WEFT is done, it will *add the relevant code to your document*. That's it—you're done!

One of the charms of WEFT is that it can be run against your entire site and "do the right thing" automatically to get your fonts working. After starting WEFT and answering a few questions, you can simply walk away.

Additional Information on WEFT and Font Embedding

Microsoft has some excellent font and typography information on its site, including step-by-step instructions on the usage of WEFT. Truly world-class stuff. If you're even remotely interested in fonts and typography, I strongly suggest visiting Microsoft's typography pages at the following URL:

```
http://www.microsoft.com/typography/
```

To download or get more information on WEFT:

```
http://www.microsoft.com/typography/web/embedding/weft/
```

Regardless of which system you're planning on using, Netscape's or Microsoft's, I strongly urge you to visit Microsoft's "Disagreeably Facetious Type Glossary" at the address below. There is a ton of wonderful information on typography and fonts in general, including the source of all that strange typography lingo.

```
http://www.microsoft.com/typography/glossary/content.htm
```

CONCLUSION

Both Netscape's and Microsoft's solutions for the font problems are good ones, but not yet perfect. I found downloading some fonts slow and distracting, taking just enough time that a normal user would lose interest and move on. Pages with embedded or downloaded fonts tend to be slower to redraw and sometimes tedious to scroll. Netscape seems to have a worse problem with this, but Microsoft isn't immune either. Microsoft has its own problems as well, including an annoying "Security Alert" window that pops up every single time you access a page with embedded fonts. As things shape up, however, you can expect these wrinkles to be ironed out and font selection become quite a bit less dangerous.

If you're interested in watching these standards form or just want to give the people involved your two cents, be sure to visit the W3C's site, which has a bunch of good information on all the contenders for the Web font standard. The W3C's font pages are at the URL below:

```
http://www.w3.org/Fonts/
```

You may also be well served to visit your local bookstore and pick up a few texts on fonts and typography, and maybe even one or two on desktop publishing. The information they contain, while probably not specific to the trials of Web page design, can be an invaluable resource for other font-related issues. If you're having trouble finding the perfect font, these books can help you figure out what you're really looking for and how to get just the right effect.

The world of fonts is a harsh one, rife with strangeness and inconsistencies. Once mastered, however, you will have the tools to create some truly world class Web pages.

CHAPTER 10

Conclusion and the Future
of Dynamic HTML

Well, that about wraps it up. We covered dynamic content, cascading style sheets, positioning, dynamic styles, and font embedding—an awful lot to cram into one book! All that is left now is to practice, experiment, and start turning out great Web documents! The rest of this chapter will tell you where to find more information, where all the example and premade code can be found, and what the future of Dynamic HTML—and the Web in general—looks like.

WEB GALLERIES, LIBRARIES, AND COLLECTIONS

There's nothing webmasters like to do more then share their inspirations, and you would be amazed at the free material floating around. Sometimes a tricky problem can be solved by a quick Web search and a few minutes of browsing. Chances are, if you're trying to do it, someone else already has and is willing to share his or her code with you. Look around! As a starting point, I've included pointers to some great collections of premade code and examples. Even if you don't find exactly what you're looking for, or aren't looking for anything in particular, these sites can give you some great new ideas and inspiration!

Style Sheets

Style sheets have been around much longer then Dynamic HTML. I remember a couple of *years* ago seeing early style sheet experiments, before the mainstream browsers even dreamt of attempting to implement them. If you're looking for style sheet resources, there's no shortage of them on the Web.

One of the best sites for style sheet information is Web Review's Style Sheet Reference Guide, located at the following address:

```
http://www.webreview.com/guides/style/index.html
```

If I had known about Web Review's Style Sheet Reference Guide earlier, it would have made writing the style sheets sections *much* easier. Everything a webmaster needs to know is there, including articles explaining compatibility issues, tutorials, references, tools, and tons of useful links.

Microsoft's Typography pages offer tons of great information on style sheets, including examples, demonstrations, and links to other resources. Microsoft also has another excellent set of style sheet "gallery" pages with a bunch more examples, including free style sheets you can use for your own documents. New styles are being added all the time, so this site is worth checking frequently.

```
http://www.microsoft.com/typography/css/gallery/entrance.htm
http://www.microsoft.com/gallery/files/styles/default.htm
```

Finally, the W3C maintains an extensive set of pages on style sheets, including all the specifications, news, press releases, and announcements. If you're really serious about style sheets, this is another must-visit site.

```
http://www.w3.org/Style/
```

Dynamic HTML

There isn't quite as much out there on Dynamic HTML yet, and what is available is still a bit confused and unorganized. A few useful starting points are listed below.

Once again, Microsoft's site has some of the best information available on Dynamic HTML, at least from the Internet Explorer point of view. My favorite pages are in the Dynamic HTML Gallery, and they include an extensive set of very impressive demonstrations and examples that can be used in your own documents. This one is well worth your time. If you still have doubts about the power of Dynamic HTML, see what the pros at Microsoft can do with it here.

```
http://www.microsoft.com/workshop/author/dhtml/
```

The Dynamic <HTML> Zone is another great site. It is supported by Macromedia, so it will be a bit biased in its recommendations, but there is enough good material here to keep you busy for quite a while! Of particular note is news of Macromedia's upcoming "Dreamweaver" web site authoring tool, which will have support for dynamic HTML.

```
http://www.dhtmlzone.com/
```

There's not much on Yahoo! yet, but I'm sure there will be soon enough. Keep an eye on Yahoo's Dynamic HTML section. I've long since given up trying to bookmark specific Yahoo! pages, so I included its "path," instead of a real URL. Go to `http://www.yahoo.com/` and follow the links to the path below, or search for "dynamic html" if you're still having trouble finding it.

```
Computers and Internet:Information and Documentation:Data For-
mats:HTML:Dynamic HTML
```

The W3C *finally* released the first draft of the new Document Object Model (DOM) and it's available online at their site. If you're interested in the nuts and bolts, this is where it's at.

```
http://www.w3.org/DOM/
```

Fonts

There are tons of free fonts and font-related information on the Web. A great place to start is Microsoft's Typography pages. See Chapter 9 for these pointers. If you're interested in collections of free fonts, try visiting Yahoo! and searching for "fonts." The Yahoo! path is below. Just go to `http://www.yahoo.com/` and following the links.

```
Arts:Design Arts:Graphic Design:Typography:Typefaces
```

There's some really great stuff here, including a lot of free fonts. Keep an eye open for TrueType in particular.

THE FUTURE OF DYNAMIC HTML (AND THE WEB!)

Right now, the specifications for Dynamic HTML and the next generation of browsers are slowly being formed and solidified. Just a couple of weeks before I wrote these words, the new Document Object Model specification's first draft was released to the public. The new HTML 4.0 specifications are also beginning to shape up, and I expect to see more progress in that area "real soon now." It seems like just yesterday we were still arguing about the HTML 2.0 specifications, and browsers were still struggling to implement HTML 1.0 properly. How quickly time flies.

There have also been some exciting new advances with a draft called XML, a potential replacement for HTML. Things are moving along at an incredible rate, and the Web will be a much different place in a year or so. Netscape and Microsoft are finally beginning to agree on what dynamic HTML really means, and when the specifications are finalized, I'm sure things will be "back to normal," or at least at an acceptable level of incompatibility, if you know what I mean. It's truly an exciting time!

A few upcoming drafts and specifications are worth mentioning here, at least briefly: XML and HTML 4.0. Keep an eye out for these two!

HTML 4.0

The next version of HTML is currently in draft form and is open for public comment and critique. Formerly known as "Cougar," HTML 4.0 will, at some point in the future, eventually replace the current HTML 3.2 specification. The current draft is being worked on by Adobe, Hewlett Packard, IBM, Microsoft, Netscape, Novell, SoftQuad, and Sun Microsystems, but anyone is welcome to participate.

The HTML 4.0 draft will attempt to address several new issues, including internationalization, accessibility, more robust tables, compound documents, style sheets, scripting, and printing. For more information, and the complete text of the draft as it currently stands, check out the W3C's site at the URL below.

```
http://www.w3.org/MarkUp/Cougar/
```

This draft is still quite away from being finished, and anything (or everything!) is subject to change at any moment. From experience, I can guarantee it will change often and without warning.

XML: Extensible Markup Language

There are some people who believe that HTML may just be a little too bloated but still not flexible enough to do the Web justice. One solution is to "convert the Web" to raw SGML, instead of HTML. No, thank you! SGML is complex, difficult to master, and while extremely flexible (HTML is "written" in SGML, after all!) all this would accomplish would be to keep high-priced consultants busy.

Another solution is to take SGML, cut out the nasty and obscure bits, simplify it a tad, and then call it XML. And that is exactly what a group at the W3C is currently doing. There's a lot going on in this area, and a visit to the W3C's XML pages would be well worth your time, if just to get yourself familiarized with what they're doing and why. You may very well find yourself working with XML sometime in the future. All the latest news and information on XML can be found at the following URL:

```
http://www.w3.org/XML/
```

In a nutshell, XML is a variation of SGML that will allow webmasters to "write" their own version of HTML. In other words, if you don't have quite the right element for the job, you can write it yourself with XML. For example, a lawyer may want to make transcripts of court cases available on the Web. Using XML, she can write specific elements to handle comments from the plaintiff, defendant, and judge. If you can't do it in HTML, you can use XML to write your own version of HTML.

Scriplets

Scriplets is a new feature of Internet Explorer 4.0 which allows you to create code which can easily be reused in other documents without all the messy hassle of cutting, pasting and rewriting. For example, if you have a complex script-driven menubar at the top of each document, instead of cutting and pasting the script dozens, or even hundreds, of times, you can write a scriptlet stored as a separate document and reference it with the <OBJECT> element.

One of the neater features of scriptlets include the ability to "encapsulate" your code into a single object and only expose certain properties and methods to the rest of your document. There is even a mechanism for quickly creating pop-up menus. It sounds like Microsoft has some big plans for scriptlets, perhaps including the ability to embed them into other Microsoft applications, such as Microsoft Word. This is an area you should watch very closely!

For more information on scriptlets, Microsoft has an excellent page and FAQ, complete with example code and a quick tutorial.

```
http://ww.microsoft.com/sitebuilder/features/scriptlet.asp
```

Scriptlets have the potential to make reusing script objects a quick and simple procedure. Check out Microsoft's site and see how scriptlets may be able to help you!

CONCLUSION

The Web is rapidly evolving, and Dynamic HTML is the next step in its evolution. As Dynamic HTML grows, there are bound to be changes, so keep your eyes open and double-check your documents with each release of Internet Explorer and Netscape Communicator. It's just a matter of time before both browsers can understand each other again, but things are going to have to be broken before they can be fixed. Stay alert, keep experimenting, and above all else, have fun!

Tables

This appendix contains various tables that may be of use, including the Unicode 2.0 C0 Controls and Basic Latin character set; a color table with hexidecimal triples, names, and RGB values; and a decimal to hexidecimal conversion table.

UNICODE 2.0 C0 CONTROLS AND BASIC LATIN (U+0000 TO U+007F)

The following table contains many characters taken from the Unicode 2.0 standard, block C0 Controls and Basic Latin in the range U+0000 to U+007F. For more information on Unicode 2.0 and the complete character set, visit their Web site at:

```
http://www.unicode.org/
```

Dec	Hex	Char	Dec	Hex	Char	Dec	Hex	Char
0	0x00	NULL	62	0x3E	>	95	0x5F	_
13	0x0D	ENTER	63	0x3F	?	96	0x60	`
27	0x1B	ESC	64	0x40	@	97	0x61	a
32	0x20	SPACE	65	0x41	A	98	0x62	b
33	0x21	!	66	0x42	B	99	0x63	c
34	0x22	"	67	0x43	C	100	0x64	d
35	0x23	#	68	0x44	D	101	0x65	e
36	0x24	$	69	0x45	E	102	0x66	f
37	0x25	%	70	0x46	F	103	0x67	g
38	0x26	&	71	0x47	G	104	0x68	h
39	0x27	'	72	0x48	H	105	0x69	i

Dec	Hex	Char	Dec	Hex	Char	Dec	Hex	Char
40	0x28	(	73	0x49	I	106	0x6A	j
41	0x29	)	74	0x4A	J	107	0x6B	k
42	0x2A	*	75	0x4B	K	108	0x6C	l
43	0x2B	+	76	0x4C	L	109	0x6D	m
44	0x2C	,	77	0x4D	M	110	0x6E	n
45	0x2D	-	78	0x4E	N	111	0x6F	o
46	0x2E	.	79	0x4F	O	112	0x70	p
47	0x2F	/	80	0x50	P	113	0x71	q
48	0x30	0	81	0x51	Q	114	0x72	r
49	0x31	1	82	0x52	R	115	0x73	s
50	0x32	2	83	0x53	S	116	0x74	t
51	0x33	3	84	0x54	T	117	0x75	u
52	0x34	4	85	0x55	U	118	0x76	v
53	0x35	5	86	0x56	V	119	0x77	w
54	0x36	6	87	0x57	W	120	0x78	x
55	0x37	7	88	0x58	X	121	0x79	y
56	0x38	8	89	0x59	Y	122	0x7A	z
57	0x39	9	90	0x5A	Z	123	0x7B	{
58	0x3A	:	91	0x5B	[	124	0x7C		
59	0x3B	;	92	0x5C	\	125	0x7D	}
60	0x3C	<	93	0x5D	]	126	0x7E	~
61	0x3D	=	94	0x5E	^	127	0x7F	DEL

BASIC COLOR TABLES

This is the basic color table, containing the original sixteen DOS colors. If the user has a color monitor, odds are these sixteen colors will look right. Of course, you can specify odd values, and probably still be safe, but some users can only display these sixteen and other colors can become mangled or dithered in strange ways.

Color Name	Hexadecimal Triple	Abbreviate Hex Triple	RGB Value
aqua	#00FFFF	#0FF	rgb(0,255,255)
black	#000000	#000	rgb(0,0,0)
blue	#0000FF	#00F	rgb(0,0,255)
fuchsia	#FF00FF	#F0F	rgb(255,0,255)
gray	#808080	#888	rgb(128,128,128)
green	#008000	#080	rgb(0,128,0)
lime	#00FF00	#0F0	rgb(0,255,0)
maroon	#800000	#800	rgb(128,0,0)
navy	#000080	#008	rgb(0,0,128)
olive	#808000	#880	rgb(128,128,0)
purple	#800080	#808	rgb(128,0,128)
red	#FF0000	#F00	rgb(255,0,0)
silver	#C0C0C0	#CCC	rgb(192,192,192)

Color Name	Hexadecimal Triple	Abbreviate Hex Triple	RGB Value
teal	#008080	#088	rgb(0,128,128)
white	#FFFFFF	#FFF	rgb(255,255,255)
yellow	#FFFF00	#FF0	rgb(255,255,0)

DECIMAL TO HEXIDECIMAL CONVERSION TABLE

You can never have too many decimal to hexidecimal conversion tables!

Dec	Hex	Dec	Hex	Dec	Hex	Dec	Hex
0	0x00	64	0x40	128	0x80	192	0xC0
1	0x01	65	0x41	129	0x81	193	0xC1
2	0x02	66	0x42	130	0x82	194	0xC2
3	0x03	67	0x43	131	0x83	195	0xC3
4	0x04	68	0x44	132	0x84	196	0xC4
5	0x05	69	0x45	133	0x85	197	0xC5
6	0x06	70	0x46	134	0x86	198	0xC6
7	0x07	71	0x47	135	0x87	199	0xC7
8	0x08	72	0x48	136	0x88	200	0xC8
9	0x09	73	0x49	137	0x89	201	0xC9
10	0x0A	74	0x4A	138	0x8A	202	0xCA
11	0x0B	75	0x4B	139	0x8B	203	0xCB
12	0x0C	76	0x4C	140	0x8C	204	0xCC
13	0x0D	77	0x4D	141	0x8D	205	0xCD
14	0x0E	78	0x4E	142	0x8E	206	0xCE
15	0x0F	79	0x4F	143	0x8F	207	0xCF
16	0x10	80	0x50	144	0x90	208	0xD0
17	0x11	81	0x51	145	0x91	209	0xD1
18	0x12	82	0x52	146	0x92	210	0xD2
19	0x13	83	0x53	147	0x93	211	0xD3
20	0x14	84	0x54	148	0x94	212	0xD4
21	0x15	85	0x55	149	0x95	213	0xD5
22	0x16	86	0x56	150	0x96	214	0xD6
23	0x17	87	0x57	151	0x97	215	0xD7
24	0x18	88	0x58	152	0x98	216	0xD8
25	0x19	89	0x59	153	0x99	217	0xD9
26	0x1A	90	0x5A	154	0x9A	218	0xDA
27	0x1B	91	0x5B	155	0x9B	219	0xDB
28	0x1C	92	0x5C	156	0x9C	220	0xDC
29	0x1D	93	0x5D	157	0x9D	221	0xDD
30	0x1E	94	0x5E	158	0x9E	222	0xDE
31	0x1F	95	0x5F	159	0x9F	223	0xDF
32	0x20	96	0x60	160	0xA0	224	0xE0
33	0x21	97	0x61	161	0xA1	225	0xE1
34	0x22	98	0x62	162	0xA2	226	0xE2
35	0x23	99	0x63	163	0xA3	227	0xE3

Dec	Hex	Dec	Hex	Dec	Hex	Dec	Hex
36	0x24	100	0x64	164	0xA4	228	0xE4
37	0x25	101	0x65	165	0xA5	229	0xE5
38	0x26	102	0x66	166	0xA6	230	0xE6
39	0x27	103	0x67	167	0xA7	231	0xE7
40	0x28	104	0x68	168	0xA8	232	0xE8
41	0x29	105	0x69	169	0xA9	233	0xE9
42	0x2A	106	0x6A	170	0xAA	234	0xEA
43	0x2B	107	0x6B	171	0xAB	235	0xEB
44	0x2C	108	0x6C	172	0xAC	236	0xEC
45	0x2D	109	0x6D	173	0xAD	237	0xED
46	0x2E	110	0x6E	174	0xAE	238	0xEE
47	0x2F	111	0x6F	175	0xAF	239	0xEF
48	0x30	112	0x70	176	0xB0	240	0xF0
49	0x31	113	0x71	177	0xB1	241	0xF1
50	0x32	114	0x72	178	0xB2	242	0xF2
51	0x33	115	0x73	179	0xB3	243	0xF3
52	0x34	116	0x74	180	0xB4	244	0xF4
53	0x35	117	0x75	181	0xB5	245	0xF5
54	0x36	118	0x76	182	0xB6	246	0xF6
55	0x37	119	0x77	183	0xB7	247	0xF7
56	0x38	120	0x78	184	0xB8	248	0xF8
57	0x39	121	0x79	185	0xB9	249	0xF9
58	0x3A	122	0x7A	186	0xBA	250	0xFA
59	0x3B	123	0x7B	187	0xBB	251	0xFB
60	0x3C	124	0x7C	188	0xBC	252	0xFC
61	0x3D	125	0x7D	189	0xBD	253	0xFD
62	0x3E	126	0x7E	190	0xBE	254	0xFE
63	0x3F	127	0x7F	191	0xBF	255	0xFF

Cascading Style
Sheets Reference

See the appropriate chapter for more information on these properties. Filters are covered in Chapter 7.

Font and Text Properties

---

font-family:	font-family: arial
	font-family: arial, sans-serif
	font-family: arial, helvetica, sans-serif
font-size:	font-size: 16pt
	font-size: larger
	font-size: x-large
	font-size: 125%
font-style:	font-style: italic
font-variant:	font-variant: small-caps
font-weight:	font-weight: bold
	font-weight: lighter
	font-weight: 900
font:	font: 24pt arial
	font: 16pt/18pt arial
	font: italic bold 32pt arial, sans-serif
letter-spacing:	letter-spacing: 0.5em
line-height:	line-height: 1.75em
	line-height: 3
	line-height: 150%
word-spacing:	word-spacing: 0.25in
text-align:	text-align: center
text-decoration:	text-decoration: underline
	text-decoration: line-through
	text-decoration: none

Font and Text Properties (*Continued*)

---

text-indent:	text-indent: 2.5em
	text-indent: 25%
text-transform:	text-transform: uppercase
	text-transform: lowercase
vertical-align:	vertical-align: super
	vertical-align: sub

Colors and Background Properties

---

color:	color: red
	color: #FF0000
	color: rgb(255,0,0)
background-attachment:	background-attachment: fixed
background-color:	background-color: green
	background-color: #00FF00
	background-color: rgb(0,255,0)
background-image:	background-image: url(myimage.gif)
background-position:	background-position: center left
	background-position: 25% 75%
background-repeat:	background-repeat: no-repeat
	background-repeat: repeat-x
background:	background: silver url(myimage.gif) no-repeat
	background: url(myimage.gif) no-repeat fixed center

Box/Layout Properties

---

border-bottom-color:	border-bottom-color: red
border-left-color:	border-right-color: #FF0000
border-right-color:	border-right-color: olive
border-top-color:	
border-color:	border-color: black
	border-color: black gray
	border-color: black blue gray white
border-bottom-style:	border-bottom-style: solid
border-left-style:	border-right-style: double
border-right-style:	border-right-style: outset
border-top-style:	
border-style:	border-style: solid
	border-style: double solid
border-bottom-width:	border-left-width: 5px
border-left-width:	border-top-width: thin
border-right-width:	border-right-width: thick
border-top-width:	
border-width:	border-width: thin medium thick
	border-width: medium
border-bottom:	border-bottom: thin solid green
border-left:	border-bottom: thick

border-right: border-right: medium double black
border-top:
border: border: medium inset red
                                     border: thin solid black
clear: clear: both
                                     clear: left
float: float: left
                                     float: none
margin-bottom: margin-top: 0.5em
margin-left: margin-left: 25px
margin-right: margin-left: 15%
margin-top:
margin: margin: 0.25in 0.50in 0.25in 0.50in
                                     margin: 1em
padding-bottom: padding-right: 5px
padding-left: padding-top: 5pt
padding-right:
padding-top:
padding: padding: 5px 10px 5px 10px
                                     padding: 0.75em

Classification and "Other" Properties

---

display: display: none
                                     display: block
cursor: cursor: hand
                                     cursor: auto
list-style-image: list-style-image: url(mybullet.gif)
list-style-position: list-style-position: inside
                                     list-style-position: outside
list-style-type: list-style-type: circle
                                     list-style-type: square
                                     list-style-type: lower-roman
list-style: list-style: disc url(mybullet.gif)
                                     list-style: square inside url(mybullet.gif)

Positioning Properties

---

clip: clip: rect(25px, 100px, 100px, 25px)
height: height: 2.5in
                                     height: 5em
                                     height: 75%
left: left: 25px
                                     left: 1em
                                     left: 25%
overflow: overflow: clip
                                     overflow: scroll
position: position: absolute
                                     position: relative

Positioning Properties (*Continued*)

top:	top: 50px
	top: 2em
	top: 10%
visibility:	visibility: hidden
	visibility: visible
	visibility: inherit
width:	width: 4in
	width: 10em
	width: 150px
	width: 50%
z-index:	z-index: 2
	z-index: 0
	z-index: -1

Layers

<LAYER>...</LAYER>

Absolutely positioned layer.

Attributes	Examples
ABOVE=	ABOVE="top_layer"
BACKGROUND=	BACKGROUND="mybackground.gif"
BELOW=	BELOW="bottom_layer"
BGCOLOR=	BGCOLOR="red"
	BGCOLOR="#FF0000"
CLIP=	CLIP=10,10,100,100
HEIGHT=	HEIGHT=90
	HEIGHT="25%"
LEFT=	LEFT=10
	LEFT="20%"
NAME=	NAME="my_layer"
PAGEX=	PAGEX=10
PAGEY=	PAGEY=10
SRC=	SRC="my_page.html"
TOP=	TOP=10
	TOP="15%"
VISIBILITY=	VISIBILITY=HIDE
	VISIBILITY=SHOW
WIDTH=	WIDTH=90
	WIDTH="50%"
Z-INDEX=	Z-INDEX=2
	Z-INDEX=1

JavaScript Properties

Property	Write?	Associated Attribute (if any)
clip.bottom	yes	CLIP=
clip.height	yes	HEIGHT=
clip.left	yes	CLIP=
clip.right	yes	CLIP=
clip.top	yes	CLIP=
clip.width	yes	WIDTH=
document	no	
layers	no	
left	yes	LEFT=
name	no	NAME=
parentLayer	no	
siblingAbove	no	ABOVE=
siblingBelow	no	BELOW=
top	yes	TOP=
visibility	yes	VISIBILITY=

Methods

Method	Examples
moveBy(*x-pixels, y-pixels*)	document.layers.myLayer.moveBy(0,-20)
moveTo(*x-pixels, y-pixels*)	document.layers.myLayer.moveTo(25,50)
resizeBy(*width, height*)	document.layers.myLayer.resizeBy(-10,-10)
resizeTo(*width, height*)	document.layers.myLayer.resizeTo(50,25)
moveAbove(*layername*)	document.layers.myLayer.moveAbove("layer_1")
moveBelow(*layername*)	document.layers.myLayer.moveBelow("layer_2")

Events

Event	Explanation
onMouseOver	When mouse moves over layer
onMouseOut	When mouse moves off layer
onFocus	When layer gets focus (is clicked, for example)
onBlur	When layer loses focus
onLoad	When layer completes loading or is drawn

<ILAYER>...</ILAYER>

Relatively positioned layer.

Attributes	Examples
ABOVE=	ABOVE="top_layer"
BACKGROUND=	BACKGROUND="mybackground.gif"
BELOW=	BELOW="bottom_layer"
BGCOLOR=	BGCOLOR="red"
	BGCOLOR="#FF0000"
CLIP=	CLIP=10,10,100,100
HEIGHT=	HEIGHT=90
	HEIGHT="25%"
LEFT=	LEFT=10
	LEFT="20%"
NAME=	NAME="my_layer"
SRC=	SRC="my_page.html"
TOP=	TOP=10
	TOP="15%"
VISIBILITY=	VISIBILITY=HIDE
	VISIBILITY=SHOW
WIDTH=	WIDTH=90
	WIDTH="50%"
Z-INDEX=	Z-INDEX=2
	Z-INDEX=1

JavaScript Properties

Property	Write?	Associated Attribute (if any)
clip.bottom	yes	CLIP=
clip.height	yes	HEIGHT=
clip.left	yes	CLIP=
clip.right	yes	CLIP=
clip.top	yes	CLIP=
clip.width	yes	WIDTH=
document	no	
layers	no	
left	yes	LEFT=
name	no	NAME=
parentLayer	no	
siblingAbove	no	ABOVE=
siblingBelow	no	BELOW=
top	yes	TOP=
visibility	yes	VISIBILITITY=

Methods

Method	Examples
moveBy(*x-pixels, y-pixels*)	document.layers.myLayer.moveBy(0,-20)
moveTo(*x-pixels, y-pixels*)	document.layers.myLayer.moveTo(25,50)
resizeBy(*width, height*)	document.layers.myLayer.resizeBy(-10,-10)

Methods (*Continued*)

Method	Examples
resizeTo(*width, height*)	document.layers.myLayer.resizeTo(50,25)
moveAbove(*layername*)	document.layers.myLayer.moveAbove("layer_1")
moveBelow(*layername*)	document.layers.myLayer.moveBelow("layer_2")

Events

None.

\<NOLAYER\>...\</NOLAYER\>

Text inside the \<NOLAYER\> element is displayed for browsers without layers support. *No attributes.*

APPENDIX D

Microsoft Style Sheeting Printing Extension

Microsoft added an interesting new feature to style sheets, allowing you to specify style sheets for screen output and other style sheets to be applied for printing only. For example, you can have one style sheet that is applied when the user views the document normally, but another style sheet that is applied only when the user prints the document. It's a neat idea, but it's non-standard and won't work in other browsers yet.

To set a style sheet for printing use, use the "MEDIA=" attribute on either the <STYLE> or <LINK> elements, as appropriate. For example, if you want one of your style sheets to be applied only when printing, you would insert the "MEDIA=PRINT" attribute. The default setting is "SCREEN," which applies the style sheet to both screen and printer output. The "ALL" setting also applies the style sheet to both screen and printer.

```
<STYLE TYPE="text/css" MEDIA=PRINT>
    P { font-family: arial;
        font-size: 32pt }
</STYLE>

<STYLE TYPE="text/css" MEDIA=SCREEN>
    P { font-family: "times new roman";
        font-size: 12pt }
</STYLE>
```

This example sets up two style sheets. The first will print all paragraphs to the printer as 32pt Arial, and the second will use 12pt Times New Roman for screen output. The ability to have two different styles, one for screen and another for the printer, is an incredibly powerful option!

As a companion for the "MEDIA=PRINT" option, two new style sheet properties have also been added: page-break-after and page-break-before. These properties allow you to give the user's printers some hints as to where good spots to break the document are. This is another *great* feature, because Web design often revolves around the "infinite page" paradigm, and printed Web pages can sometimes be broken in very strange spots. The page-break-before property tells the user's printer to start a new page *before* printing the element, and the page-break-after property says it's fine if the new page is started *after* printing the element.

The page-break properties accept one or two of the following values: auto, always, left, or right. The "auto" value tells the printer that this is a good spot to do a page break, but only if necessary. If you want the printer to *always* do a page break at this point, use the "always" value. Sometimes it is valuable to do an additional page break in order to resume printing on a left or right page. For example, chapters in a book are almost always started on the *right* page. By specifying "left" or "right," you can tell the printer to do an additional page break if it is required to resume printing on a left-hand or right-hand page.

```
<STYLE TYPE="text/css" MEDIA=PRINT>
    BR.pbreak { page-break-after: always }
    BR.chapter { page-break-after: always right }
</STYLE>
```

This example defines two classes for the <BR> element. The "pbreak" class will always perform a page break and start printing on the very next page. The "chapter" class identifies the next page as the start of a new chapter and will therefore resume printing on the right-hand page. The <BR> element seemed logical to use for page breaks, but you can apply these properties to any printable element. For example, the <H1> element could page break always to the right, indicating a new chapter, and the <H2> element could always page break to the next available page.

The page-break properties aren't implemented yet, but they should be in the next release. Keep an eye out for them. The "MEDIA=" attribute *does* work, however, and has a lot of potential. When printing, remember that your filter: properties are always ignored, including visual filters.

Index